STUDIES IN INTERNATIONAL RELATIONS

Edited by
Charles G. MacDonald
Florida International University

A ROUTLEDGE SERIES

STUDIES IN INTERNATIONAL RELATIONS
CHARLES G. MACDONALD, *General Editor*

PROMOTING WOMEN'S RIGHTS
The Politics of Gender in the
European Union
Chrystalla A. Ellina

PROMOTING WOMEN'S RIGHTS
THE POLITICS OF GENDER IN THE EUROPEAN UNION

Chrystalla A. Ellina

Routledge
New York & London

Published in 2003 by
Routledge
29 West 35th Street
New York, NY 10001
www.routledge-ny.com

Published in Great Britain by
Routledge
11 New Fetter Lane
London EC4P 4EE
www.routledge.co.uk

RoutledgeFalmer is an imprint of the Taylor & Francis Group.
Printed in the United States of America on acid-free paper.

10 9 8 7 6 5 4 3 2

Library of Congress Cataloging-in-Publication Data

Ellina, Chrystalla.
  Promoting women's rights : the politics of gender in the European Union / by Chrystalla Ellina.
    p. cm. — (Studies in international relations)
  Originally presented as the author's thesis (Ph. D.)—University of Missouri-St. Louis, 1999.
  Includes bibliographical references and index.
  ISBN 0-415-94435-X (alk. paper)
  1. Women's rights—European Union countries. 2. Women—Government policy—European Union countries. 3. Women's rights—International cooperation. 4. International organization. I. Title. II. Studies in international relations (Routledge (Firm))
HQ1236.5.E97 E45 2003
305.42'094—dc21   2002036779

Contents

v

Acknowledgments

I WOULD LIKE TO THANK A NUMBER OF PERSONS AND ORGANIZATIONS FOR their help in completing this book. An international fellowship awarded by the American Association of University Women (AAUW) Educational Foundation in 1998-99 made possible the fieldwork in Brussels. A graduate assistantship at the Department of Political Science at the University of Missouri-St. Louis enabled me to conduct preliminary research. I am grateful to my dissertation committee, Martin J. Rochester, Joyce Mushaben, Kenny Thomas and Frances Hoffman who read and commented on the draft, as originally presented in the form of a dissertation. I am indebted to all the interviewees who provided the primary material for this research in Brussels, at the European Commission, Barbara Helfferich then at the European Women's Lobby and Suzanne Seeland at EUROPS. I also thank Routledge for their initiative in reviewing this book, Charles MacDonald, the editor of the series Studies in International Relations, Farideh Kamali and John Shea for the smooth process their professionalism ensured. I am deeply indebted to Boyd Anderson who has proofread the entire manuscript and supported me throughout the process.

Abbreviations

AP	Action Programme
CAP	Common Agricultural Policy
CEDAW	Convention on the Elimination of All Forms of Discrimination Against Women
CEEP	European Center of Public Enterprises
CFSP	Common Foreign and Security Policy
CNA	Cyprus News Agency
COREPER	Committee of Permanent Representatives
CREW	Center for Research on European Women
CSF	Community Support Framework
CSW	Commission on the Status of Women
DG	Directorate-General
EAGGF	European Agricultural Guidance and Guarantee Fund
EB	Eurobarometer
EC	European Community
ECJ	European Court of Justice
ECOFIN	Economic and Financial Council of Ministers
ECSC	European Coal and Steel Community
ECU	European Currency Unit
EEA	European Economic Area

EEC	European Economic Community
ENOW	European Network of Women
EO	Equal Opportunities
EOC	Equal Opportunities Commission (UK)
EP	European Parliament
EPD	Equal Pay Directive
ERDF	European Regional Development Fund
ESF	European Social Fund
ETD	Equal Treatment Directive
ETUC	European Trade Union Confederation
EU	European Union
EURATOM	European Atomic Energy Community
EUROPS	European Office for Programme Support
EWL	European Women's Lobby
FAO	Food and Agriculture Organization
FIFG	Financial Instrument for Fisheries Guidance
GATT	General Agreement on Tariffs and Trade
GDP	Gross Domestic Product
IGOs	International Governmental Organizations
ILO	International Labour Organization
INSTRAW	International Institute for the Advancement of Women
IR	International Relations
IWY	International Women's Year
MEP	Member of the European Parliament
MP	Member of Parliament
MTEP	Medium Term Economic Programme
OECD	Organization for Economic Co-operation and Development
NAFTA	North American Free Trade Agreement
NAP	National Action Plan
NGOs	Non-Governmental Organizations
NOW	New Opportunities for Women
OJ	Official Journal
OP	Operational Programme

QMV	Qualified Majority Voting
SAP	Social Action Programme
SEA	Single European Act
SMEs	Small and Medium-sized Enterprises
SPD	Single Programming Document
SSD	Social Security Directive
TA	Technical Assistance
TEU	Treaty on European Union
TUC	Trades Union Congress
UK	United Kingdom
UN	United Nations
UNESCO	United Nations Educational, Scientific, and Cultural Organization
UNICE	Union of Industrial and Employers Confederations of Europe
UNIFEM	United Nations Development Fund for Women

Introduction

INTERNATIONAL INSTITUTIONS PLAY AN INCREASINGLY IMPORTANT ROLE in policy arenas once considered strictly within the realm of national politics. National level policymaking is no longer sufficient for analyzing such diverse policy sectors as environmental, fiscal and monetary policies. Social policy, often considered as a "core area of national sovereignty" (Pierson 1996, 148) and zealously guarded by states eager to protect and proclaim their national identity, is not immune from these developments.

This book examines the impact of international institutions on women's rights policies by focusing on the European Union (EU)[1] as a case study in order to illustrate the influence and the ways in which international factors affect women's rights as a global policy concern. At the supranational level, I focus on the European Union's (EU) gender policy in order to provide empirical evidence on the role of supranational institutions in initiating policy change and ameliorating the status of European women. I concentrate on gender policy in the Structural Funds, the major source of funding for European social policy, in order to demonstrate the ways in which specific EU programs influence national policies. I also examine the influence of international institutions on Cyprus, a state seeking admission into the EU, in order to determine whether the EU can act as a catalyst for change in social policy in candidate countries that are resistant to change.

THE EUROPEAN UNION (EU) AND ITS PRINCIPAL INSTITUTIONS

The current fifteen-member EU "is the most important institutional manifestation of the process of European integration" (Sbragia 1999, 471). Its origins lie in the post-World War II desire to restructure the relationships that had historically produced major wars and, in particular, to integrate Germany into a cooperative Europe. The 1950 Schuman Plan, named after the French Foreign Minister Robert Schuman, was a manifestation of this shift in European geopolitics. Schuman's Plan was the basis for the creation of a European organization integrating the coal and steel industry as a concrete measure of French-German reconciliation. In addition to France and Germany, four other countries (Italy, Belgium, Luxembourg and the Netherlands) established the European Coal and Steel Community (ECSC) by signing the Treaty of Paris in April 1951. Jean Monnet, the French general commissary for the Plan of Modernization and Equipment at the time, was instrumental in articulating a vision that was both transnational and supranational in nature. Monnet believed that supranationality was necessary for the efficient functioning of the new organization and in order to avoid interstate power struggles. Supranationality was institutionalized in the High Authority, the main structure with the power to make decisions above national governments.

The 1958 Treaties of Rome incorporated the ECSC with the two newly established Communities, the European Economic Community (EEC) and the European Atomic Energy Community (EURATOM). The three Communities came to be known as the European Community (EC), and by 1967 shared a single bureaucracy. The objective of the EEC, as expressed in the Treaty of Rome, was to create a common market and common agricultural policy by allowing the free movement of people, goods and services.

In 1973, the United Kingdom (U.K.), Denmark and Ireland joined the EEC in the first expansion of the organization. In the mid-1980s, the expansion included Greece, Spain and Portugal in an effort to consolidate their transition from dictatorship to democracy. The enlarged EC amended the Treaty of Rome with the 1987 Single European Act (SEA), also known as the "1992 project" which referred to the deadline for eliminating all non-tariff barriers. The SEA allowed for qualified majority voting for all legislation necessary in creating an internal market. The 1993 Treaty on European Union (TEU), also known as the Maastricht Treaty, changed the name of the EC to that of the European Union (EU). The TEU modified the structure of the Community and created three "pillars," each representing different institutions. The first pillar covers economic and social policymaking. The second pillar includes the Common Foreign and Security Policy (CFSP), and the third pillar refers to justice and home affairs. Whereas the "old" Community institutions are responsible for the first pillar, decision making in the last two pillars involves primarily the Council of Ministers.[2] As the primary intergovernmental organ, the Council of Ministers has the exclusive right of initiating policy that requires unanimous voting.

With the addition of Sweden, Finland and Austria, the 15–member EU signed the Treaty in Amsterdam in June 1997 that was entered into force on May 1, 1999. In view of further expansion to the East and South, the Treaty of Amsterdam concerns institutional reforms aiming to speed up decision-making. This treaty calls for more democratic control through the coopera- tion of EU institutions and national parliaments. It permits the possibility for some countries to move together in increasing cooperation in order to avoid "slow movers" becoming an obstacle to further integration, and encourages new actions within the second and third pillars. The most recent treaty signed in Nice in February 2001 has not yet entered into force as of this writ- ing.[3]

The 1958 Treaty of Rome as amended by the SEA, the TEU, and the Treaty of Amsterdam established a unique, sophisticated, and, some say, "much too complex" institutional framework. In the context of the first pil- lar, the Council of Ministers is the main decisionmaking body responsible for the adoption of legislation initiated by the Commission (described below). It embodies national interests and plays a role in providing policy guidelines. Since the signing of the TEU, it is also the primary organ in the context of the intergovernmental second and third pillars. The Council consists of the respective minister from each member state in addition to a representative from the Commission. There is a separate Council to represent each policy sector such as the environment, agriculture, transport etc. ECOFIN, the Council of Economics and Finance Ministers, is considered one of the most important and powerful councils. The voting in the Council of Ministers is weighted according to population size. The U.K., Germany, France and Italy have ten votes each, whereas smaller countries such as Denmark, Ireland and Finland have three votes. Qualified majority voting requires sixty-two out of a total eighty-seven votes. The Committee of Permanent Representatives (COREPER), composed of the fifteen ambassadors to the EU, and a staff of national civil servants, prepares the work of the councils together with the Council's secretariat.

The European Council is the other intergovernmental institution and
plays more of a strategic role in providing broad guidelines and direction for
the future while overseeing and monitoring the work of the three pillars.
The European Council is composed of the heads of state or government
from the member states in addition to the President of the Commission. The
biannual meetings at the end of each Presidency began in the mid-1970s but
did not become a formal part of the institutional framework until the 1987
SEA. Each member state holds the Presidency for a six-month period on a
rotating basis. The Presidency is responsible for representing the EU exter-
nally and chairing the meetings of both the European Council and the
Council of Ministers.

The Commission is the initiator and supervisor of legislation as well as
the manager and executor of EU policies. The Commission consists of twenty members who form the college of Commissioners. Each member state
appoints one Commissioner with the exception of the larger states—
Germany, France, Spain, Italy and the U.K.—which have two appointments.
Each Commissioner is responsible for one policy area which may involve
more than one Directorate-General. There are twenty-three Directorates-
General (DGs) that are the principal administrative agencies; each DG is
assigned specific functional tasks.

In comparison to national parliaments, the European Parliament (EP)
has limited powers, although it has acquired considerable influence since the
1987 SEA and has further expanded its power through the subsequent treaty
revisions. The 626–member assembly, directly elected since 1979, has the
authority to reject, amend or approve legislation. The EP also approves
Commission appointments and agreements with non-EU states, receives
petitions from European citizens, appoints an ombudsman and tables questions to the Commission and the Council. It moreover serves with the
Council of Ministers as the budgetary authority of the EU.

The European Court of Justice (ECJ) is composed of fifteen justices,
drawing one from each member state. The ECJ is responsible for applying
and interpreting EU law. The Court can invalidate legislation adopted by the
Commission, the Council of Ministers and national governments if found
incompatible with EU law. It can also render judgments on the interpretation of EU law and deliver opinions on agreements with non-EU countries.
The Commission, individuals, and other member states can bring action
against those actors failing to comply with treaty obligations. Articles 169
and 170[4] entitle the Court to rule on infringements and fine states for non-
compliance (Article 171). National courts can also consult with the ECJ by

using the procedure known as *preliminary ruling* in order to request the inter-pretation and applicability of EU law.

In comparison to other international organizations, the EU provides a case characterized by more fully developed institutions with the authority to initiate, formulate, implement and monitor policy compliance of the mem-ber states.[5] EU law takes precedence over national law and is binding on member states. Unlike other international organizations that lack the power to enforce treaties, the EU has the legal mechanism to hold states account-able for implementing legislation by means of the European Court of Justice (ECJ). Although state non-compliance is persistent (Mendrinou 1996), the EU remains "far more legally authoritative and institutionally sophisticated than any other international body" (Sbragia 1999, 469). The diversity of terms used to describe the EU reflects the difficulty in explaining an entity with features that are at once unique but also embedded in existing systems of organization (Sbragia 1992, 22). The EU is described as "a mere forum for interstate bargaining" (Moravcsik 1993), "the most advanced regional organ-ization" (Axelrod and Vig 1999, 72), an "emergent multitiered system of gov-ernance" (Pierson 1996, 158; Pierson and Leibfried 1995, 6), "a partial poli-ty" (Sbragia 1992 13), and "at once an international organization and the proto-government for some future political entity" (Peters 1992, 77). Regardless of the differing opinions, the fact remains that the EU already has a rich history and a legislative and judicial record from which to illustrate supranational agency in the particular field of women's policies which is one of "the most developed of the EU's social policy programmes" (Hoskyns 1996, 1).

"Students of a wide range of governmental activities, have found that they can no longer understand the domestic processes and outcomes that interest them without addressing the role of the EC" (Pierson 1996, 124). Following this recent line of European Union research, and contrary to tra-ditional policymaking studies that focus solely on national politics to account for policy outcomes, I argue that one has to include other levels of analysis. One can meaningfully use international and regional levels of analysis because the variety of issues which touch upon women's conditions increas-ingly transcends national boundaries. The United Nations (UN) Women's Conferences and the international networks of women activists born of these conferences have contributed to the realization that issues such as domestic violence, secondary political status and socioeconomic violations of women's human rights affect women worldwide regardless of their economic, social and cultural differences. The inclusion of the international and regional level of analysis is necessary because of the role international institutions play in agenda setting, policy legitimization and formulation.

CHAPTER ORGANIZATION

In chapter 1, I review the relevant theories pertaining to international relations (IR) and European integration in order to situate this study of EU gender policy within the existing body of literature. I build on existing analytical frameworks in order to critique and modify those aspects, which may not provide insight into the study of European social policy. I start by defining two scholarly traditions in IR, realism and globalism, and examine their assumptions and evaluate whether they can accommodate the role of the EU as a supranational policymaker. I then focus on two major theories developed for the study of the EU, neofunctionalism and intergovernmentalism.

I continue by presenting other approaches that have been used in understanding national level policymaking processes and are now extended for the study of the EU. I review historical institutionalism, rational choice institutionalism, the "garbage can politics" model of organization and the policy and epistemic communities approach. As many scholars emphasize the uniqueness and complexity of the EU (Richardson 1996, 3; Mazey 1996, 25), they try at the same to understand this dynamic organization by borrowing and combining diverse theories from American and British politics (Richardson *et al.* 1996; Leibfried, Pierson *et al.* 1995). Many EU scholars reject the idea that a single theory can sufficiently account for the development of the EU (Cameron 1992, 30; Hoskyns 1996, 19). In examining the *Development of the European Idea*, Sonia Mazey summarizes these tendencies and declares that "no single theoretical perspective can encapsulate the totality of European integration" (Mazey 1996, 25).

Last, I propose a theoretical framework for the study of European gender policy. Given that my larger object of inquiry is the role of international institutions, this study necessarily goes against the basic realist view that states are the most important actors in international politics (Maghoori 1982, 14). This study is more in line with the idealist or globalist view since it acknowledges the importance of international organizations in the international system. However, my study of the EU as a policymaker goes farther than merely establishing that international institutions are important actors, and it attempts to examine the supranational policy process in a specific sector and its eventual impact on states. I challenge the main intergovernmentalist assumptions regarding the role and the importance of the relevant actors and their influence on policies. I draw from neofunctionalism since it sought to explain the role of supranational actors in European integration, the development of unintended consequences and the possibility of policy "spillover." I extend neofunctionalism with a historical institutionalist analysis. Historical institutionalism, as re-discovered in American politics (Evans *et al.*1985; March and Olsen 1989), comparative politics (Steinmo *et al.* 1992), and European Union studies (Sbragia 1992; Leibfried and Pierson 1995; Garrett and Tsebelis 1996) has the potential to explain the ways in which international institutions are important. Historical institutionalism focuses on the autonomy of institutions in affecting social policy development, the impact of international institutions on the formation and goal identification of social group actors, the feedback effect of policies, and the role of institutional rules and routines in organizing the process (Evans *et al.* 1985, March and Olsen 1989). The principal propositions of this study are that states are not the primary actors, that institutions are not instruments of states, and that policies are not the direct outcome of member-state preferences.

Chapter 2 traces the history of gender policy in the EU starting with Article 119 of the Treaty of Rome. This Article guarantees the principle of equal pay for equal work regardless of sex: "Each member state shall during the first stage ensure and subsequently maintain the principle that men and women should receive equal pay for equal work." The original negotiators of Article 119 in the Treaty of Rome could not have easily predicted the consequences of the inclusion of the "equal pay" provision. As most studies of the Treaty of Rome negotiations attest, the inclusion of Article 119 was simply a negotiating tool to appease French fears of industrial competitive disadvantage. This "concession" did not appear particularly dangerous or controversial at the time, given that the nation state had full competency over gender policy. The negotiators could have hardly predicted that this Article would provide the basis for the future development of policies in favor of women and the transfer of competency from the state to the EU. Based on Article 119's "legacy," the EU developed nine Directives on gender equality, four Action Programs and several court cases. The expansion of policy competence beyond the equal pay provision of Article 119 was in the historical institutionalist sense "unanticipated."

This chapter employs Kingdon's (1984) decision-making model originally applied to describe the national policymaking process in order to understand the long-term development of EU gender policy. I review the forty-year history of EU gender policy through Kingdon's *problems, policies and politics "streams."* In addition to defining the institutional context and the evolution of gender policy, I examine European policy in connection with global developments and existing regimes.[6] I consider the temporal proximity of the first three EU Directives in conjunction with the UN Decade of Women (1975–85) and the UN Women's Conference in Mexico City in 1975. I also consider established principles and norms as expressed in International Labor Organization (ILO) treaties, UN conventions, the UN Women's Conferences, non-governmental organizations (NGO) and international governmental organizations (IGO) activities. I consider the international influence as well as the interaction between international and regional institutions in providing a specific policy environment. This chapter's historical treatment of EU gender policy contributes to establishing the instrumentality or autonomy of supranational institutions, their role in structuring the policy process and actors, and the influence of past policy on future policy definition, which is further elaborated in chapter 3.

Chapter 3 uses two cases from the history of EU gender policy discussed in chapter 2 to illustrate that historical institutionalism offers a more appropriate theoretical approach in studying supranational policy than intergovernmentalism. The first case examines the development of the concept of *pay* and the second the transfer of Article 119 to a different section of the Treaty of Rome. Both cases emphasize that member-state preferences are not the only determinants of EU gender policy and that unintended consequences beyond national control can play an important role. Autonomous supranational institutions such as the Commission also hinder national control of EU policy. The Commission's autonomy depends on its ability to take advantage of institutional rules in order to assure policy development and to structure the policy environment by establishing an interest group constituency.

Chapter 4 concentrates on equal opportunities policy in the Structural Funds in order to demonstrate the influence of supranational institutions on national policies and the impact of specific EU programs. The European Social Fund (ESF), one of the four Structural Funds, is the major source of funding for European social policy. I examine two of its financial tools available to the Commission for promoting equal opportunities in the member states: mainstream ESF funding and Community Initiatives. In terms of mainstream ESF funding, I examine the case of France for the period 1994–99 in order to assess the role of the Commission in the planning and implementation of French equal opportunity policy. France, one of the six original members of the ECSC and one of the most powerful member states, is more likely to defend its national preferences if different from supranational policy. The impact of EU equality policy on France that is contrary to national preferences would thus make the case of supranational autonomy stronger.

The second financial instrument, Community Initiatives, are programs "whose guidelines are established by the Commission according to European priorities" (European Commission 1997, 6). I examine the New Opportunities for Women (NOW) program, an initiative that specifically targets women, in order to identify the ways in which the Commission influences national employment policy. The Commission's role in mainstream ESF programs and Community Initiatives in financing, policy programming, and implementation offer the opportunity to examine the influence of supranational institutions on national social policies and particularly in developing and improving employment opportunities for women.

Chapter 5 examines the case of Cyprus, in order to determine whether the EU can act as a catalyst for social policy change in candidate countries because they are anticipating EU membership. Cyprus applied for EU membership on July 4, 1990; together with five other countries form Eastern and central Europe,[7] it started accession negotiations on March 31, 1998. Among the six "first-wave" EU applicants,[8] Cyprus is the only country that did not experience Communist rule and that more closely resembles the socioeconomic conditions of some of the member states. Cyprus shares cultural similarities with Greece and a legal tradition with Britain. However, in terms of gender equality policy, Cyprus lags behind EU policy. The Cypriot case will respond to the question whether international institutions, in general, and the European Union, in particular, can play a progressive role in social policy, either compelling a state to change discriminatory policies or to initiate policy addressing social concerns in countries that are resistant to change.

RESEARCH METHODOLOGY

I use the case study method of one supranational organization, which may offer insights into the policy process of other types of international organizations. The total absence of social policy concerns, in general, and feminist considerations, in particular, from the GATT and NAFTA negotiations raises interesting questions for the future of economic agreements and common markets. The inclusion of environmental provisions in the above treaties reveals that the issues considered relevant in economic agreements among states are evolving and expanding. Given its already rich institutional history and expansive definition of economic concerns, the EU could have a "spillover" effect on other current and future economic communities.

My study combines the use of primary and secondary sources with open-ended interviews conducted in Belgium and Cyprus.[9] Primary documents are now widely available in electronic form on the European Union's Internet server *Europa* and in EU depository libraries around the world.[10] I use EU documentation produced by all the institutions involved in policymaking, such as the European Commission, the Council of Ministers, the European Parliament (EP) and the European Court of Justice (ECJ). Within each institution, I concentrate on the relevant units dealing with women's policies. Regarding the Commission, I analyze documents emanating from the following Directorates-General (DGs):[11] 1. DG V Employment, Industrial Relations and Social Affairs, particularly the Unit V/D/5 Equal Opportunities for Women and Men; 2. DG X Information, Communication, Culture and Audiovisual Media, specifically the Women's Information Service; 3. DG XXII Education, Training and Youth, specifically the Directorate B on Co-operation on Vocational Training.

I substantiate EU primary and secondary document examination with on-site interviews conducted with policymakers involved in gender policies in Brussels, supplemented by my observation of the Women's Rights Committee meetings of the EP in January 1999. In Brussels, the list of interviewees includes administrators at the European Commission, members of European women's organizations and independent consultants to the Commission. At the Commission, I interviewed individuals in four Directorates-Generals (DG): DG V, DG IX, DG X and DG XXII. I conducted most interviews with administrators at DG V, which is the primary policymaking institution for gender policy. Within DG V, I interviewed individuals in several Directorates. At Directorates B and C, dealing with National Employment Monitoring and ESF Operations, the interviews concerned the Community Initiatives NOW and operations of the ESF regarding women's training. At Directorate D, dealing with Social Dialogue, Social Rights and Equality Issues, I spoke with several individuals at the Equal Opportunities Unit on European equality law, mainstreaming equal opportunities, and enlargement. In addition to DG V personnel, I interviewed administrators at DG X (Information) Women's Information Sector, at DG IX (Personnel and Administration) and at DG XXII (Education, Training and Youth). Outside the Commission, other interviewees include members of European-based lobby organizations as well as technical consultants assisting the Commission in the implementation of the NOW program. For chapter 5 and the Cyprus case, I conducted additional interviews with governmental officials in Cyprus in May 1998.

This book hopes to bridge several distinct bodies of literature in international relations, international organizations, comparative politics, public policy and women's studies in order to understand an emerging phenomenon, the intersection of international, regional and domestic politics in an international system that is both global and fragmented. Using two levels of analysis, regional and national, I seek to provide a further understanding of the supranational policy process and its impact on national policies. I combine evidence from primary and secondary documentation complemented by on-site interviews with political actors involved in gender policy.

NOTES

[1] The term European Union (EU) was adopted by the Maastricht Treaty in 1991, which was ratified in November 1993. I employ the term European Community (EC) to refer to the institution pre-Maastricht and European Union (EU) for the post-Maastricht period.

[2] For the organizational structure of the EU, see McCormick, John 1996. *European Union: Politics and Policies.* Boulder: Westview Press (p.207).

[3] "The Treaty of Nice will enter into force on the first day of the second month after the lodging of the ratification instrument by the member state which is the last to complete this formality" (http://europa.eu.int/comm/nice_treaty/). The last member state to complete the ratification procedure, Ireland, voted in favor of the Treaty in a second referendum on October 19, 2002.

[4] As the period covered in this book precedes the adoption of the Treaty of Amsterdam, the book follows the article numbering system of the prior treaty in force.

[5] The EU has the power to make binding decisions by using four legal instruments: regulations, directives, decisions, and recommendations.

[6] I adopt Krasner's definition of a regime as consisting of "principles, norms, rules and decision making procedures" (Krasner 1983, 2).

[7] The other five countries are Hungary, Poland, Estonia, the Czech Republic and Slovenia.

[8] The December 1999 Helsinki European Council added seven other countries to the "first-wave" group: Bulgaria, Latvia, Lithuania, Malta, Romania, and Slovakia. Turkey was given a "candidate status."

[9] See Appendix A, for a list of the interviewees.

[10] Measures to increase access to EU documents became a policy objective after the Maastricht Treaty. That objective took form with the 1994 Commission decision on public access to Commission documents and a joint Commission and Council of Ministers code of conduct.

[11] The DG numbering and organization refers to the structure of the European Commission in place at the time of the interviewing in January 1999.

PROMOTING WOMEN'S RIGHTS

Chapter 1
Theoretical Perspectives

T HE CONSTANT AND RAPID CHANGES IN THE NATURE OF EUROPEAN integration have contributed to the characterization of the European Union (EU) as a "moving target" resembling a "rolling mystery train" (Falkner 1996, 233). This rapid institutional evolution and the complex policymaking process have supported the increasing acceptance among EU observers that there is no single theoretical framework for the study of the EU (Bache 1998, 16; Cameron 1992, 30; Hoskyns 1996, 19; Mazey 1996, 25; Richardson 1996, 4). The effort to synchronize research agendas with a dynamic institution at times seems to outpace the development of theoretical and empirical studies: "The new institutional layer is added before the previous one is completely understood" (Tsebelis and Kalandrakis 1997, 1).

My examination of the impact of the European Union (EU) on women's rights policies requires three different but not separate, theoretical debates. The first section of this chapter situates this study within the larger debate in international relations (IR) theory between realism and globalism or transnationalism, otherwise known as the "third debate" (Maghoori 1982). Some of the defining differences of these theories involve the relative importance given to the role of the state and international institutions in the international system, the degree of interdependence, cooperation and potential global governing arrangements. These differences are central for the theoretical context of this study as to the role of the state and institutions in the international system and the potential for global, international or regional policymaking.

The second section examines two competing theories in the study of European integration—intergovernmentalism and neofunctionalism. This scholarly debate has its roots in IR theory and continues the inquiry into the role of states and institutions. The increasing complexity of the EU multi-level policy process instigated the search for alternative or complementary theoretical approaches: "The complexity of the EU policy process means that we must learn to live with multiple models and learn to utilize concepts from a range of models in order to at least accurately describe the policy process" (Richardson 1996, 20). The third section summarizes different approaches that have been used in understanding national level policymaking processes and are now being extended for the study of the EU. I review historical institutionalism, rational choice institutionalism, the "garbage can politics" model of organization and the policy and epistemic communities approach. In the last section, I propose a theoretical framework for the study of European gender policy.

REALISM AND GLOBALISM

The opposition between realism and globalism represents a "tendency to dichotomize all differences" in the evolution of the IR discipline since the inter-war period (Rosenau 1982, 2). The dichotomous debate and the classification of authors in broad schools of thought are in many ways artificial. This dichotomy first implies that there exists a common definition of theoretical paradigms and that scholars follow one or the other without transgressing the rigid lines between them. Often there is disagreement on classifying certain scholars within theoretical traditions and scholars themselves object to classifications of their works by others that do not correspond to their self-identification. Some scholars, for example, classify Waltz (1979) as a neorealist because of his emphasis on a systemic approach to international politics in his major work *Theory of International Politics*. One may also consider Waltz as a successor to the earlier realist tradition most commonly associated with Morgenthau's (1948) *Politics Among Nations: the Struggle For Power and Peace* that adopts as key concepts the balance of power and self-interest. First published in 1948, this work is considered one of the major and defining works of the period.

Secondly, the division suggests that the two traditions are static references for IR scholars and remain stable regardless of historical circumstances. However, theoreticians "change over time in conjunction with changes in international circumstances" (Kegley 1995, 3). The traditions have not only been altered over time, as Maghoori's (1982) organization in three chronological debates reveals, but they have splintered into sub-varieties. The emphasis on dichotomous debates may mask the diversity among their individual components such as neorealism, structural realism, neoliberal institutionalism and globalism. The definition of the competing theoretical paradigms is controversial (Kegley 1995, 3), and many scholars "display hybrid characteristics" (Clark 1989, 67). Despite these reservations, the general organization into three chronological debates among competing paradigms is a useful analytical tool and "a device for the convenience of the observer" (Clark 1989, 67). The adopted device may also focus our attention on the dominant features of the tradition rather than on the distinct differences among scholars. In the context of the "third debate," one such dominant difference is the role that states and international institutions play in international politics and the possibility for supranational policy.

Maghoori (1982) organized the theoretical debates into three chronological periods. During the period between the two world wars, realists and idealists disagreed on questions of maintaining world order. In the second period, defined as the 1950s and 1960s, the differences were methodological, separating traditionalists from behavioralists. The so-called "third debate" between realists and globalists arose in the late 1960s, and focused on the nature of the international system and the dominant actors in a context of interdependence. The other two labels describing the two views within the "third debate," state-centric and transnationalists, reveal that the role and the place of the state in the international system is of defining importance. A study of supranational policy necessarily introduces another important actor in the system and does not automatically allow the state to be the unique and primary locus of decision. By examining the role of an institution like the EU in policymaking, this study also addresses the role of the state.

One of the main differences between realists and globalists is indeed the role and the primacy of the state in the international system. Realists focus on the role of self-interested states competing for power (Grieco 1988).[1] Grieco's (1988) definition of realism concentrates on the anarchic nature of the system and states' concern for power and self-interest. For realists, the state remains the most important actor in world politics. While not denying the role of the state, globalists recognize the importance of non-state actors such as international organizations and multinational corporations. The theoretical and empirical question, namely, whether we have experienced a decline in the importance of the state, is reminiscent of the scholarly debate about the decline of American hegemony (Strange 1987). The realist view of states as autonomous entities defined by geographical boundaries and distinctly separating domestic and foreign policy is incongruent with any study of supranational policy.

Another distinction between realists and globalists is the difference in values and beliefs, a legacy perhaps of the inter-war "first debate" among the earliest realists and idealists. The globalist expectation of cooperation through international organizations contrasts with the realist picture of states competing for power, and portrays different values and beliefs. The globalist view of world politics is based on beliefs in the following: the goodness of human nature and the capability of cooperating, the possibility of progress, the reform of the anarchical system to avoid war by institutionalizing international society, and war and justice requiring international action. On the other hand, realism is defined by the prevalence of power, an anarchic system requiring sufficient military capabilities, distrust of international organizations and international law, and stability as a result of the balance of power (Kegley 1995, 4–5). Realists and globalists differ in their readings of history and expectations for the future. Realists see the future international order based on states interacting through diplomacy and force. Globalists regard states as capable of improving their interactions through international institutions (Rochester 1986, 81–82).

Clark (1989) defined the underlying optimism and pessimism characterizing the "third debate" based on the philosophy of Rousseau and Kant. Clark (1989) suggests that one can define globalism as "utopianism" because of its belief in reforming the international system, promoting improvement, attaining change through human agency, and viewing rationalism and politics as a mixed-motive game. Realism is associated with power politics, denial of progress, mutual trust and rationality, and a deterministic view of the world. European gender policy appears to be situated within the globalist value system since it accepts the capability of cooperation among states through international institutions. In sharing the globalist assumption that international institutions can promote "progress," I examine whether the EU can become the preferred locus of policy for some countries. In the specific area of gender equality, the EU has developed important progressive policies that could greatly benefit countries of the "periphery" such as Greece and Cyprus.

Jacqueline Nonon (1998), who has been at the Commission since 1958, views the EU's action in social policy as "avant-garde." Nonon was very closely involved in the development of the first directives for women in the 1970s. She was the head of the Equal Opportunities Unit in DG V, then called the Women's Bureau, which was established in 1976. In introducing a recent collection of documents regarding the EU's policies on women,

Nonon recognizes that there is a normative goal behind the EU's activity (Nonon 1998, 4). She suggests that the EU is motivated by a desire to succeed in an "avant-garde" policy area in order to show that European integration can be the instigator of social progress. My examination of EU gender policy is in accordance with globalist values. I view the EU not only as an intergovernmental forum promoting cooperation but also as an external agent for social change, despite its predominantly single market orientation.

Some realists attempted to readjust their theoretical framework to account for the dramatic increase in international organizations since World War II that indicates a greater degree of cooperation among states. Realists introduced the regime concept in IR theory in an effort to modify and expand the state-centric perspective (Krasner *et al.* 1983, 356). This modification strives to address and reconcile international collective action with the realists' assumptions on the centrality of sovereign states and their motives for cooperation. Regimes are defined as "sets of implicit or explicit principles, norms, rules and decision making procedures around which actors' expectations converge in a given area of international relations" (Krasner 1983, 2). The regime literature attempts to explain the international system as more than an aggregate of sovereign states. The reformulated perspective is expressed in the "tectonic plates" metaphor: "one plate can be envisioned as the distribution of power among states, the other as regimes and related behavior and outcomes" (Krasner 1983, 357).

Some regime theorists acknowledge interests, power, diffuse norms and knowledge as causes of regimes (Puchala and Hopkins 1983; Young 1983) and reject the idea that states are the only causal factors in regime creation. However, in accordance with realist views, most scholars consider state interests and state power as the basic causal variables with regimes acting as intervening variables (Keohane 1983; Stein 1983). Regime theory considers states as purposeful agents who "use international institutions as deliberate instruments to improve the efficiency of bargaining between states" (Moravcsik 1993, 507). In creating international institutions, states are viewed as making a calculated decision in order to overcome collective action problems. These problems include reliability of information, transaction costs and costs of enforcing agreements under uncertainty: "regimes facilitate agreements by raising the anticipated costs of violating others' property rights, by altering transactions costs through the clustering of issues, and by providing reliable information to members" (Keohane 1984, 97). The intentional action of states does not account for the participation of non-state actors such as non-governmental organizations (NGOs) and multinational corporations (MNCs) in regimes that seek to question or hinder the state's monopoly. Even if we accept that states create international governmental organizations (IGOs) in order to increase their own efficiency in negotiating agreements, this does not guarantee that such organizations will remain dependent on the original relationship. The instrumentality of regimes and their dependency on national interests and power contrasts with the increasing role NGOs play in the environmental or human rights regime, for example, independently of or contrary to the state's interests.

The realist-globalist debate in IR theory, expanded by the contributions of regime theory, differs in the choice of level of analysis, the primacy of the state, the role of non-state actors, the reading of history and proposals for the future. Generally, globalists do not challenge the realist premise as to the importance of states but are willing to question the notion of sovereignty as an absolute value and guiding force in the international system.

The realist-globalist debate provides the basis for the development of new theoretical labels among Europeanists: "the starting point for understanding theoretical developments in the study of the EU is with IR" (Bache 1998, 17). Neofunctionalism and intergovernmentalism, the two main theoretical traditions dominating the study of European integration, have their roots in the "third debate" of IR theory. Rooted in the globalist theoretical tradition, neofunctionalism regarded supranational and subnational actors as influential in advancing European integration. Intergovernmentalism shares common assumptions with realism such as the primacy of sovereign states.

NEOFUNCTIONALISM AND INTERGOVERNMENTALISM

The direction and the growth of the EU studies have closely followed the development and the institutional innovations of the organization. The theoretical debates mirror the historical evolution of the institution, with periods of enlargement and optimism enhancing scholarly interest. Research activity then decreases during periods of Euro-sclerosis and Euro-pessimism.

Neofunctionalists dominated the first period of European integration after the signing of 1957 Treaties of Rome, which incorporated the European Coal and Steel Community (ECSC) with the two newly established Communities, the European Economic Community (EEC) and the European Atomic Energy Community (EURATOM). By 1967, the three Communities shared a single bureaucracy and were collectively called the European Community (EC). Neofunctionalists sought to explain the integrative process that began with the ECSC in 1952 and led to the establishment of the EEC in 1958. Neofunctionalists were interested in explaining "how and why they (states) mingle, merge and mix with their neighbors so as to lose the factual attributes of sovereignty while acquiring new techniques for resolving conflict between themselves" (Haas 1970, 610 quoted in Bache 1998, 17). Neofunctionalists developed the concept of functional and political "spillover" to predict relations among European states. Member state cooperation in one economic sector would lead to functional "spillover" and integration in other sectors. The creation of the ECSC in 1952 around a specific economic and technical sector would provide a basis for the development of common structures and interests among member states. Political "spillover" refers to the expectation that once functional spillover occurs, national actors who have benefited from the spillover process would pressure for more integration that would eventually lead to political union (Haas 1958).

Neofunctionalist studies in the 1950s and 1960s reflected not merely a formal interest in supranational organizations but also normative considerations in advancing European integration (Haas 1958; Lindberg 1963). The characterization of the periods of EU history as either optimistic or sclerotic and pessimistic reveals the normative biases. Regional integration, institutional expansion and treaty proliferation at the European level are viewed as positive developments; maintaining the status quo or increasing national sovereignty at the expense of the EU are considered "sclerotic."

The 1965 "Empty Chair" crisis marked the beginning of the decline of neofunctionalist theory. The crisis was result of a French dispute over the funding of the Common Agricultural Policy (CAP) and a conflict regarding "Community competence and institutional powers" (Dinan 1994, 55). French President Charles De Gaulle attempted to limit the Treaty of Rome's supranational provisions, and the conflict resulted in a French boycott of the Council of Ministers. The 1966 Luxembourg Compromise resolved the crisis at the expense of the organization's supranational powers by requiring unanimity for issues that member states consider of important national interest. The crisis and paralysis of the institutions during the French boycott showed the power of member states capable of hindering further integration. The "disintegration" that resulted from the crisis contradicted the neofunctionalist expectation that "spillover" would lead to progressive integration. In the mid-1970s, Ernst Haas (1975) epitomized the decline of neofunctionalism in his article on "The Obsolescence of Regional Integration Theory."

Intergovernmentalism overtook the realist state-centric assumptions and became the main response to neofunctionalism. Hoffmann (1966) was one of the earliest intergovernmentalists to oppose neofunctionalism. He argued that national governments were the most important actors and ultimately determined decision-making. On issues of national importance, governments would act as "gatekeepers" in order to protect and promote national preferences.

In the 1990s, Moravcsik (1993) became one of the leading advocates of intergovernmentalism. He attempted to refine intergovernmentalism by extending the neorealist approach beyond viewing states uniquely as unitary actors whose preferences are wealth maximization, security provision and power enhancement (Moravcsik 1993). Although Moravcsik (1995) shared the traditional realist assumption that states are rational actors, he differed from earlier intergovernmentalists such as Hoffmann (1966) by emphasizing the domestic development of foreign policy preferences. His alternative approach, "liberal intergovernmentalism," borrows from theories of international political economy (Moravcsik 1993; 1995). The approach is characterized as liberal because it incorporates economic interdependence as a factor influencing national interest formation. It is labeled intergovernmental because of its approach to international negotiation. Moravcsik summarized his approach by stating that "the EC can be analyzed as a successful intergovernmental regime designed to manage economic interdependence through negotiated policy co-ordination" (Moravcsik 1993, 474).

Intergovernmentalism, as adapted by Moravcsik's liberal intergovernmentalism, views the EU as an arena for diplomacy and bargaining among states: "The EC has developed through a series of celebrated intergovernmental bargains" (Moravcsik 1993, 473). States are the only important political actors, while social actors participate indirectly through the domestic structures of the member states. States conduct policy by way of direct negotiation and limited delegation of authority. The main objective is to maximize gains for each individual state, and policy is therefore explained by concentrating on members' interests (Moravcsik 1993; Lange 1993).

One of the "celebrated intergovernmental bargains" was the negotiation of the Single European Act (SEA). Moravcsik (1992) explained the SEA as the result of "conventional statecraft," mainly involving the three largest countries—France, Germany and Britain—each motivated by specific national interests. The intergovernmentalist treatment of states as the ultimate arbiters neglects the role of non-state actors. Cowles (1994; 1995), for example, argued that although states were important, multinational enterprises were critical in setting the agenda of the Single Market program. Her account examined the role of the European Round Table of Industrialists (ERT) in mobilizing at the national and supranational levels in order to influence the European regulatory framework (Cowles 1994; 1995).

Despite its assumption that states behave rationally, liberal intergovernmentalism rejects the realist premise of fixed preferences and allows for variation in state behavior at the international level, depending on the configuration, and/or pressures from domestic social actors expressed through the intermediary of political institutions. As relates to negotiations, the state is not viewed as a unitary "billiard ball" but as an aggregation of societal actors' preferences formed during the process of national preference definition. Although Moravcsik admits that both national and transnational factors influence societal actors' interests, the process remains clearly inter-state because all interests are expressed through the domestic polity (1993, 483). In this pluralist process where social groups determine outcomes, the liberal intergovernmentalist approach allows for "agency slack" in cases where groups' interests do not clearly determine state policy. In a principal-agent relationship, "agency slack" refers to the amount of discretion governments have to define national interests where "societal pressure is ambiguous or divided" (Moravcsik 1993, 484). "Agency slack" is the only divergence from a pluralist perspective which allows a certain autonomy to national leadership but not to supranational officials.[2] The states' incentive to coordinate policies and cooperate comes from the desire to decrease "negative international policy externalities" which inevitably arise from economic interdependence. When national policies involving devaluation or trade barriers impose costs on the societal groups of another state, states attempt to manage externalities by coordinating and harmonizing policies. For example, competitive devaluation and negligent pollution standards are costly to foreign social groups. Consequently, this approach claims to be capable of predicting the amount of co-operation or conflict among states according to the distribution of costs affecting societal actors.

With regard to supranational institutions, intergovernmentalists generally view their role as minimal. Moravcsik asserts that the EC structure does not weaken the power of states but strengthens it in two ways. First, strong institutions are used as efficient negotiation and bargaining channels. Second, supranational institutions support national leadership by legitimizing domestic policies against the interests of particularistic domestic groups. "The unique institutional structure of the EC is acceptable to national governments only insofar as it strengthens, rather than weakens, their control over domestic affairs, permitting them to attain goals otherwise unachievable" (Moravcsik 1993, 507). The institutional structure of the EU is viewed as another regime that decreases bargaining costs in repeated negotiations among states. However, regime theory cannot fully explain the fact that the EU is unlike any other international institution. The EU is unique because the states delegate sovereign powers to institutions and "pool" their sovereignty in cases of qualified majority voting. Liberal intergovernmentalism extends regime theory by attempting to account for the EU's extraordinary features. The EU is viewed as a deliberate creation of the nation state that is willing to reduce the costs of future negotiations and political risks through delegation. In a rare agreement with neofunctionalists and historical institutionalists, Moravscik admits that the enforcement powers of the ECJ might have gone beyond the original intentions of the states: "the decisions of the Court clearly transcend what was initially foreseen and desired by most national governments" (Moravcsik 1993, 513). A specific falsification does not have to invalidate a general theory. Therefore, Moravcsik considers the ECJ case as deviant and an "anomaly" (1993, 513) and the factors that led to the ECJ's role as "idiosyncratic" to the European Union (Burley and Mattli 1993).

The institutional structure of the EU is still evolving and as such this organization is sometimes called "a polity in the making" (Sbragia 1992, 22). The ratification of the Single European Act (SEA) in 1987, the Treaty on European Union (TEU) in 1993, and the Treaty of Amsterdam in 1997 have inaugurated a period of rapid development, bringing frequent treaty revisions, institutional innovations, and expansion. In the context of rapid changes in Western and Eastern Europe in the late 1980s and 1990s, the EU institutions may give the impression of "racing desperately to stay abreast of events and in coordination with one another" (Peters 1992, 75). The EU's evolution has sometimes been considered "uneven and erratic" (Mazey 1996, 25) and the political system unstable, given that "the basic institutional structure is still very much in dispute" (Richardson 1996, 4). The 1999 resignation of all twenty Commissioners, preceded by what was widely considered a power struggle between the EP and the Commission, indicates that the role of institutions in the policy process is still in a developing stage.

For example, the SEA and TEU amendments have considerably enhanced the EP's role in EU policymaking. Although the role of the EP in the original Treaty of Rome was rather limited, the SEA increased the EP's right to participate in policy-making through the co-operation procedure, as did the TEU by way of the co-decision procedure. The co-operation procedure entitles the EP to hold two readings of policy proposals. The EP has the right to propose amendments, which, if accepted by the Commission, can only be rejected by the unanimous decision of the Council. Under the co-decision procedure, which applies only to policy areas related to completion of the single market, the free movement of workers and consumer protection, the EP has the right to a third reading of the proposals. In the event that the Council rejects the EP's amendments from the second reading, the Council and the EP must attempt to settle their differences in the Conciliation Committee. If that Committee fails to reach a compromise between the two institutions, the Council may proceed and approve the proposal by itself. However, the EP can still reject the proposal if an absolute majority of the members of parliament (MEPs) is reached. These significant revisions of the policymaking process along with other new rules, such as the introduction of qualified majority voting in the Council of Ministers over matters concerning the single market, have altered the institutions and the course of EU studies. Before these revisions were enacted, the EP had been dismissed as a "talking shop," while now an increasing number of studies concentrates on the EP procedures alone (Tsebelis 1994, Kreppel 1997; Tsebelis and Kalandrakis 1997). An evolving and more complex institutional structure has stimulated an increasing number of in-depth institutional studies.

Rapid changes, a relatively recent history, and the complex policy process involving multiple actors operating at subnational, national and supranational levels complicate the "problem of theorizing EU policy-making" (Bache 1998, 25). Moravcsik (1993) has responded to the "theoretical problem" by extending the theory of intergovernmentalism to that of liberal intergovernmentalism. Others have borrowed from theoretical frameworks originally formulated to explain national processes, in Anglo-American political science such as historical institutionalism, rational choice institutionalism, "garbage can" politics and the policy community approaches.

RECENT APPROACHES TO THE STUDY OF EU POLICYMAKING

HISTORICAL INSTITUTIONALISM AND RATIONAL CHOICE INSTITUTIONALISM

The "rediscovery" of institutions in American political science in the late 1970s brought new research perspectives to the study of comparative politics in general (Steinmo *et al.* 1992) and the European Union in particular (Sbragia 1992; Leibfried and Pierson 1995; Garrett and Tsebelis 1996). Rational choice institutionalists and historical institutionalists refocused the research agenda on the study of the EU while continuing to inform their analyses with neofunctionalist insights (Pollack 1997).

In American political science the "return to history" is more than simply one of the elements associated with the "new institutionalism" (Robertson 1993). The new institutionalist approach examines institutions as independent actors that change over the long term, shaping future developments and requiring, by definition, an historical analysis (Robertson 1993, 9). Policies not only affect institutions in the relevant period but also have a long-term effect by constraining or facilitating future policies through institutions. Institutional legacies are considered important in the same way that court decisions set precedents for future judicial decision making in national and international law.

Institutions, as organizational structures, are governed by rules; rules are reflected in the behavior of the Weberian "officials" (March and Olsen 1989). March and Olsen define rules as the "routines, procedures, conventions, roles, strategies, organizational forms, and technologies around which political activity is constructed. We also mean the beliefs, paradigms, codes, cultures, and knowledge that surround, support, elaborate, and contradict those roles and routines" (March and Olsen 1989, 22).

Historical institutionalist analyses of EU integration concentrate on institutional evolution and path dependence, arguing that one cannot concentrate solely on the intentions of the original designers to account for the current functioning of institutions (Pierson 1996, 131). Path dependence refers to "the ways in which initial institutional or policy decisions, even suboptimal ones, can become self-reinforcing over time" (Pierson 1996, 145). Policies and institutional arrangements have long-term consequences because they raise the costs of adopting alternative ideas and encourage development towards a specific "path" (Pierson 1996, 145). [3]

Historical institutionalists critique three main intergovernmentalist premises: the centrality of sovereignty, the instrumentality of institutions, and the concentration on "grand bargains" such as the major treaties (Pierson 1996, 128). The historical institutionalist challenge focuses on the existence of "gaps" in the control of states over the EU institutions. Gaps are defined as "significant divergences between the institutional and policy preferences of member states and the actual functioning of institutions and policies" (Pierson 1996, 131). Gaps emerge because of institutional autonomy, politicians' short term interests,[4] the development of unanticipated consequences, and changes in the member states' policy preferences (Pierson 1996). Environmental policy is probably one of the most obvious examples where cooperation in one functional area may "spillover" into another. The original treaty did not refer to the environment until the 1987 SEA. The EU has become now an important international actor in this area, has an increasing amount of authority over environmental national policies, and has instituted a Commissioners' portfolio and a Directorate-General (DG) specifically for the environment. In gender policy, the original policy over equal pay has expanded to cover other issues such as violence against women, women in decision making, sexual harassment and women's health.

Once these gaps emerge, the states find it difficult to regain their control over the institutions and policies because of organizational resistance by EU actors, the difficulty of reform ensured by institutional rules, sunk costs, and the price of exit (Pierson 1996, 142). Treaty revision requires unanimous agreement by all member states, ratification by national parliaments and sometimes by electorates. The possibility that all fifteen member states, their parliaments and electorates will agree on redesigning the treaties is small: "the price of any attempt to exit from previously agreed but presently undesired aspects of the EU simply is prohibitive" (Pierson and Leibfried 1995, 12).

Historical institutionalism shares with neofunctionalism common premises: the importance of supranational actors, spillover and unintended consequences. However, historical institutionalism extends neofunctionalism by adding an analysis of the constraints of member states: "the evolution of rules and policies along with social adaptations creates an increasingly structured polity that restricts the options available to all political actors" (Pierson 1996, 147).

In addition to historical institutionalism, rational choice institutionalism informs a growing number of recent EU studies (Garrett 1992; Garrett and Weingast 1993; Tsebelis 1994). Pollack's (1997) rational choice institutionalism promises to overcome the differences between intergovernmentalism and neofunctionalism. His study of the EU borrows the delegation model from functionalism (1997, 128). Pollack builds a bridge between the two competing schools by accepting both the primacy of the state and supranational autonomy (1997, 101). He considers three sets of questions in examining institutional autonomy. First, he addresses the question of the types of functions that member states delegate to European institutions. Based on principal-agent models of delegation, Pollack concentrates on four functions. The delegated functions are monitoring state compliance of treaties, solving problems due to uncertainty and incomplete contracting, adopting regulations requiring independent non state actors, and initiating proposals in order to overcome inefficiency of a majoritarian system.

The second question in examining institutional autonomy centers on whether institutions are capable of assuming their delegated functions independent of state intervention. Pollack argues that the "agency" of institutions depends on the functioning of the principals' (states) control mechanisms, which he claims vary according to the institution and the issue (1997, 101). The mechanisms at the members' disposal are the ECJ's review, reauthorization of Council legislation, the possibility of treaty amendments, and comitology oversight procedures. Comitology refers to the delegation of legislative powers from the Council to the Commission based on the amendment of Article 145 in the SEA that gives the Commission powers of implementation (Dinan 1994, 222). Comitology represents "the numerous committees linking the Council of Ministers and the Commission, with further links to national bureaucracies" (Peters 1992, 8). The Comitology Decision of July 13, 1987 codified the working in committees and defined three types of oversight committees: advisory, management and regulatory.

The third question concentrates on the Commission's role in agenda setting. Pollack argues that the Commission's formal agenda-setting role depends "on the voting and amendment rules in the Council of Ministers" (1997, 102). On the other hand, in setting the informal and substantive agenda, supranational institutions enjoy informational advantages.

GARBAGE CAN POLITICS, POLICY COMMUNITIES AND EPISTEMIC COMMUNITIES

Just as EU historical and rational choice institutionalist analyses borrowed a theoretical framework from American political science, other concepts were also introduced in EU studies. The most recent study of EU policymaking uses concepts from American, British and international politics such as "garbage can politics," "policy communities/networks," and "epistemic communities" (Richardson 1996). In the United States, the "garbage can" metaphor was originally developed by Cohen, March and Olsen (1972) and later expanded by Kingdon (1984) to describe a particular model of decision making. In a "garbage can" model, an organization does not proceed based on a coherent policy process. Cohen, March, and Olsen described an organization as "a collection of choices looking for problems, issues and feelings looking for decision situations in which they might be aired, solutions looking for issues to which they might be the answer, and decision-makers looking for work" (Cohen *et al.* 1972, 2 quoted in Richardson 1996, 12). Kingdon's analysis of public policy is a reformulation of the "garbage can" model into what he describes as "process streams." The three streams of problems, policies and politics flow separately but join together at an opportune time. Solutions, problems and political forces are coupled, aided by the appearance of a "policy window" (Kingdon 1984, 21).

The "policy communities/networks" literature developed in reaction to "old institutionalism" which studied public policy only in relation to the role of formal institutions. In one of the earlier works on policy communities, *Governing Under Pressure*, Richardson and Jordan (1979) examined the informal relationships of British policy actors and processes in accounting for policy outcomes. The term was meant to convey the "stability of relations and stability of actor participation" (Richardson 1996, 7). In the United States, first Heclo's (1978) seminal work on Washington politics, and then Baumgardner and Jones' (1993) work focused on dynamics, rather than stability. However, both British and American scholars introduce novel ways to understand the policy process. Heclo (1978) calls policy communities "issue networks" but both terms try to capture the informal processes and actors involved in specific policy sectors. At the international level, Haas (1992) defined the concept of "epistemic communities" as " a network of professionals with recognized expertise and competence in a particular domain and an authoritative claim to policy-relevant knowledge within that domain or issue-area" (1992, 3). "Epistemic communities" point to the same degree of specialization within a somewhat identifiable group of policy actors and thus are comparable to Heclo's issue networks. In his study of American public policy, Heclo (1978) refers to "specialized subcultures composed of highly knowledgeable policy-watchers." (1978, 49).

The similarity of the two concepts, "epistemic communities" and "issue networks," reveals that national and international processes are not as distinctly separated as the delineation of the different scholarly literatures might suggest. The blending or combination of what were until now very separate research agendas might lead to new understandings in the study of an organization such as the EU, which combines traditional and unique features (Sbragia *et al.* 1992). The combination of both national and international features in the EU's institutional structure reveals a certain tension and reflects the theoretical disagreements among scholars. The traditional separation between national and international levels of analysis breaks down when dealing with the EU. However, this new multi-level analysis is not easily integrated within traditional perspectives.

A THEORETICAL FRAMEWORK FOR EUROPEAN GENDER POLICY

The review of the major theoretical debates within IR, as it pertains to the EU, and historical institutionalism in particular, provided the opportunity to assess their applicability for the study of supranational gender policy. This study is in line with idealism or globalism because it acknowledges the importance of international organizations in the international system. I challenge the main intergovernmentalist assumptions regarding the role and the importance of the relevant actors and their influence on policies. The critique regarding the relevant actors, their importance in the system and their effect on policy outcomes draws from neofunctionalism attention to the role of supranational actors in European integration. I extend neofunctionalism with a historical institutionalist analysis in order to examine the role of the relevant actors and the development of policy as a process "unfolding over time" and not just as an analysis of "synchronic determinants of policy" (Pierson 1996, 131).

The principal propositions of this study are that states are no longer the primary actors in EU policymaking, that institutions are not merely instruments of states, and that policies are not the direct outcome of member-state preferences. Although I do not reject the significant role of the state, I argue that it has lost many of its traditional attributes, such as its absolute sovereignty and autonomy as a policymaker in a number of policy areas. In order to challenge intergovernmentalism and test the above propositions, I focus on social, and specifically gender, policy. The issue is important because it represents an arena where the role of the state has been considered dominant and the role of supranational institutions moderate. If the EU does appear to play a significant role in this policy arena traditionally reserved within the national realm, this study will provide evidence of the changing position of supranational institutions vis-à-vis states and their influence on national policymaking.

I examine the history of EU gender policy, in order to provide evidence for the above propositions, suggesting that beyond states, international institutions are autonomous agents that influence policy outcomes often against member states' preferences. I use a historical institutionalist perspective to explain the factors that intervene between member states' preferences and policy outcomes. These factors are institutional autonomy vis-à-vis states, the institution's ability to structure the policy process, the influence of past policies, the development of unintended consequences, and the possibility of policy "spillover." Because of its state-centric assumptions, intergovernmentalism would have us ignore the role of international and supranational institutions in influencing policy. Intergovernmentalism also heavily discounts the development of unanticipated consequences that create what Pierson (1996) calls "gaps" between member state control and supranational institutions. These "gaps" allow the latter to engage in autonomous action in influencing policy. Historical details have consequences that affect states' interests in the long term in ways that cannot be anticipated at the time policy instruments are being negotiated. Hoskyns conducted a number of interviews with national officials from EU member states and found that "those who negotiated the original provisions had no idea what force they would prove to have or the legislative upheaval they would provoke" (Hoskyns 1996, 306). Just as court decisions set precedents, past policies and institutional legacies facilitate, and constrain, current and future policy.

I provide further evidence for the proposition that institutions are not merely instruments of states by focusing on the role of supranational institutions in influencing national policy through the use of EU financial instruments. The EU financing capability with respect to national programs allows supranational institutions such as the Commission to promote an agenda independent of that of various member states. The evidence supporting the independent role of supranational institutions in influencing national policies would be further enhanced if their influence also extended to non-member states. This supports my hypothesis insofar as candidate countries have full knowledge of the increased supranational autonomy yet still voluntarily surrender their sovereignty to allow for external influence over their national policies. The long term-development of EU gender policy, and the impact of supranational institutions on national policy in member-states and candidate countries questions the intergovernmentalist state centric assumptions on the primacy of the state and instrumentality of institutions. I propose a policymaking system where supranational institutions increasingly affect policy at the EU, national and international levels and promote social change in issues that have been traditionally reserved to nation states.

In the next chapter I present the development of EU gender policy between 1958 and the 1997 Amsterdam Treaty, examining the EU policy process in light of Kingdon's (1984) reformulated "garbage can" model of decision making. The flexibility and fluidity in Kingdon's organizational system is useful in explaining a policy system that includes national, international and supranational institutions and actors. The examination of EU gender policy will focus on the role of states and institutions and their responsibility in determining policy outcomes.

NOTES

[1] The purpose of Grieco's article is to challenge neoliberal institutionalism based on realist theory. His article thus reviews the orthodox strands of the traditional realist such as Morgenthau, Waltz, Aron and Gilpin.

[2] Moravscik responded to criticisms on the role he assigned to supranational officials in his original formulation of liberal intergovernmentalism. In a 1995 "rejoin-

der" article, Moravcsik states that "it would be absurd to assume...that supranational officials do not matter" (1995, 612). However, he insists that the main factor determining European integration is the "intergovernmental demand for policy ideas" and not the "supranational supply of those ideas" (Moravcsik 1995, 618).

[3] For work on path-dependence regarding technological change, lock-in effects because of costs of exit and increasing returns, in economics see Arthur 1988, North 1990; in political science, Krasner 1989.

[4] ". . . long term consequences are often the by-products of actions taken for short-term political reasons" (Pierson 1996, 136).

Chapter 2
The Evolution of Gender Policy in the European Union

THE ORIGINS OF GENDER POLICY IN THE EUROPEAN UNION (EU) REST with Article 119 of the Treaty of Rome, guaranteeing the principle of equal pay for equal work regardless of sex. Article 119's focus on equality only as it pertains to employment is one of the original parameters that constrains and defines the framework within which future EU gender policy can be negotiated. Ostner and Lewis view the employment focus of EU gender policy as "a needle's eye" that filters and constrains policy (1995,177). The domination of economic considerations over social concerns has greatly influenced further developments. Although the primacy of economic concerns persists, future policy may "spillover," as neofunctionalists expect, in issue areas lying outside the original definition of the Rome Treaty. Since 1958, there have been three revisions of the original Treaty, added to nine Directives, several "soft" law policies such as resolutions, recommendations and action programs, and over sixty court cases.[1]

This chapter examines the history of EU gender policy since 1958 and argues that member state preferences alone have not determined the policy outcomes of this period. I draw from historical institutionalism to identify the factors that affect policy outcomes beyond member states' control. These factors are institutional autonomy vis-à-vis states, the institution's ability to structure the policy process, the influence of past policies, the development of unintended consequences, and the possibility of policy "spillover." Historical details have consequences that affect states' interests in the long term in ways that cannot be anticipated at the time of negotiation of policy instruments.

I organize the long-term development of EU gender policy using a decision-making model originally conceived to describe the policymaking in the United States as a process of three independent "streams" (Kingdon 1984). The streams of *problems, policies and politics* flow separately until they join at an opportune time to create policy change: "solutions become joined to problems, and both of them are joined to favorable political forces" (Kingdon 1984, 21). I view the period of change as a punctuation of a policy system in an apparent equilibrium (Baumgardner and Jones 1993). I employ Kingdon's (1984) "coupling of the streams" metaphor, as well as Baumgardner and Jones' (1993) concept of "punctuated equilibrium" to describe the same policymaking process that produces policy change and institutional creation. The new institutional structures created during the period of rapid change are the "devices" that enable a policy system to "settle into a period of incrementalism" (Baumgardner and Jones 1993, 15). Institutions structure further policy development and participation, giving the impression of an equilibrium "that can be changed only by changing the institutions themselves" (Baumgardner and Jones 1993, 238).

With the inclusion of Article 119 into the 1958 Treaty of Rome, the two streams of problems and policies were in place waiting for the appearance of the third stream of politics to expand gender policy in the form of directives. The 1970s were the "critical juncture," a period in which the three streams joined together to produce policy change. The appearance of a policy window and the presence of policy entrepreneurs facilitated this coupling (Kingdon 1984, 21). The policy change produced by this "coupling" of the process streams, or the "punctuation," took the form of strong directives,[2] landmark court decisions, and institutional creation. Following the punctuation of the 1970s, the new institutional structures contributed in maintaining the period of relative stability.

Incrementalism characterizes this period of apparent stability beginning with the passage of the 1979 Social Security Directive (SSD) and ending approximately with the Maastricht Treaty. The new rules in place under the Social Protocol allowed for the adoption of three further directives in 1996–97: "the politics of the EU is also about constantly changing the '"decision rules' of the system" (Richardson 1996, 20). The new punctuation of the mid-1990s, although not as thorough as that of the 1970s, has the potential to change the policy system further "by changing the institutions themselves" (Baumgardner and Jones 1993, 238). The force behind this potential for institutional change is the concept of mainstreaming, the integration of a gender perspective into all EU policies.

I first examine Kingdon's "problem stream" and the ways within which the condition of gender inequality came to be placed on the EU agenda.

THE PROBLEM STREAM

"Social conditions do not automatically generate policy actions" (Baumgardner and Jones 1993, 23). The problem stream governing the policy process involves the recognition and acceptance of conditions previously considered "unproblematic and inevitable" as problems (Edelman 1988, 12). The condition of pay inequality between men and women is not defined as a problem unless "we come to believe that we should do something" about it (Kingdon 1984, 115). As one of Kingdon's interviewees[3] remarked on the subject of problem recognition, "if you have only four fingers on one hand, that's not a problem; that's a situation" (Kingdon 1984, 115). Let us examine the context in which the condition of gender inequality was defined as a problem strictly within the realm of paid employment, which resulted in Article 119.

THE ORIGINS OF ARTICLE 119

As noted above, the origins of EU gender policy lie in Article 119 of the Treaty of Rome which guarantees the principle of equal pay for equal work regardless of sex: "Each member state shall during the first stage ensure and subsequently maintain the principle that men and women should receive equal pay for equal work." A consensus exists among analysts that the inclusion of Article 119 in the Treaty was not due to the negotiators' feminist concerns but to rather to economic considerations (Warner 1984; Mazey 1988; Ostner and Lewis 1995; Hoskyns 1996; Hubert 1998). French negotiators had insisted on the inclusion of this article in order to avoid competitive disadvantages for their industrialists. Since equal pay legislation had already been enacted in France, a lowering of tariff barriers would have given an advantage to industries in other countries that would have presumably continued to underpay women. In France, the wage differential for men and women was 10%, compared to 30–40% in the other five negotiating countries (Sullerot 1975, 102). The immediate French concern rested with the textile sector employing primarily a female labor force (Warner 1984).

THE TREATY NEGOTIATIONS AND THE WIDER CONTEXT

The dominance of the French position in including an equal pay provision in the Treaty is situated within a wider political and economic context. In the mid-1950s, France's faced a number of foreign policy challenges resulting from its participation in the 1956 Suez Canal crisis and the 1954–1962 Algerian war of independence. In 1956, the French Parliament rejected the Paris Treaty, which would have established a European Defense Community, and this development particularly worried Belgium, the Netherlands and Luxembourg. The Benelux countries wanted to ensure peace and cooperation between France and Germany, fearing the failure of the Paris Treaty could have led to a renewal of Franco-German hostilities. Robert Marjorin and Paul-Henri Spaak, key participants in the treaty negotiations, have written about the pressures and constraints of the period (Marjorin 1986; Spaak 1969). Marjorin was one of the key actors in the French delegation and knew that industrialists in France were hostile to the creation of a common market and especially afraid of the destruction of the protective national barriers. The inclusion of an equal pay provision was considered as compensation to the industry for the consequent lowering of tariffs. As the coordinator of the Treaty negotiations, the Belgian Foreign Minister Spaak was pressured by the necessity of completing the Treaty negotiations while a French government in favor of European integration was still in power (Hoskyns 1996, 45). The United States also supported the creation of a Common Market and the strengthening of Western Europe in hopes of creating a strong commercial partner and a bloc against the Soviet Union. These conditions created a favorable environment and made the concession to the French and the conclusion of the negotiations possible.

FRANCE AND EQUALITY POLICY

France's historic contribution to EU gender policy might appear paradoxical insofar as France was one of the last countries in Europe to give women the right to vote; with the exception of Greece, it still has one of the lowest percentage of women in Parliament among the fifteen member states. Before women acquired the right to vote in 1944, parliament rejected four legislative proposals regarding women's suffrage. The context in which the provisional Parliament in Algiers rejected the last enfranchisement proposal conveys the deputies' attitudes on women's rights. According to French historian Michele Perrot, as late as 1944 a deputy argued that the Parliament ought to wait for the return of the prisoners of war before enfranchising women (Hubert 1998, 47).[4] The reason in support of this delay was that "in the absence of the authority of their natural tutor, women voters would feel distraught" (Perrot quoted in Hubert 1998, 47).[5] French women eventually acquired the right to vote in April 1944 "not by the magnanimity of the legislators of the parliamentary republic but by decree of General Charles de Gaulle" (Offen 1994, 161). The 1946 Constitution of the Fourth Republic provided for equal rights for women, and the 1958 Constitution of the Fifth Republic reconfirmed this provision.

The comparatively late enfranchisement of French women contrasts with the early history of the suffrage movement in France. In 1900 an international congress on women's rights was convened in France, and in 1901 a bill extending municipal and legislative suffrage to unmarried women was introduced in the Chamber of Deputies where it failed (Offen 1994, 158). In 1906, a different bill was proposed aiming to give all adult women the right to vote in municipal and departmental but not national elections. During the inter-war period, the Chamber of Deputies had approved four women's suffrage proposals, all of which were blocked because republican senators believed that enfranchised women might endanger the secular republic, since women were perceived to be Catholic with conservative leanings. The reasons for granting women's enfranchisement in France in 1944 are different from those in countries like the United States and Great Britain where the women's suffrage movement was a strong force for change. French women had organized for the right to vote as early as 1909 with the *Union Française pour le Suffrage des Femmes* (UFSF), which was an affiliate of International Woman's Suffrage Alliance. However, most historians describe women's enfranchisement as a calculated move by General De Gaulle and a result of the unique circumstances faced by the provisional government (Scott 1996, 162). De Gaulle hoped that women's perceived conservative vote would balance the feared domination of the Communists in the new government. Women's suffrage also provided an opportunity for the new government to differentiate itself from the discredited Vichy regime and the Third Republic's failures. France hoped to rehabilitate the legacy left by the Vichy regime by aligning the country with the other Western democracies that had already granted women voting rights. The provisional government also wanted to send a message of unity by overcoming the past institutional struggle between the Chamber of Deputies and the Senate, the main reason why past proposals had failed (Scott 1996, 163).

The very late enfranchisement of French women and the apparent domination of political over feminist concerns in granting women the right to vote contrasts with the image of France as the originator of gender equality legislation in the EU. Following women's enfranchisement, France passed a decree in 1946 striking down the concept of "female salary" (Stetson 1987, 142). The same year, the preamble of the Constitution stated that "the law guarantees to women equal rights with men in all spheres." In 1950, a law required collective bargaining agreements to respect equal pay without, however, imposing any sanctions for unequal pay for the same work. Another law introduced a minimum wage (SMIG) intended to apply equally to men and women. The motives behind these equality provisions are "ambiguous" (Hubert 1998, 53). After the war, the French left had supported a program of reducing poverty and increasing social equality. In their dual role as workers and mothers, women could contribute to the post-war reconstruction. As workers, they could compensate for the labor force shortage and as mothers, they would help to repopulate a country devastated by war (Hoskyns 1996, 54). The French State's dual treatment of women, at once traditional and emancipated, contributes to the "ambiguousness" of the French provisions. Although there was no women's movement pushing for the above reforms, women were active during this period as they participated in the strikes and bread riots of 1946–47 (Hoskyns 1996, 54). Regardless of the motives and the effectiveness of the provisions, the existence of an equal pay requirement at home was sufficient to convince French industrialists to require EU action in this field.[6] However, the negotiations over Article 119 were influenced not only by national but also by international factors. An EU policy that appears at first as innovative and historic in its consequences actually marked a continuation of past institutional legacies at multiple levels of governance.

THE INTERNATIONAL LABOUR ORGANIZATION (ILO) CONVENTION AS THE BACKDROP FOR ARTICLE 119

Most realist and neorealist analyses in international relations dismiss the influence of the United Nations (UN) or other international organizations on public policy at the national or international level. However, the case of the International Labour Organization (ILO) Convention in relation to Article 119 illustrates not only the influence of international institutions on national and regional policy but also the need to study policy at more than one level of analysis. The ILO influenced the adoption of Article 119 of the Rome Treaty both through the 1956 Ohlin Report and through 1951 ILO Convention No. 100. The Report and the Convention influenced the Treaty of Rome negotiations by providing an existing context from which to borrow definitions of and solutions to the problem, draw expertise and resources and serve as an independent arbitrator of the conflict between France and the five other negotiating countries.

The Ohlin Report was named after Bertil Ohlin, a Swedish economist who had also served as Minister of Commerce in Sweden. In early 1955, the ILO asked Ohlin to chair a group of economists to study the social aspects of European economic integration. The report was to address the conflict between the mainly French and the German views over European Community (EC) regulation of divergent social policies. The French position maintained that EC regulation was needed to harmonize indirect labor costs that would otherwise distort competition. The Germans held that there was no need to harmonize indirect labor costs since other factors, such as taxation and productivity also influenced competitiveness (Ostner and Lewis 1995, 162). Published in 1956, the Report reached the conclusion that market forces would settle the existing differences in social costs among member states (Hoskyns 1996, 49; Hubert 1998, 49). The Report's minimalist approach in social affairs supported the German view and was in line with the position of states resistant towards allowing curtailment of their national prerogatives. The report did mention that in specific industrial sectors, EC intervention would nonetheless be needed to correct certain distortions to competition such as unequal pay for men and women as well as paid vacations. The inclusion of unequal pay as an example of potential distortion of competition was "significant" (Hoskyns 1996, 49). It provided the rationale for the Treaty of Rome negotiators in responding to French demands that led to the eventual adoption of Article 119.

Yet, the mention of equal pay in the Ohlin Report was neither accidental nor innovative but rather reflected a continuation of the 1951 ILO Equal Remuneration Convention No. 100. In a historical institutionalist sense, past policies have long-term effects by constraining or facilitating future policies. The debates over the ILO Convention had already familiarized the relevant ministries in each country with debates over equal pay, which in turn, facilitated negotiations over Article 119 (Hoskyns 1996, 54). Interviewed by Hoskyns in 1994, Michel Gaudet, one of the legal drafters of the Treaty of Rome and head of the legal service of ECSC, stated that "the other countries would have not accepted equal pay just because France wanted it. It was already a legitimate issue in the public domain" (Hoskyns 1996, 54).

As early as 1951, the ILO Equal Remuneration Convention had provided for "equal remuneration between male and female workers for work of equal value." The ILO affirmed the principle of equal opportunities[7] in its 1944 Declaration of Philadelphia.[8] The UN's 1948 Universal Declaration of Human Rights likewise included equal pay for men and women. However, the principles for the 1951 ILO Equal Remuneration Convention had been incorporated much earlier into the 1919 preamble of the ILO Constitution. As Kingdon has suggested, one might engage in a pattern of "infinite regress" in trying to find the origins of policies (1984, 77).

Agnès Hubert (1998) refers to Vogel-Polsky's account of how the principle of equal pay came to be included in the ILO Constitution. Eliane Vogel-Polsky was a Belgian women's rights advocate and the lawyer who brought the first equality case before the ECJ in 1968, testing the scope of Article 119. In her research on *tripartisme*[9] in the ILO, Vogel-Polsky herself was unable to determine the reasons for the inclusion of the equal pay provision in its Constitution based on the organization's own documentation. Vogel-Polsky wrote to Marguerite Thibert in search of an answer, since the latter had been present at the 1919 negotiations (Hubert 1998, 51).[10] Thibert was a French militant socialist who had joined the ILO staff in 1926 and established the Women's Service, which she then headed (Lubin and Winslow 1991, 31). She was one of the very few women in policymaking positions during the early days of the ILO. Thibert told the story of how a delegation of trade unionists met with the negotiators and demanded that the principle of equal pay be included in the Constitution. The trade unionists based their demands on the belief that employers, accustomed to female labor during the war, might claim that "work was done equally well by women" and thus downgrade men's salaries upon their return to civil life (Hubert 1998, 51). Thibert's testimony gives the impression that, as was the case with the Treaty of Rome, fear of imbalanced competition was the main reason behind the inclusion of gender equality into the ILO's Constitution.

Many women leaders came to the 1919 Paris Conference to lobby for their own proposals that included the issue of equal pay. Margaret Bondfeld, a British member of the Trades Union Congress (TUC), was instrumental in convincing a delegate of her country, George Barnes, to include women's provisions in the ILO's Constitution (Lubin and Winslow 1991). Barnes was Bondfeld's colleague in the labor movement. The Commission of International Labor Legislation that established the ILO, composed entirely of men, accepted Barne's amendments as proposed by Bondfeld. One amendment required that delegates should have at least one woman advisor when discussing issues regarding women's labor (Article 3 of the ILO Constitution). The other amendment to Article 9 obligated the ILO director to employ women on the organization's staff (Lubin and Winslow 1991, 21; Whitworth 1994, 125).

In addition to Bondfeld, many other women's delegations arrived in Paris to lobby the Conference but "arrived late in the proceedings and submitted a disparate set of demands that lacked focus" (Lubin and Winslow

1991, 21). The International Council of Women (ICW), the Belgian delegate Van Den Ples of the Conference of Allied Women Suffragists, and Americans Mary Anderson and Rose Schneiderman of the National Women's Trade Union League (NWTUL) presented equal pay for equal work proposals (Lubin and Winslow 1991, 21–23) during the Conference. Lubin and Winslow (1991) do not link the women's lobby efforts with the equal pay provision, despite Bondfeld's direct influence on the ILO Constitution. In fact, they do not discuss the inclusion of the "principle that men and women should receive equal remuneration for work of equal value," leaving Thibert's testimony as the only known historical source. However, the two authors very briefly give credit to the women's lobbying for the inclusion in the Constitution of "a system of inspection in which women should take part," referring to the inspection of the equal pay provision (Lubin and Winslow 1991, 1). A multiplicity of similar proposals from different national and international women's organizations regarding equal pay shows that the issue was already creeping onto the public agenda, and was transforming it from a "condition" to a "problem." These proposals might not have had the direct influence Thibert assigns to the unionists' concerns over distortions to competition, but they indirectly influenced the agenda by formulating and publicizing the issue.

The equal pay principle in the ILO Constitution did not materialize until the 1951 Equal Remuneration Convention. This Convention was prepared with the collaboration of the UN Commission on the Status of Women (CSW), established in 1946. The ILO collaborated with the CSW to study women's economic rights and took into consideration the CSW's recommendations regarding the Equal Remuneration Convention (UN 1995, 19).

This understanding of the origins of Article 119 of the Rome Treaty as a basis for future EU gender policy necessitates a regressive journey at multiple levels of analysis: national, regional and international. In order to determine how the condition of women's unequal pay became a problem on the EC's supranational agenda, it was first necessary to situate the Treaty of Rome within the wider European political context and to evaluate the pressures constraining and/or facilitating the negotiations. Second, France's close association with Article 119 links the history of equality policy to the national level. Developments at the international level involve the ILO's role, connecting Article 119 with the Ohlin Report, the Equal Remuneration Convention and the 1919 ILO Constitution. The condition of gender inequality became a public problem amenable to a policy solution. At the international level, a solution was already attached to the problem to produce policy by 1951 (ILO Treaty). At the EU level the problem was still waiting for the appearance of the other two independent streams of policy and politics.

THE POLICY STREAM

Kingdon describes the second stream as a "primeval soup" in which ideas "float around" before a few come to dominate and are then selected for final decision-making (1984, 123). The policy stream metaphor describes "the processes by which proposals are generated, debated, redrafted, and accepted for serious consideration" (Kingdon 1984, 151). Policy proposals are debated within policy communities, defined as loose groupings of expert individuals in a particular policy area. Individuals who advocate specific proposals are labeled policy entrepreneurs (Kingdon 1984, 129).

ADOPTION OF ARTICLE 119

Catherine Hoskyns (1996) describes the process by which the first EU policy solution was attached to the problem of unequal pay in the form of a treaty. Hoskyns has established a chronology of Article 119's textual development by examining the preparatory documents (*travaux préparatoires*) of the Council of Ministers archives (1996, 55).[11] The early draft of the article on equal pay was weak, as it did not obligate states to implement it directly and was considered jointly with other existing differences in social costs among the negotiating countries. By the fall of 1956, equal pay was being examined independently of other social cost provisions and in greater length than occurred in the first draft. The new draft on equal pay mirrored the ILO provisions by requiring equal pay "for equal work and work of equal value by the time the Foreign Affairs Ministers met in October 1956. The new version also imposed a time frame for implementation and directly obligated the states. The negotiators accepted this text and assigned a Committee of Social Experts to finalize it with a reservation regarding the inclusion of the phrase "work of equal value." Hoskyns credits French pressure for this renewed activity in the fall of 1956 and the new draft on equal pay (1996, 56). The publication of the Ohlin Report in the same year must have also strengthened the French position and provided the basis for the new draft.

The text prepared by the Committee of Social Experts differed from the ILO Convention in its exclusion of the phrase "work of equal value." Rather, it followed the ILO definition of pay as encompassing "everything that the employee receives directly or indirectly, whether in cash or in kind"

(Hoskyns 1996, 56). In early February 1957, this version of the text, now named Article 46, was incorporated in a Treaty section dealing with measures distorting competition. Approved by the member-states delegates, it was adopted on February 20, 1957. Final adoption was modified when Article 46 was later renamed Article 119 and was transferred from the "Distortions to Competition" section to the "Social Policy" section of the Treaty.

Despite her careful reconstruction of the chronology of Article 119's adoption, Hoskyns was unable to find documents explaining this sudden development (1996, 57). The author suggests that pressure exercised on the coordinator of the Treaty negotiations Spaak might explain the sudden transfer of Article 119 (Hoskyns 1996, 57). In January 1957, Spaak had received a delegation of labor organizations and ECSC Assembly members asking for worker involvement in Community decision-making and for strengthening social policy in the Treaty (Hoskyns 1996, 48). This intervention seems to be at the origin of Article 117 as part of a distinct social policy title. Article 117, as adopted, promotes "improved working conditions and improved standards of living for workers" while favoring "the harmonization of social systems." In addition to Article 117, Hoskyns maintains that it is "likely" that the transfer of Article 119 is explained "by the need to strengthen the social policy section after the pressures on Spaak" (1996, 57). Article 101 replaced the section on competition distortion[12] and assigned to the Commission responsibility for dealing with these matters.

POLICY DEVELOPMENTS AFTER ARTICLE 119

"Article 119 undoubtedly provided EC policy-makers and the women's lobby with a necessary juridical hook on which to hang their demands for further EC sex equality legislation" (Mazey 1998, 138). This juridical base in the Treaty represented a potential source for expanding gender policy given favorable circumstances in the political stream. As primary legislation, treaties offer a source and a justification for the development of secondary legislation such as Directives. Directives are one of the legal instruments allowing the EU to make binding decisions, rendering objectives compulsory but leaving it up to the member states to translate them into national legislation. Directives are defined as "means to a goal" (Ostner and Lewis 1995, 158) and must be based on a specific treaty article in order to justify action.

To what extend did Article 119 provide the "necessary juridical hook" that Mazey (1998, 138) and others studying the history of EU gender equality policy present it to be? Although Article 119 has become the reference for many European Court of Justice (ECJ) gender equality cases, it has not supplied the direct basis for most equality Directives. In the period 1975–92, all Directives but one[13] were based either on Article 100 (Equal Pay Directive) or Article 235 (Equal Treatment and Social Security Directives). A combination of Articles 100 and 235 provided the basis for the 1986 Directives on Occupational Social Security and on the Self-employed. Article 100 allows for the development of secondary legislation for subjects concerning the functioning of the common market. Article 235, known as the "everything else" clause (Mushaben 1994 10), allows action in order to meet "unforeseen needs." Since the adoption of the Maastricht Treaty, three Directives have been justified in terms of the Social Protocol (on Parental Leave, Burden of Proof and Part-time Work). The open-ended provisions of Articles 100 and, especially, 235 make it possible for even issues ignored in the establishing Treaty to be introduced in future amendments. One example is secondary legislation addressing environmental issues, introduced for the first time under Article 235 in 1972. It was not until the 1987 that environmental issues were given a treaty base (Article 130) by way of the Single European Act (SEA). The environmental case suggests that had Article 119 not been adopted at the outset, gender equality issues could have emerged on the EU agenda based on Article 235.

The fact that Article 119 lay dormant for more than a decade shows that the mere presence of a legal or a juridical tool does not necessarily translate into policy implementation and expansion. The lack of implementation also shows that the context in which "conditions" came to be defined as "problems" affects the chances of a problem and a proposal becoming a successful policy. As mentioned in the discussion of Article 119's origins, the domination of economic and tactical concerns and the lack of consideration regarding women's interests compromised the impact of the Article in the short term. The period between Article 119's inclusion in the 1958 Treaty and the adoption of the first gender directive in 1975 was not favorable for implementation and further policy development. Not all the "independent streams" in the policy process were present or sufficiently "coupled" to produce policy change.

Article 119 did not spark further policy expansion at the supranational level until the 1975 Equal Pay Directive (EPD). The only exception to this period of inactivity regarding women's issues is the 1967 Medium Term Economic Programme (MTEP), which merely "encouraged" women to enter the labor force. At the national level, however, Article 119 inspired two cases originating in Belgium.[14] First, Vogel-Polsky sought to test the application of Article 119 by initiating the landmark *Defrenne* cases in 1968. The court history of the first EU gender equality case spanned an entire decade, starting with the first case in 1968 and lasting until 1978 with a ruling on the final case. Gabrielle Defrenne, an airhostess with the Belgian airlines, Sabena, was forced at the age of forty to change jobs within the company at a loss of income; such policies did not apply to men. During the ten-year period, Vogel-Polsky prepared three separate cases of which she won only the second. The first (Defrenne 1) raised the issue of unequal pensions, the second (Defrenne 2) attacked lower wages based on gender-specific jobs, and the third (Defrenne 3) addressed working conditions and retirement age. It was in the 1976 *Defrenne 2* decision that the ECJ established the "direct effect" of Article 119; this means that "Article 119 could be invoked by individuals against the State (direct vertical effect) as well as against individuals (direct horizontal effect)" (EP 1998, 9).

The second case is one of the first indications of the "Europeanisation of political processes" (Hoskyns 1996, 65). Women in a Belgian arms factory in Herstal went on strike demanding equal pay in 1966. Given that Belgium had not taken measures for translating Article 119 into national legislation by mid-1966, the Herstal strikers based their demands on EC legislation. Hubert (1998, 62) and Hoskyns (1996, 67) refer to the placards used during the demonstrations demanding the "application of Article 119," as the first visual manifestation of the Europeanization of national policies.[15]

The Herstal strike and the *Defrenne* cases in Belgium did not, in the short-term, inspire hosts of lawyers, activists or trade unionists in other member states to take advantage of European law to improve national conditions. The isolated nature of the Belgian incidents, the absence of broader policy directives until 1975, and the possibility that Article 235 could, hypothetically, have allowed EU legislation at a later stage, tend to decrease the importance assigned to Article 119. However, in the legislative arena Article 119's significance was not in serving as the direct foundation for the equality Directives but in placing the issue on the European agenda, legitimizing the problem, providing solutions, and strengthening the position of policy initiators. Article 119 set the framework within which the 1970s Directives would be negotiated and adopted.

THE 1970S DIRECTIVES AND THE POLICY STREAM

In tracing the origins of Article 119, I have shown that ideas and proposals for equal pay in Europe date back, at least, to the 1919 ILO Constitution. The first of the 1970s gender Directives to expand Article 119 also finds its roots in the 1951 ILO Equal Remuneration Convention. The 1975 Equal Pay Directive (EPD) shares the same language with the ILO Convention by referring not only to "equal pay for equal work" but also to "work of equal value." The proposal for "work for equal value" was "floating around" during the Treaty of Rome negotiations but it did not succeed in attaching itself to the proposed solution. Still, the idea remained in the "primeval soup" to resurface in the 1970s and the negotiations over the Equal Pay Directive (EPD).

As was the case with the EPD, proposal ideas for preparing the Equal Treatment Directive (ETD) have their origins in the work of other international organizations. From the mid-1960s onward, the Organization for Economic Co-operation and Development (OECD) as well as the Council of Europe, began comparing sex-segregated statistics, analyzing trends and publishing reports on the subject of female employment (Klein 1965; Kok 1967; OECD 1970; Hoskyns 1996, 26). In addition to initiating research and analysis, these organizations created a group of expert women whose knowledge of the subject would later be used to influence national and EU policies. One of these experts was French sociologist Evelyn Sullerot (1968) whose work on the *History and Sociology of Female Work* was influential in two ways. First, Sullerot's work drew attention to the neglected subject of women's paid and unpaid work, contributing to an expanding pool of ideas and proposals. Second, her work established her as an authority in the subject, an expert that institutions in need of information on women's policy could consult (Hoskyns 1996, 26). In 1968, the Commission asked Sullerot to investigate women's employment in the then six member states. Her report published in 1970, introduced recommendations for women's policy going beyond equal pay (Sullerot 1970). The use of concepts such as "the structural nature of women's disadvantage" (Hoskyns 1996, 84), job segregation, and reconciliation of work and family enriched the "policy primeval soup," contributing to the development and definition of policies that would have been unthinkable during the first decade of the EC. It was no longer sufficient to address pay equity only once women entered the labor force. The emphasis on structural discrimination drew attention to obstacles and barriers that prevented women from entering the labor force; "the strong emphasis on barriers to women's participation in the labour market" influenced and shaped the policies of both the EC and the OECD (Hoskyns 1996, 30). The new emphasis found concrete expression in the 1976 ETD that prohibits sex discrimination in "access to employment, vocational training, promotion and working conditions."

THE WOMEN'S POLICY COMMUNITY

According to Kingdon's policy stream framework, individuals such as Sullerot participate in, and debate their proposals within, a community loosely organized around a particular policy area. The community focusing on women's policy was still in its infancy in the late 1960s and the first half of the 1970s, the period when the first two directives were debated and adopted. During this phase of development, the policy community appears to have been composed of a group of dedicated individuals, not of organized groups and institutional entities.

The main structures for gender issues in the Commission—the Equal Opportunities Unit (originally named the Women's Bureau) in DG V and the Women's Information Service in DG X—were not established until 1976. There was, therefore, no gender-specific institutional structure during the negotiations for the first two strong directives. Non-governmental groups, another potentially important element of a policy community, were also missing during this period. Many women's organizations were already active at the national level at the time; however, such groups either rejected the mainstream EC institutions or were substantially unaware as to the possibilities offered at the supranational level (interview with Seeland).[16] The only women's organization active at the EC level at the time was the Women's Organization for Equality (WOE), more of a "consciousness-raising" group founded in 1971 (Hoskyns 1996, 130). The group's EC-institutional focus did not develop until 1978 with the rise of a WOE's subgroup, the Women's European Action Group (WEAG).

Despite the lack of specific institutional structures and organized groups addressing women's policies at the EC level, dedicated individuals succeeded in influencing the agenda during this early period. These individuals were able to channel their activities and influence policy by taking advantage of access points in the existing institutional structure. For example, the Commission facilitated institutional access to individuals by inviting experts to participate in consulting as hoc committees. Jacqueline Nonon was one important member of the nascent policy community. From her position at DG V, Nonon organized the Ad Hoc Group on Women's Work and influenced its composition. The Commission's DG V formed this group, which was composed of national representatives whose task was to prepare the ETD. She "used her influence" to make sure that the individuals nominated by the members states would be women interested in the issues (Hoskyns 1996, 101). Nonon further influenced the agenda by using an existing institutional practice, the formation of ad hoc groups, to facilitate the introduction of women's perspectives into the ETD draft.

Outside the formal institutions, lawyer Eliane Vogel-Polsky, trade unionist Emilienne Brunfaut and sociologist Evelyne Sullerot participated in the women's policy community by structuring their activities through existing institutions. Perhaps Eliane Vogel-Polsky could best fit Kingdon's description of a policy entrepreneur; policy entrepreneurs are "advocates for proposals" and found not only in governmental settings but also in interest groups and research organizations (Kingdon 1984, 129). The defining characteristic of policy entrepreneurs is "their willingness to invest their resources-time, energy reputation, and sometimes money-in the hope of a future return" (Kingdon 1984, 129). As the lawyer of the landmark *Defrenne* cases, Vogel-Polsky "invested" a lot of her resources in actively seeking a test case for Article 119. Her individual traits, her enthusiasm and tenacity over a ten-year court saga were crucial in opening the ECJ doors to other cases and thus to influencing legislation. Vogel-Polsky carefully organized her action in order to take advantage of the EC's institutional structure. She utilized the mechanism of preliminary ruling to allow a change of venue from national courts to the ECJ. She recognized that given the supremacy of EC law, a verdict by the supranational ECJ could enforce changes of national law. A cabinet member of the Employment Minister Ernest Glinne, Vogel-Polsky represented Belgium in the Ad Hoc Group on Women's Work in 1974. Influential in proposing a draft directive that combined both equal opportunities and special treatment for women (Hoskyns 1996, 102), she structured her independent contribution to women's rights within the institutional framework of the Commission. It was the Ad Hoc Group that gave to advocates like Vogel-Polsky the opportunity to "mainstream" their policy proposals.

While Vogel-Polsky "used" the Ad Hoc Group, Belgian trade unionist Emilienne Brunfaut influenced the EC agenda, and specifically the drafting of the EPD, through the "Article 119" group. In 1966, Brunfaut had worked for the Herstal women, the first strike to demand the application of EU gender equality law. She also became the permanent representative for Belgium in the "Article 119" group, set up by the Commission in 1961 to examine the implementation of Article 119. The group continued to meet and was later consulted in the preparation for the EPD directive. During the first stage, the Commission prepares a draft directive after consulting with "expert" groups and committees such as the "Article 119" group. According to Hoskyns (1996, 88), Brunfaut and the other trade unionists were instrumental in introducing "work of equal value" in the EPD. The Commission still loyal to its 1958 definition of equal pay did not include "work for equal value" in the draft EPD. Formal institutions such as the Commission structured the participation of the larger policy community with the result that outside experts were allowed to enrich the "primeval soup" and influence policy definition at the initial stage of the policy process.

Sullerot's participation in the policy community was also structured through EC institutions. Recall that the Commission had asked Sullerot in 1968 to write a report on women's employment and also solicited policy recommendations once the report was published in 1970. At this stage, Sullerot consulted with Nonon, a cooperation that reveals the interconnections of institutional and non-institutional actors of the policy community (Hoskyns 1996, 100). As a result of their cooperation, the 1971 social policy guidelines referred to women's work that went beyond the narrow confines of equal pay (Hoskyns 1996, 100).

THE POLITICS STREAM

In Kingdon's depiction of the policy process, ideas float around in a "policy primeval soup" until they find the opportunity to couple with the "political stream" (1984, 21). Entrepreneurs in the policy community attempt to couple problems and policy proposals; policy change is more likely when the "independent stream" of politics joins the other two streams of "problems" and "policies" (Kingdon 1984, 20). The politics stream is "composed of such things as public mood, pressure group campaigns, election results, partisan or ideological distributions in Congress and changes of administration" (Kingdon 1984, 152).

In the late 1960s and early 1970s, the political stream was composed of many of the elements identified in the above definition. During this period, many member states experienced a change of government and partisan or ideological distributions in legislatures. In Germany, the Social Democrats came to power in 1969 with the new Chancellor Willy Brandt bringing a new social policy perspective. In the same year in France, De Gaulle retired and was succeeded by Pompidou. Although both the Pompidou government in France and the Heath government in Britain were conservative, their commitment to Europe meant that they were willing to compromise on certain EC issues. De Gaulle's retirement also resulted in the opening of negotiations with three EC applicant countries, Denmark, Britain and Ireland. At the 1972 Paris Summit, Brandt, Pompidou and Heath showed a "strong commitment to a renewed social policy" (Hoskyns 1996, 80). In this "new context for social policy" (Hoskyns 1996, 879), the leaders of the summit asked the Commission to prepare a social initiative which resulted in the 1974 Social Action Programme (SAP).

"Agendas are changed because some of the major participants change" (Kingdon 1984, 160). At the institutional level, additional personnel from the three new EC member states arrived at the Commission in 1973. At DG V, Irish Patrick Hillery became Commissioner, with British Michael Shanks as the Director-General. This change in the top hierarchy of DG V was significant since the newcomers' lack of experience with EC affairs meant that they "came with much less baggage" (Hoskyns 1996, 81). Working at DG V at the time, Nonon confirms Hoskyns' evaluation of the effect of the new leadership in DG V. Nonon recognized the role of the new "Anglo-Saxon" hierarchy in women's policy development, in breaking away from traditionalist practices in Brussels and introducing a new style of administration (1998, 5).

Favorable conditions in the political stream facilitated the adoption of the first two directives in the early 1970s; one such condition, the change of the major participants also assisted the approval of the Social Security Directive (SSD). Although by 1977 a draft had already been prepared, the arrival of Dutch socialist Henk Vredeling as Commissioner for Social Affairs was an important development for the SSD's success. Before becoming Commissioner, Vredeling had been a member of the European Parliament (MEP); in 1968, he had submitted motions at the EP regarding the women's strike at Herstal. Vredeling "went out of his way to support further EC legislation in favor of women" (Hoskyns 1996,76). Former Dutch member of parliament (MP) Nel Barendreght became Vredeling's *chef de cabinet*. With past experience as an advocate and campaigner on equal pay issues, Barendreght supported the Commissioner's interest in women's issues in general, and the SSD in particular (Hoskyns 1996, 110).

In the late 1960s and early 1970s, the government changes in Germany and France and new administration at the Commission coincided with the presence of another element of the politics stream, the rise of pressure group campaigns. The feminist movement in all the member countries initiated a strong pressure group campaign to demand policy changes in all aspects of life. "Feminist ideas, values and policy demands constituted a major, new challenge to long-established, cultural attitudes and traditions" (Mazey 1998, 131).

EU GENDER POLICY DEVELOPMENTS AND INTERNATIONAL REGIMES

The development of EU policy instruments and the actions of relevant policy actors took place in a context of global developments. The combination of activities within states, as well as within regional and international organizations, suggests the establishment of what Krasner has defined as a regime: "principles, norms, rules and decision making procedures" (Krasner 1983, 2). Principles of equality and norms of justice expressed in UN or ILO treaties, the creation of institutional structures, and the organization of international conferences point to the beginning of an international women's rights regime.

Demands of the national feminist movements did not rise independently of international developments. National, regional and global policies do not develop in isolation of each other. Women's mobilization at the national level was concurrent not only with the passage of the first two EU Directives but also with the UN Decade of Women and the UN Women's Conference in Mexico City in 1975. In 1972, the UN's Commission on the Status of Women (CSW) was instrumental in proclaiming 1975 as the International Women's Year (IWY); the years 1975 to 1985 became the UN Decade for Women, complemented by the first World Conference for Women held in Mexico in 1975. According to Tinker and Jacquette, the combination of these activities contributed to elevating women's issues "to the level of international diplomacy" (1987, 419).

The almost simultaneous developments at the national, EC, and international level were not coincidental. Given the large number of states participating in the Conference and the visibility of the event, governments felt obliged to portray their countries positively, however symbolic their proposals for women's rights appeared. The trend of states preparing "showpiece" policies (Baldez 1997, 46) for the purpose of presenting them in international conferences has continued in the 1980s and 1990s including the most recent 1995 UN Women's Conference in Beijing. Among most member nations, "UN activities led to increased mobilization among women, heightened visibility of women's issues and the announcement of policy initiatives to address women's concerns" (Baldez 1997, 24).

Britain is one example where national "showpiece" policies concerning women have been developed in the context of international conferences. Many British Members of Parliament (MPs) saw the passage of the Sex Discrimination Act in 1975 as a publicity event designed specifically for the International Women's Year (Gelb 1989).[17] At the EU, the International Women's Year caused a "certain sense of urgency" (Hoskyns 1996, 86); the Directives were "timed to coincide with the 1975 United Nation's Year of the Woman" (Warner 1984, 150). In a 1984 interview with Hoskyns, Nonon was "insistent upon the importance" of the UN activities in the passing of the first two gender directives: "It would be useful for the EC to have 'something to say' at the [UN] inaugural conference" (Hoskyns 1996, 95).

THE 1970S PUNCTUATION

These developments in the political stream facilitated the joining of the three independent streams that, in turn, triggered policy change (Kingdon 1984, 174). The UN events may have "opened" the "policy window" that allowed problems, policies and politics to join together: "a window opens because of change in the political stream" (Kingdon 1984, 174). Although other factors in the politics stream may have contributed to change, concurrent changes in women's policies all over the world, from Australia to Europe and Canada seems to be responsible, at the very least, for the timing of the changes.

While Kingdon (1984) uses the merging of the three streams to describe the process of agenda accessing and agenda setting, Baumgardner and Jones (1993) viewed change in the American policy process as a punctuated equilibrium. Punctuations, also described as "waves of enthusiasm," "bursts," or "spasms of change" are preceded and followed by apparent equilibria (Baumgardner and Jones 1993, 3).

The 1970s are considered as the years of "intensification" with regard to EU gender policy (Hoskyns 1996a, 17) due to the passage of the three strong directives (EPD, ETD and SSD) and the establishment of the direct effect for Article 119. The first Directive on equal pay (75/117) redefines and extends the principles of Article 119. The second Directive, the Equal Treatment Directive (ETD, 76/207) sought to redress job segregation and discrimination by sex from the time workers enter the labor force. It was issued to address inequality in recruitment, promotion and training. The third Directive (79/7) concerns statutory social security schemes covering sickness, invalidity, occupational diseases, working accidents, and unemployment. Retirement age and survivor's benefits are not included. The third Social Security Directive (79/7) is the last of a string of policy instruments developed during the punctuation or the "stream coupling" period in the 1970s.

In addition to policies, new institutional structures are created during the period of change and then "settle into a period of incrementalism" (Baumgardner and Jones 1993, 5). Although Baumgardner and Jones view equilibria in political systems as rare, they accept that stability and incrementalism can follow periods of change (1993, 15).

PUNCTUATION AND INSTITUTIONAL CREATION

The punctuation of the 1970s, the period starting with the proclamation of IWY in 1972 and culminating with the Mexico Conference in 1975, resulted in a "process of institutionalization of women's rights" (Hubert 1998, 70) at the national, regional and international levels. Once created, the new institutional structures are preserved "structuring further participation, creating apparent equilibria that can be changed only by changing the institutions themselves" (Baumgartner and Jones 1993, 238). Following the 1975 Mexico Conference, women's ministries were established in some countries, and in others offices were created within existing ministries (Social Affairs or Labor). At the international level, women's centers were attached to the UN Regional Economic Commissions in Africa, Latin America, Asia and the Pacific, Europe and the Middle East. Women's concerns were also pursued within national agencies for development. Following the 1973 Foreign Assistance Act, USAID created the agency of Women In Development (WID). Other development agencies followed the American initiative, such as the Commonwealth Secretariat. UN resolutions also created women's offices within most UN agencies such as the World Bank, UNESCO, ILO and FAO. Following UN resolutions passed at the Mexico Conference, two new agencies were created within the UN system: the Voluntary Fund for the Decade of Women (now UNIFEM) and the International Institute for the Advancement of Women (INSTRAW).

For EC countries, the 1970s were also a time of change for women's rights with many countries establishing equal opportunities institutions and passing relevant legislation. Among the member states, in 1975 alone, Belgium, Denmark, France, Germany, the Netherlands and the U.K. created institutions and/or passed legislation for women. Institutional creation was followed in Denmark with the establishment of the Equal Status Council and in the U.K. with the Equal Opportunities Commission. A year earlier, Ireland's Anti-discrimination Act set up Equality Officers in the Labour Court. In the legislative arena, Belgium passed a decree making equal pay binding on all employers. France passed an equal treatment law addressing hiring, dismissal and protection of pregnant workers. In Germany, a judgment of the Federal Constitutional Court required the improvement of women's pensions within the next decade. Ireland and the Netherlands passed Equal Pay Acts, and the U.K. adopted a Sex Discrimination Act.

EC-LEVEL INSTITUTIONAL CREATION

A year after the Mexico Conference, the Commission acquired two structures dedicated entirely to women: the Equal Opportunities Unit in DG V
and the Women's Information Service in DG X. The Equal Opportunities
Unit (then called Women's Bureau) was established in 1976 with Nonon as
its first head. Nonon was personally dedicated to improving women's status,
a tradition that subsequent heads of the Unit, such as Agnès Hubert, continued. Although the Equal Opportunities Unit has a policymaking role, its
position is not very high in the Commission's hierarchy. Both Nonon and
Hubert left their posts for higher positions although they remained involved
with gender equality issues. Unlike the DG X's Women's Information
Service, personnel of the Equal Opportunities Unit are specialists in gender
issues, and some are hired as "national experts." These women are very quick
to identify themselves as interested in the issues. They distinguish themselves from career administrators who change positions across different
departments not necessarily because of their substantive interest in the issues
in which they are involved (interview with Havnoer). The department was
originally assigned to monitor implementation of the Equal Treatment
Directive (ETD), changes in the European Social Fund (ESF) and to design
future policies. Its workload has increased steadily with each new policy proposal for directives and other secondary legislation. Its budget and personnel
have also increased dramatically, especially in the first part of the 1990s. In
the period 1992–95, its budget grew from 4.8 million ECUS to 8.5 million,
and its personnel expanded from a staff of 15 to 25 persons (Hubert 1998,
79).

The second institutional creation within the Commission is the
Women's Information Service, established in 1976 to disseminate information about women's policy and the EU to women in the member states.
Fausta Deshormes was responsible for setting up the Service in DG X and
publishing the newsletter *Women of Europe*. She attributes the decision to
organize such a structure "to the echoes caused" by the 1975 International
Women's Year, coupled with "requests from women's associations and the
women's press" (Deshormes 1992, 51). In 1987, the Women's Information
Service was associated with the unit providing information to two other
social groups, trade unions and young people. More than twenty years after
its creation, the task of the service remains the same: "Although women are
an integral part of the society, they still need extra help because for various
reasons they are not as well informed as men. So we are making an extra

effort to ensure women's access to information in the same way as men access information" (interview with Pau).

The Information Service was originally assigned—and still possesses—a very small staff, and its position was quite low in the DG X hierarchy. The staff's qualifications lie more in the field of communication and information, not in the area of women's issues *per se*. Despite many public proclamations of the need to inform Europe's women, the Service has remained under-staffed and neglected (interview with Pau). Had it been adequately staffed and provided with sufficient resources from the outset, this Service might have influenced women's opinion of the EU and averted some of the nega-tive and national referenda on European integration.

Informing European women became more important after the discov-ery of a gender gap in support of European integration: "1994 apparently was the year of the gender gap in Europe" (Liebert 1997, 1). Norwegian women campaigned against the entry of their country in the EU. As a result of a 1994 referendum, Norway did not become an EU member. In the same year, women in the other applicant countries—Sweden, Finland, and Austria—mobilized against entry into the EU. In 1992, the first Danish ref-erendum failed to ratify the Maastricht Treaty, with 44% of women voting against and 21% abstaining. In France, the Maastricht referendum approved the Treaty with only a very slight majority (55% of women younger than 35 years old voted no) and after the government had invested considerable resources in influencing public opinion in favor of ratification. In Switzerland, 60% of women voted against entry in the European Economic Area (EEA). A 1994 Eurobarometer (EB) opinion poll showed that "gender disparities" in support of the EU were higher than 10% in five countries: Denmark, Greece, Norway, Sweden and France, (Liebert 1997, 2). Disparities in other member states ranged between 7–10%. Spain and the Netherlands were the only countries where men and women's support did not differ greatly. A 1996 EB survey on support for equal opportunities showed that a minority of the respondents had any knowledge of EU and national equality measures (EB 1997). This disparity exists despite the fact that equal opportunity policies count among the most developed of EU social policies.

A DG X official confirmed that "the results of the Maastricht ratifica-tion and the reaction of European citizens were a bit of a shock" (interview with Pau). The DG X official observed: "the institutions realized that the cit-izens needed to be consulted and that the Union cannot work without the participation of the citizens. They developed more policies for communica-tion, information, transparency and access to information" (interview with

Pau). It appears that the Commission, at least in terms of information, did not take seriously the signals sent by European women. The staff of this service remains small, only three persons, and the resources minimal (interview with Pau). Unlike many of the Equal Opportunities (EO) Unit's staff in DG V who identify themselves as feminists and who have a personal interest in women's rights, the personnel in the Women's Information Service are communications professionals (interview with Stratigaki).

INCREMENTALISM AND THE 1980S

With the new "venues" in place, the 1979 passage of the Social Security Directive (SSD) signaled the end of the punctuation and the "de-coupling" of Kingdon's independent streams. The 1980s are generally described as "hard times" for EU women's policies (Hoskyns 1996a 18). The development of new policies concerning women was blocked in a context of high unemployment, deregulation, government cuts and an expansive service sector requiring a "flexible" workforce. In 1979, conservative Margaret Thatcher was elected prime minister in Britain and remained in power for a decade marking a new era in British and European politics. Thatcher gave her name to the political ideology known as Thatcherism that referred to limited government intervention in the economy and society, belief in market forces as a cure to economic difficulties, privatization, and strong foreign policy. Thatcher curtailed social policy development both in Britain and at the EC.

However, the institutional structures created during the years of expansion helped to maintain and preserve past acquisitions (interview with Seeland). The two directives born of this period did not actually address new issues but rather concerns inherited from past policies. Just as the SSD addressed issues raised with the *Defrenne* 1 case, a new 1986 directive on occupational social security schemes covered issues raised by the 1979 SSD. As historical institutionalists might expect, policies have a feedback effect (Evans *et al.* 1985; March and Olsen 1989): "Social processes...generate elaborate feedback loops and interaction effects." These feedback effects of policies intervene to alter the outcome intended by decisionmakers thus questioning the intergovernmentalist premise that policy outcomes are the direct result of member state preferences.

The new 1986 equality Directive (86/378)[18] addresses private occupational pension schemes, an issue that was specifically left out of the 1979 SSD which only covered statutory schemes. The second directive of 1986 (86/613)[19] concerned equal treatment of the self-employed, such as women working in family enterprises as "assisting spouses" or women in agriculture. The self-employed directive focused on sectors of the work force not covered by the 1976 ETD and the 1979 SSD.

With the exception of the two 1986 directives which partly complemented 1970s policies, the rest of the period is characterized by non-binding resolutions and recommendations, as well as blocked Commission proposals. Resolutions are "statements of principle" that the Council of Ministers can adopt on the recommendation of the Commission. Recommendations can be adopted by EU institutions to express their views and preferences. Neither is legally binding on member states. Over the 1980s, Council of Ministers resolutions to promote equal opportunities approved the first and second Action Programmes (APs) in 1982 and 1986.[20] The Action Programmes on equal opportunities are means for proposing and monitoring policy initiatives, supporting research and networking (Hoskyns 1996, 142). The Equal Opportunities Unit in the Commission coordinates these types of multiannual programs. Throughout the 1980s, other resolutions targeted female unemployment (1984), equal opportunities in education (1985), and the reintegration of women into working life (1988).[21] The Council adopted one recommendation on promoting positive action in 1984 and the Commission announced one on women's vocational training in 1987.[22]

The embrace of non-binding policy instruments contrasts with the failure of other Directive proposals. Commission proposals on part-time work (1981), parental leave (1983), the implementation of social security schemes (1987), and burden of proof (1988) were not approved by the Council.[23] A proposal for a mere non-binding resolution on sharing family and occupational responsibilities (1989)[24] also failed to secure approval. In the 1980s, the U.K. opposed and used its veto to reject all social policy proposals. Other countries might have opposed the parental leave directive and other social policy provisions. However, it is likely that the U.K.'s systematic veto conceals other member states' opposition: "several governments, including the U.K., were on the record as determined to block any legislation which interfered with the rights if employers or attempted to regulate the labour market" (Rutheford 1989, 309). The U.K. was the only country to veto the Parental Leave Directive, but Belgium and the Netherlands also voiced their opposition. The 1980s' unfavorable climate and the definition of family issues as outside EU prerogatives combined to prevent gender policy development.

Despite the negative climate of the 1980s for the development of EC gender policy, the Commission continued to prepare a steady stream of proposals. Although many proposals were blocked, and others were passed only on a non-binding basis, the Commission managed to sustain what has been achieved, defend against any backlash and to build a base for future expansion. It was the institutional structure that kept the interest in gender policies alive, at a time when the feminist movement in Europe was considered to have "gone underground" (Hoskyns 1996a, 18).

POLICY COMMUNITY-1980s

For most of the decade (1982–90), Odile Quintin headed the DG V's Equal Opportunities Unit. Quintin focused on building support for gender policies by establishing networks of experts, such as the "law network," as a source of information, consultation and research. In contrast to the earlier policy community in the 1960s-1970s, composed mostly of committed individuals, the 1980s saw the emergence of a larger organization-based community. The Commission created support by funding the creation of European organizations in addition to the networks of experts. In 1983, the European Network of Women (ENOW) was established, thanks to a DG V grant awarded to another group, the Center for Research on European Women (CREW) for that purpose.

This decade saw the creation of two gender-specific institutional structures at the Commission and the European Parliament (EP). Within the Commission, the DG V's Advisory Committee on Equal Opportunities was established in 1981; it was composed of representatives from national equal opportunities agencies. The EP's Ad Hoc Committee on Women's Rights was set up soon after the first direct elections in 1979 that resulted in the increase of female representation from 5% to 16%. Simone Veil's election as the EP's President combined with the increasing presence of female MEPs, created a favorable environment for the creation of the Committee. As minister of health in the French government, Veil had been the sponsor of the 1974 abortion bill named after her (*La Loi Veil*). The Ad Hoc Committee became a permanent committee in 1984 and has increasingly become a strong policy actor both as an institution and as a venue to individual MEPs.

Socialist Yvette Roudy became the first chair of the Women's Rights Committee. Roudy's subsequent career is an illustration of the increasingly close ties of the women's policy community that blends national and European level policy actors. In the 1960s, Roudy founded a feminist group of non-communist women of the left, which later merged with the Socialist Party. Roudy acquired European level experience first as an MEP and later as a cabinet member representing France in the Council of Ministers. She participated in the Council in her capacity as a Minister of Women Rights, a position she acquired with the 1981 socialist victory in France. As a Council member, Roudy was influential in the passage of the Resolution that approved the Action Programme 1 (AP1) (Hoskyns 1996, 144). At the same time Roudy was contributing to EU policy, she was working on drafting an equal employment law for women in France that became known in 1983 as *La loi Roudy*. The Ministry of Women's Rights also organized training and educational programs for girls. Mazur considers the impact of Roudy's reforms in France as "symbolic" (1995, 88). However, the focus on employ-ment reveals that European and French developments were not developing in isolation. In the same year that Roudy influenced her European colleagues in the Council of Ministers in passing the first Action Programme (AP), she was developing French policy borrowing or sharing "discourse" used in the European arena. Her combined experiences at the European and national levels contributed to loosening the barriers perceived to surround national social policies.

Individuals such as Roudy, newly founded European organizations such as ENOW, and institutional structures in DG V and the EP sustained a certain level of attention to gender policy in the "cold climate" of the 1980s (Hoskyns 1996, 140). Non-binding policy instruments such as the AP1 were important in providing the "policy primeval soup" with ideas; with a shift to favorable conditions in the other "policy streams," these ideas would eventu-ally inform and influence the agenda. Many of the policies introduced with the first AP were to find more concrete development in the next decade. The AP1 embodied the ETD's legacy in combining special and equal treatment for women by addressing positive action, vocational choices and desegrega-tion of the labor market. It introduced new issues, such as the impact of new technology on women and policies affecting immigrant women, and also contained unsuccessful proposals such as the parental leave directive. More than a provider of policy ideas for future development, the first AP was important in providing a policy model to emulate. Subsequent programs continued to be characterized by a multi-annual engagement of member states, pre-defined objectives and integration of lessons learned from earlier programs. Following the first and second AP, programs were also approved in 1991[25] and 1995 for five-year periods.

THE 1990S: FROM INCREMENTALISM TO A NEW PUNCTUATION?

Policy development in the first part of the 1990s continued to resemble the 1980s with the incremental passage of non-binding recommendations and resolutions. However, past policies embedded in the Action Programmes expanded the repertoire of women's issues beyond those strictly associated with the labor market. This gradual expansion of EU gender policy to include non-market related issues has also occurred in regard to citizenship rights (Wiener 1999). The 1993 Maastricht Treaty has incorporated specific political rights for EU citizens that do not depend on the individual's capacity as a worker. Since the ratification of the Maastricht Treaty, EU citizens have rights of residency, free movement, petition, diplomatic protection and the right to vote and stand as candidates in municipal and European Parliament (EP) elections in their state of residence. Wiener characterized this evolution in citizenship policy as "a change from market citizen, or *bourgeois* to EU citizen, or *citoyen*" (1999, 142).

With an expanded repertoire of women issues, the second part of the decade was a period of intense policy development, suggesting the appearance of a new period of punctuation and the joining of the problem, policy and politics streams. The problems and policies of the 1980s took advantage of new institutional rules and favorable developments in the politics stream. The rejected Commission proposals of the 1980s were successfully re-introduced resulting in a series of directives in the second part of the 1990s. This new period has the potential to trigger major institutional reforms that could drastically change the framework for gender policy through the mechanism of mainstreaming.

INCREMENTALISM AND ISSUE EXPANSION

Most women's rights advocates do not consider Action Programmes (APs) as important as directives (interview with Seeland). However, the AP funding of research and projects provided a "venue" to actors in the wider policy community and allowed women's perspectives on issues to appear on the EU agenda. These issues included new and old concerns of the women's movement, such as childcare, pregnancy, and sexual harassment. The issue of childcare appeared on the EU agenda with the creation of a network by the Equal Opportunities Unit. The European Childcare Network's efforts resulted in a comparative report of childcare in the member states (Moss 1988). Article 119's market-oriented legacy and the employment focus of EC gender legislation constrained and directed this report. This report concentrated on finding out whether different practices in the member states "disadvantaged certain groups of women and prevented the emergence of a fair labor market" (Hoskyns 1996, 156). Although the report did not lead to a directive, the Council adopted a Childcare Recommendation in 1992.[26]

Sexual harassment was a relatively new issue on the European agenda and was not defined as a policy "problem" until the 1980s. In 1983, the British Trade Union Congress published a sexual harassment code and the Industrial Tribunal tried the first case dealing with the issue. At the EC level, the Council's 1984 resolution on positive action, included reference to the "dignity of women in the workplace" (Collins 1996, 26). Two years later, an informal Council of women's rights ministers also discussed the issue. The first concrete measure came with a 1990 Resolution[27] presented during the Irish Presidency, asking the Commission to deal with the issue (Collins 1996, 27). The Commission responded with a 1991 Recommendation[28] defining sexual harassment as sex discrimination that limits women's labor force participation. The only binding equality policy of this period is the 1992 Directive on "safety and health at work of pregnant workers and workers who have recently given birth or are breastfeeding."[29]

Table 1. Women in the European Parliament (EP) 1989 and 1994

State	Women MEPs in 1989 (%)	Women MEPs in 1994 (%)
Belgium	16.7	32
Denmark	37.5	43.8
France	22.2	29.8
Germany	32	35.4
Greece	4.2	16
Ireland	6.7	26.7
Italy	12.3	10.3
Luxembourg	50	33.3
Netherlands	28	32.2
Portugal	12.5	8
Spain	15	32.8
United Kingdom	14.8	18.4
EP average	19	25.3
EU average	11	15

Sources: Hoskyns, Catherine. 1996. *Integrating Gender: Women, Law and Politics in the European Union.* London, New York: Verso, p. 222 and Mushaben, Joyce. 1998. "The Politics of *Critical Acts*: Women, Leadership and Democratic Deficits in the European Union" *The European Studies Journal*, XV No. 2, p. 83.

The 1992 Directive inaugurates a period during which institutions have been able to take advantage of new rules in treaty revisions allowing them to re-introduce failed the 1980s proposals. These proposals were adopted as directives in the second part of the 1990s, a period characterized by favorable developments in the politics stream. One such development was the increase in women's representation in the EP after the 1994 elections.

The percentage of women MEPs increased from 19% to 26%, a level well above the EU average of 15% (see Table 1). A year later, the new Commission included five women among the twenty Commissioners, the highest number in the history of the EU.[30]

The EU national average of female parliamentary representation remained lower than the EP's despite the 1995 accession of Sweden and Finland, the two countries with the highest percentage of women MPs in the world. Nonetheless, admission of Sweden, Finland and Austria to the EU changed the framework for gender policy insofar as the Scandinavian countries brought into the EU a longer experience and stronger tradition with regard to gender equality policies. The arrival of nationals from these countries in Brussels meant that the Scandinavian experience could directly influence all EU institutions. The former Swedish Commissioner for Internal Affairs and Immigration, Anita Gradin, showed a personal interest in gender policies and immediately became a member of the newly founded group of Commissioners on Equal Opportunities (interview with Havnoer). The former German Commissioner for Regional Policies, Monica Wulf-Mathies, became the second female member of the four Commissioners participating in this group.

Outside the Commission, the European Women's Lobby (EWL), an umbrella organization of national and European women's organizations founded in 1990, was quickly becoming an important policy actor. As was the case with the 1970s punctuation, policy change in the second part of the 1990s coincided with positive international developments. The EU participated in the 1995 UN Women's Conference in Beijing as "one voice," representing the fifteen member states with a delegation from the Commission and the EP under the Spanish Presidency of the Council. The preparation of a common EU position, integrating the diversity of the fifteen member states resulted in proposals that proved "more acceptable" to Conference participants. Their pre-negotiated common position avoided national idiosyncrasies and gave the EU a leadership position at the Conference (Hubert 1998, 3). The visibility of the UN Conference and the opportunity to showcase policies and positions created a favorable climate for EU-level policy developments.

NEW RULES AND THE 1990S DIRECTIVES

The 1987 SEA and the 1993 Social Protocol introduced new rules facilitating the adoption of directives, which the Council of Ministers had failed to approve throughout the 1980s. The SEA replaced unanimity with qualified majority voting (QMV) for legislation regarding the single market (Article 100A) as well as with regard to health and safety at work (Article 118A). The Commission prepared the 1990 proposal for a Pregnancy Directive based on the new health and safety Article in order to circumvent British opposition.[31] The Directive was adopted in 1992, although it was watered down from the original proposal.[32] The Commission had proposed sixteen weeks of paid maternity leave but the Directive as adopted allows only for fourteen weeks "with remuneration at the level of statutory sick pay" (Mazey, 1995, 603).

These provisions would greatly benefit some European women, such as Portuguese workers and especially English women, previously entitled to only six weeks of paid maternity leave. However, this Directive falls beyond the standards of other countries; France, for example, mandates sixteen weeks of maternity leave. The prospect of European equality directives lowering national standards may partly explain the discontent of French and Nordic women over the Maastricht ratification and Europe in general. However, EU social legislation allows states to maintain national legislation that is more favorable, a provision that many women opposing the EU seem to ignore or do not trust. In order to show the extent of the misunderstanding, Hubert refers to the prominent French lawyer and feminist Gisele Halimi, who proclaimed on the evening of the Maastricht referendum results "that Brussels would force the French government to reduce the legal maternity leave from 16 to 14 weeks" (1998, 30).

Beyond the SEA, the 1993 Social Protocol introduced another set of new rules that allowed for the successful re-introduction of Directives that had failed in the 1980s. The 1993 Social Protocol, of which the U.K. opted out, is based on the 1988 Charter of Fundamental Social Rights. The Social Protocol established a "code of practice" and allows qualified majority voting (QMV) in issues dealing with living and working conditions, training and equal opportunities, gender equality, underprivileged groups, and health and safety protection. The Social Protocol also allows the "social partners," management and labor, to conclude joint framework agreements which the Commission then submits to the Council as draft directives (Article 4.2). Directives on parental leave, burden of proof and part-time work were re-introduced, taking advantage of the U.K.'s absence since the latter had blocked such proposals in the past.

First proposed in 1984, the Parental Leave Directive was initially rejected because of British opposition.[33] The Commission re-introduced the proposal, and, using the Social Protocol's Article 4(2), began consultation with the social partners' representative organizations, UNICE, CEEP and ETUC[34] in mid-1995. The social partners concluded a framework agreement on parental leave in December 1995 that was subsequently adopted by the Council as a Directive in June 1996. The social partners wanted to define the minimum requirements by establishing individual parental leave rights for all workers. The three-month leave is non-transferable from one parent to another. Workers are protected against dismissal in applying for parental leave and are also allowed time off for urgent family reasons.

The Directive regulating the burden of proof in cases of sex discrimination[35] was originally proposed in 1988 and also failed to gain Council approval, again due to British opposition. Previously, the burden of proof in discrimination cases had rested with the plaintiff; the plaintiff often had great difficulty in proving such cases because relevant documents were usually in the employer's possession. The new directive allows plaintiffs to go to court under the "presumption of discrimination" and transfers the burden of proof to the employer, who must show that no discrimination took place. The directive also provides a definition of indirect discrimination.

Originally proposed in 1981, the Directive on part-time work was adopted on December 15, 1997, the same day as the burden of proof Directive, and was based on a framework agreement among the social partners. The objective is to redress discrimination faced by part-time workers, the majority of whom are women.

THE AMSTERDAM TREATY

The Social Protocol's new rules aiding the passage of the above directives were annexed in the Maastricht Treaty and applied to all member states except the U.K.. The Labour government's victory in the 1997 British elections facilitated the signing of the Amsterdam Treaty and the incorporation of the Social Protocol in the Treaty. Signed in 1997, the Treaty thus ensured a uniform EU social policy with U.K. participation. The Social Protocol's incorporation into the new Treaty formalizes the role of organizations representative of management and labor as the social partners in the policy process. Article 118b (now Article 139) obligates the Commission to consult the social partners before submitting a social policy proposal. The partners may also conclude framework agreements; they have, indeed, used these new prerogatives with regard to the parental leave and part-time work Directives.

The Social Protocol also helped to extend Article 119 in the Amsterdam Treaty (renamed Article 141 in the new Treaty) to include positive action measures (affirmative action). Article 119's new added paragraph allows for the coexistence of equal treatment and positive action. The new paragraph enables member states to maintain and adopt "measures providing for specific advantages in order to make it easier for the under-represented sex to pursue a vocational activity or to prevent or compensate for disadvantages in professional careers." Article 119 is also broadened by the inclusion of the principle of equal pay not only for equal work but also for work of equal value. As discussed earlier, work for equal value was originally included in the ILO Equal Remuneration Convention, excluded from the Treaty of Rome, yet eventually added to the 1975 EPD. The revised Article 119 expands the EP's role by extending the co-decision procedure to include equal opportunities and equal treatment implementation.

Another innovation of the Amsterdam Treaty in terms of gender equality pertains to the new Title VIII on employment. This title encourages member states and the Community to "work towards developing a coordinated strategy for employment" in order to bring about the new Article 2 objectives that include equality between men and women. As an indication of the importance assigned to employment, the heads of state and government decided at the June 1997 Amsterdam European Council to implement the new procedures before the Treaty took effect in May 1999. In November 1997, the European leaders decided to launch the new employment strategy at the "Jobs Summit" in Luxembourg, the first summit of this kind ever convened. Member states must ensure that national employment polices follow EU guidelines; however, there is no mechanism to punish non-compliance. While the new Title is careful to reassure states that they maintain their national prerogatives, it defines employment policy as "a matter of common concern." In order to emphasize the importance of the issue, the European Council is assigned to review EU employment annually and to adopt Conclusions.[36]

In the Luxembourg process, as it is now known, the Commission takes the initiative for the preparation of annual employment guidelines that member states will consider in the preparation of their national employment policies (European Commission 1999a, 10). Based on the European Council Conclusions, the Council adopts the guidelines by qualified majority after consultation with the EP, the Economic and Social Committee (ESC), the Committee of the Regions and a newly founded Employment Committee. The member states prepare annual reports on the measures adopted according to the EU guidelines. Both the Commission and the Council examine the national reports and prepare the Joint Employment Report to be considered at the December European Council. The Commission may also issue a recommendation for revising the next year's guidelines. The Council may then make further recommendations to specific member states regarding their employment policy. Finally, the Council will repeat the process by adopting the following year's guidelines based on the European Council's Conclusions. Although the principal intergovernmental organs, the European Council and the Council of Ministers, are directly involved in this new procedure for employment guidelines, the Commission retains important responsibilities of initiative, follow-up, implementation and evaluation.

Member states carried out this new obligation in 1998 when, for the first time, they prepared National Action Plans (NAPs). In the NAPs, member states describe national measures for creating employment and addressing the EU Employment guidelines (European Commission 1999, 12). The Commission's review of these first NAPs determined that member states focused more on guidelines for *employability* and *entrepreneurship* and did not sufficiently address *equal opportunities* (European Commission 1999, 13).[37] The Commission shared its assessment of the 1998 NAPs with national authorities and social partners in a seminar in July 1998. A common issue among the member states was the lack of childcare services, a subject taken into consideration by the June and December 1998 European Councils. The 1999 guidelines devoted a specific section to the need for "reconciling work and family." With the new Luxembourg process in place, the state is no longer the dominant actor defining national employment policy. Supranational institutions are increasingly involved in policymaking.

Beyond the incorporation of the Social Protocol, Article 119's expansion, and the Employment Title, the Amsterdam Treaty adds three new gender-related articles. Article 2 includes equality between men and women as a "Community task" now on equal footing with economic convergence and employment promotion. Article 3(2) introduces a legal standing for the concept of *mainstreaming* (see below) by obligating the EU to "eliminate inequalities, and to promote equality between men and women" in all its "activities." These new articles are somewhat weakened by the contents of Article 6a which, first, requires unanimity and not qualified majority for Council measures combating sex discrimination and, secondly, restricts the EP's participation to the consultation process rather than co-decision procedure (EP 1998, 36).

MAINSTREAMING

Institutions "remain in place for decades, structuring further participation, creating apparent equilibria that can be changed only by changing the institutions themselves" (Baumgardner and Jones 1993, 238). Policy developments in the 1990s in the form of treaty revisions and directives took place in the context of *mainstreaming*, the new buzzword in Brussels.[38] The concept of mainstreaming has the potential to change dramatically the framework for gender policy through institutional reforms and the possible elimination of women-specific structures in the EU.

The Commission's definition of gender mainstreaming found expression in a 1996 Communication. Gender mainstreaming entails:

> the systematic integration of the respective situations, priorities and needs of women and men in all policies and with a view to promoting equality between women and men and mobilizing all general policies and measures specifically for the purpose of achieving equality by actively and openly taking into account, at the planning stage, their effects on the respective situation of women and men in implementation, monitoring and evaluation.[39]

In other words, all Community organs will now be required to take into consideration a gender perspective in policymaking. Hubert, who had headed the Equal Opportunities Unit during 1992–96, criticized this long definition as a combination of "official statements of auto-satisfaction and intention of good will" (1998, 120). The EP criticized the absence of a timetable and any concrete measures in the Communication and found the definition "difficult to understand and to distinguish the different elements which compose" the term (EP 1997).

The concept of mainstreaming was introduced in the third Action Programme for Equal Opportunities, but it was not heavily promoted until 1995 and the UN Beijing Conference (European Commission 1990). The entry of two more Nordic countries in 1995 contributed to this development; the latter had insisted on the inclusion of mainstreaming as an EU priority for the UN World Conference (Hubert 1998, 118). As a result of the EU's strong position on the matter, the concept has been included in the Beijing Platform for Action (European Commission 1997a, 115). With its inclusion in a UN document, mainstreaming "emerged as a major strategy to promote equal opportunities for women and men in the global arena" (European Commission 1998, 6). Following the Beijing Conference, mainstreaming became the focus of the Fourth Action Programme for Equal Opportunities covering the period 1996–2000 as well as a vehicle for implementing the Platform for Action (European Commission 1997a, 123). During a 1998 session of the UN's Commission on the Status of Women (CSW),[40] the U.K. Presidency (representing the EU) declared mainstreaming to lie "at the heart of the Platform of Action" (European Commission 1999, 10). According to one mainstreaming expert at the Commission, the concept's acceptance at the international level and the EU's impact on the

Conference is "maybe because it [mainstreaming] appeared quite innocent in comparison to other difficult issues such as inheritance, sexual, reproductive and abortion rights" (interview with Havnoer). The EU was less successful in promoting its position on these other issues but "mainstreaming was not perceived as very threatening" (interview with Havnoer).

In adopting mainstreaming at the EU level, the Commission emphasized a top-down approach. Former Social Affairs Commissioner Padraig Flynn declared that "top-level commitment is a sine qua non for success"[41] during a public hearing on mainstreaming before the EP's Women's Rights Committee. Although Flynn was not known for his commitment to gender equality (interview with Helfferich), his speech echoed the Commission's formal commitment to mainstreaming. The top-down approach to implementation rested on the direct involvement of Commission President Jacques Santer, who established and chaired the Commissioners' Group on Equal Opportunities in 1995. The Group's function is "to stimulate debate and ensure that the concern for equal opportunities for women and men is built into all Community activities" (European Commission 1997a, 18). A second structure, an inter-departmental group, was set up to assist the Commissioners Group in preparing and monitoring mainstreaming at the Commission. This resulted in the appointment of gender mainstreaming officials in each Directorate-General (DG) in order to promote the concept in their respective services (interview with Havnoer). The common characteristic among these established structures is that they are all staffed by existing personnel, not by newly hired experts. These administrators have responsibilities not necessarily related to gender mainstreaming; thus many are not enthusiastic about increasing their workloads with new functions that are little understood (interview with Havnoer). Mainstreaming has increased the number of actors concerned with equal opportunities horizontally, since all Directorate-Generals (DGs) are now involved in gender equality policy. It has also increased the number of actors vertically given the involvement of the Commission's top hierarchy including the President, the Commissioners, and the Director-Generals.

However, Commission officials at DG V and women's rights advocates fear and suspect that this strategy will be used in order to dissolve women-specific structures among the EU institutions such as the Equal Opportunities Unit (interviews with Helfferich, Havnoer and Seeland). These policy advocates, who originally accepted the strategy with some hesitation, now realize "it is actually used as a backlash instrument" (interview with Helfferich). One of the major policy actors of the Brussels women's policy network was categorically opposed:

I do believe that in two or three years time there will definitely be a move to abolish the Equal Opportunities Unit and abolish the specific gender institutions like the Women's Rights Committee. You abolish it [gender-specific institution], you mainstream it somewhere. There is no need for an the Equal Opportunities Unit anymore because you have main-streaming throughout the Commission. That will be a major backlash (interview with Helfferich).

Mainstreaming may endanger the future of gender-specific institution-al structures. However, predictable organizational resistance may prolong the existence of the endangered structures. During the period of resistance, an organization at risk like the Equal Opportunities Unit may adopt suffi-cient mechanisms protecting existing policy against a potential "backlash." A Norwegian expert at the Equal Opportunities Unit views the issue in two ways and refers to the necessary control procedures which could ensure the successful implementation of mainstreaming:

On one side, there is always a danger that mainstreaming might mean dissolving of responsibilities, nobody to be specifically responsible, everybody to be responsible in general, nobody gets evaluated . . . and nobody checks the documents, checks the output. . . . For example, in Norway this has been in some instances the case (interview with Havnoer).

Although acknowledging the potential "danger," this mainstreaming expert sees criticism of the new approach as a defensive reaction of an orga-nizational entity seeking to preserve its power:

With the mainstreaming strategy it means that the Equal Opportunities Unit, the head of that unit or director, will no longer be solely responsi-ble for that policy area, so it means that you lose visibility, you lose con-trol in a way. I think that in some member states you see a reluctance to take up mainstreaming by those responsible for equal opportunities, partly for fear that it will have unfortunate consequences, but also I think maybe because of this fear of losing control (interview with Havnoer).

The Commission insists that mainstreaming is "complementary to positive actions" (European Commission 1997a, 16): "Mainstreaming opens up a two-track or a dual system towards equality of opportunity" that includes mainstreaming on one track, and positive action in favor of women on another (European Commission 1998a, 34). The Commission has based its dual-track strategy on practical experience gained at the national level and, more specifically, in Sweden and Norway. A Swedish expert on gender mainstreaming, Birgitta Aseskog, shared her country's experience during the EP's public hearing on the subject.[42] Indeed the Equal Opportunities Unit specifically hired a Norwegian expert to oversee mainstreaming. Sweden actively has promoted mainstreaming since 1994, while Norway has pursued the integration of equal opportunities in central administration policies since 1986 (interview with Havnoer). As mentioned above, the entire Nordic group had influenced the EU position at the Beijing conference. Norway participated in the preparatory process for the UN Conference as member of the European Economic Area (EEA)[43] and an EU candidate country (interview with Havnoer). Both Swedish and Norwegian experts insist on the importance of a dual-track strategy:

> I think we can't avoid it [mainstreaming] because we can't change socie-
> ty by only working on the sides. But what we stress, what we always
> stress, is the dual or the two-track strategy which means that we should
> never abandon specific measures of positive action, programs, legislative
> measures *et cetera* in parallel with redefining mainstream policy (inter-
> view with Havnoer).

Another interviewee used the Swedish experience to illustrate "that if you have mainstreaming without the necessary mechanisms and the speci-ficity for women, women will be once again the losers" (interview with Helfferich).

Despite such criticisms, the Commission emphasizes the success of mainstreaming by identifying the employment guidelines as its "clearest and best example."[44] Following the Luxembourg process, the 1998 European Employment Guidelines for member state use in developing national employment policy included equal opportunities among the four main pil-lars. The other three pillars are employability entrepreneurship, and adapt-ability. Mainstreaming was included in the 1999 guidelines "which means that they [member states] are also obliged to mainstream a gender perspec-tive and equal opportunities into all the other guidelines" (interview with Havnoer). This acquires increased visibility at the EU's highest level since it must be discussed at the annual European Council meetings among heads of state or government. Expert Ann Havnoer suggests that the mainstreaming requirement for all four guidelines strengthens the implementation of equal opportunities in the national employment policy; member states could more easily ignore equal opportunities as a separate guideline without the main-streaming obligation. The evaluation of the 1998 National Action Plans (NAPs) showed that most member states' reports emphasized "more mainstream traditional guidelines," such as employability and entrepreneurship, at the expense of equal opportunities (interview with Havnoer).

The relative progress of mainstreaming, as implemented in the employment guidelines, does not reassure most skeptics. Women advocates justify their skepticism towards mainstreaming because the concept's introduction coincided with a period of budget cuts in public administration (Hubert 1998, 116). This was the case not only at the European level but also at the national level (the Netherlands, Spain, Ireland) and the regional level (Emilia-Romagna, Catalogne). According to Hubert, "mainstreaming has often hidden under a cloak of progress, the intention to reduce, if not abolish, the administrative services dedicated specifically to equality and with them, positive action" (1998, 116). Mainstreaming has been considered a successful strategy as implemented in the employment guidelines. However, mainstreaming may also become the catalyst for a major "reform," prematurely dismantling gender-specific policies and institutions.

Skeptics' fears were further substantiated in the fall of 1998 when the EP, "in an effort to streamline" its operations, proposed to "abolish the Parliamentary Committees that do not perform any legislative tasks" (European Women's Lobby (EWL), 1998). The Committee on Women's Rights would have been included in this "streamline," despite the fact that it was "expected to have more legislative power after the ratification of the Treaty of Amsterdam" (EWL, 1998). The EWL and other women's organizations organized a successful campaign to defend the existence of the parliamentary Committee (EWL, 1998a). With 2,700 member associations in the member states, the EWL mobilized its membership to avert the abolition of the Women's Rights Committee which some of its own members even wanted (interview with Helfferich). Their campaign was successful because the EWL capitalized on its European-wide membership: "we have the means to mobilize a lot of voters and that is now understood [by MEPs], and because that is understood we have some influence" (interview with Helfferich). However, the EWL declared victory with the reservation that "the threat seems to have been averted for the moment" but not eliminated (EWL, 1998a). Women's advocates realize that this one-time victory is only temporary; many believe that "institutional arrangements like the Committee on Women's Rights will disappear" (interview with Helfferich). The campaigns to preserve institutional structures known to support women-specific policies means that major actors dedicate a great amount of energy to defending the status quo and not in furthering policy development. Barbara Helfferich stressed: "we are fighting like hell against this. The campaign for the Committee on Women's Rights is part and parcel of it. We are just fighting off things, we are not advancing anymore."

The existence of another gender-specific structure, the DG X's Information for Women's department, also appears to be in dispute. The old debate within the feminist movement between equal or special treatment for women continues in a department that targets women as a special group. One DG X official declared, regarding the future of the department: "we have also an ambition, and the ambition of this section is to become obsolete, because if we become obsolete, we would have fulfilled our function extremely well. They would not need us any longer. If we achieve that, it will be great" (interview with Pau). The future of this type of structure is not only discussed in the context of mainstreaming but also as part of DG X's position in the Commission. First, in the context of mainstreaming, the theoretical "integration of a gender perspective in all EU policies" questions the necessity of gender-specific structures. Second, the future of the women's information service is doubtful in the context of DG X's future in general. Since DG X is in charge of information for policies produced in other DGs, other policymaking DGs who have their own information services challenge its existence as a separate DG: "if you are a policymaker, you have to inform about your policies" (interview with Pau). Given the current "re-thinking of the functioning" of the Commission as a whole, the future of the Women's Information Service is uncertain: "they are re-thinking the Commission of the new millennium, modern administration and how it is going to be restructured" (interview with Pau).

As skeptics feared, mainstreaming has already been used to cut budgets that were earmarked for women at the policy level. A budget line dedicated to equal opportunity projects in the Socrates education program at DG XXII (Education, Training and Youth), for example, was deleted in favor of mainstreaming. The Commission's Progress Report on mainstreaming admitted that it was "unclear" what the effects of this approach on equal opportunities in education might be (European Commission 1998f). In discussing the Commission's report, the Committee on Women's Rights criticized budget cuts under the guise of mainstreaming. The Commission's own mainstreaming expert admitted that DG XXII's action was "a premature measure to take with a view to the early stage in which mainstreaming finds itself. You have to make sure the responsibilities are fixed, that measures are evaluated with gender proofing, at least before taking away what existed before" (interview with Havnoer). All women-specific institutional structures are still in place, but their existence seems at risk. Although it is too early to evaluate the impact of mainstreaming, other DGs are beginning to follow the DG XXII's lead in cutting budgets earmarked for women's programs. For example, the DG V has not renewed the "Employment" program, which allocated specific funds for women's training for the period 1994–99. The new program called EQUAL does not earmark funds for specific groups for the period 2000–2006. EQUAL's objective is to combat "discrimination and inequalities in connection with the labour market" (European Commission 1999b). However, unlike "Employment" that allocated specific funds for women, youth, and disabled people, EQUAL has a common budget for all "disadvantaged" people (interview with Livingstone). Mainstreaming has the potential to reform the current policy environment before perhaps settling in a new period of incrementalism.

CONCLUSION

In this chapter, I examined the long-term development of EU gender policy by presenting the different phases in the policy process as three independent policy streams. In the first stream, I traced the origins of Article 119 to determine how a condition became accepted as a problem amenable to a solution in the policy realm. In the policy stream, the presence of ideas in the "policy primeval soup" and policy entrepreneurs prepared solutions to be exploited at the opening of a window by way of developments in the politics stream. The three streams joined together in the 1970s, producing policy change and creating new institutions. The joining of the process streams, or the "punctuation," took the form of strong directives, landmark court decisions, and institutional creation. The new institutional structures inaugurated a period of incrementalism from the end of the 1970s until the beginning of the 1990s. The mid-1990s punctuation, facilitated by new institutional rules, has the potential to change the policy system "by changing the institutions themselves" (Baumgardner and Jones 1993, 238) through the concept of mainstreaming.

The history of EU gender policy revealed that the intergovernmentalist emphasis on the primacy of member states is problematic. Policy outcomes are not solely the result of member state preferences, and the EU is more complex than a mere intergovernmental forum where state interests directly define policy outcomes. In many cases, as with the inclusion of Article 119 and the rejection of the 1980s proposals, member states' interests were the primary concerns. However, even in those cases, the influence of past policies and other institutions was also important in structuring, defining and determining policy outcomes.

This chapter's historical institutionalist analysis identified three factors that affected policy outcomes beyond member states' control: supranational autonomy, institutions structuring the policy process and the influence of past policies. An intergovernmentalist perspective would have ignored the multiple relationships among international institutions. This was the case with the ILO and the EU during the Treaty of Rome negotiations, the ILO and the UN's Committee on the Status of Women (CSW) in preparation of the Equal Remuneration Convention, and UN Women's Conferences influence on national and EU policy development. The ILO became a venue for policy proposals such as equal pay, giving voice to national and international women's organizations that perceived "the problem" as an international one. The principle formulated in the 1919 ILO Constitution did not find a concrete expression in policy until 1951. However, the ILO Constitution internationalized and legitimized an issue until the post World War II circumstances allowed the issue to resurface with the founding of the UN and the establishment of the CSW. By establishing institutional expertise on the matter, the ILO influenced policy development in another international institution. The ILO's institutional legacies provided the parameters within which Article 119 could be negotiated. It provided the policy definitions, the institutional expertise, introduced the problem in the public agenda and familiarized national administrators with the issue. Institutions like the ILO played an important role by influencing other international institutions such as the EU.

At the EU, supranational institutions like the Commission have played an important role in structuring the environment, influencing the formation and goal identification of individuals in the women's policy community. The Commission structured the participation of outside experts such as Vogel-Polsky and Sullerot who contributed to the expansion of the issue beyond the original treaty. The "spillover" of gender policy beyond equal pay can partly be explained by the fact that one institutional actor, Nonon, used her official position to influence the composition of the working group preparing the Equal Treatment Directive (ETD). Article 119's original economic focus still guides and constrains policy development. However, policy did "spillover," as neofunctionalists would have predicted, in issue areas lying outside the original Treaty definition, i.e., parental leave and sexual harassment. The Commission maintained an interest in women's policies throughout the negative climate of the 1980s, a position contrary to policy priorities of the member states. Institutional rules and routines such as qualified majority voting (QMV) have been used creatively to re-introduce proposals in the 1990s and to re-organize the policy process. In the next chapter, I focus on two obstacles impeding national control of EU policy, unanticipated consequences and autonomous behavior by EU supranational institutions.

NOTES

[1] For a chronological table of EU gender policy development, see Appendix B.

[2] The three directives are the Equal Pay Directive (EPD), the Equal Treatment Directive (ETD) and the Social Security Directive (SSD).

[3] Kingdon conducted interviews with decisionmakers in health and transportation policy.

[4] Perrot and Hubert were participants at a University of Louvain-la-Neuve conference, March 20, 1996.

[5] All the translations of French and Greek texts will be mine.

[6] Hoskyns (1996, 55) refers to Tribolati's 1958 study on female salaries in the EC countries ("Salaires féminins dans les pays du Marché Commun," *Informations Sociales*, Sept. 1958). Tribolati is skeptical about the effectiveness of equal pay provisions (except for the SMIG) based on the fact that collective agreements did not cover the majority of working women in France.

[7] "…All human beings, irrespective of race, creed or sex, have the right to pursue both their material well being and their spiritual development in conditions of freedom and dignity, of economic security and equal opportunity…"

[8] Declarations are "designed to make formal statements, often addressed to the world at large or to special groups." The ILO Conference in Philadelphia "used this form to enunciate the ILO Social Mandate in the postwar world" (Lubin and Winslow 1991, 5).

[9] In the ILO structure, each member state participates with delegates representing the government, employer's and worker's organizations.

[10] The ILO was established in 1919 during the Paris Peace Conference, which ended World War I. The Treaties of Peace included the ILO Constitution as Part XIII.

[11] Hoskyns examined documents in *Conference intergouvernemental: Historique des articles 117 à 120 du traité instituant la CEE.*

[12] The section Distortions to Competition was then deleted from the draft of the Treaty of Rome.

[13] The 1992 Pregnancy Directive was based on health and safety, Article 118a.

[14] One may wonder whether the physical location of EU institutions in Brussels increased awareness of EU policies among Belgians.

[15] Hubert (1998) does not specify her source. While admitting to have found no photographic evidence, Hoskyns (1996) uses interview material from one of the participants in the strikes (Janine Niépce) as well as secondary sources such as the detailed description of the strike (Marie-Thérèse Coenen. 1991. *La grève des femmes de la F. N. en 1966.* Brussels: Pol-His).

[16] For a list of interviewees, see Appendix A.

[17] Gelb (1989) bases her observation on the work of Vallance (1979) on women MPs in Britain (Vallance, Elizabeth. 1979. *Women in the House.* London: Athlone Press).

[18] OJ L 225, 12 August 1986.

[19] OJ L 359, 19 December 1986.

[20] OJ C 186, 21 July 1982, p. 3 and OJ C 203, 12 August 1986, p. 2.

[21] Council Resolution (CR) of 7 June 1984 on action to combat unemployment among women, OJ C 161, 21 June 1984, p.14; CR of 3 June 1985 on equal opportunities for girls and boys in education, OJ C 166, 5 July 1985, p. 1; CR of 16 December 1988 on the reintegration and late integration of women into working life, OJ C 333, 28 December 1988, p. 1.

[22] Council Recommendation 84/635/EEC of 13 December1984 on the promotion of positive action for women, OJ L 331, 19 December 1984, p. 34; Commission Recommendation 87/567/EEC of 24 November 1987 on vocational training for women, OJ L 342, 4 December 1987, p. 35.

[23] Commission Proposal for a Council Directive on part-time work, COM (81) 775, 22 December 1981; On parental leave and leave for family reasons, COM (83) 686, 22 November 1983; On completing the implementation of equal treatment for men and women in statutory and occupational social security schemes, COM (87) 494 final, 23 October 1987; On the burden of proof, COM (88) 269 final, 27 May 1988.

[24] Proposal for Council Resolution of 8 June 1989, blocked by the U.K. June 12 1989.

[25] European Commission. 1990. Equal Opportunities for Men and Women-the third Medium-term Action Programme 1991–95, COM (90) 449 final; The Fourth Medium-term Action Programme on Equal Opportunities for Men and Women 1996–2000, adopted by Council Decision of 22 December 1995, OJ L 335 of 30 December 1995, p. 37.

[26] Council Recommendation 92/241/EEC of 31 March 1992 on childcare, OJ L 123, 8 May 1992, p. 16.

[27] Resolution adopted on 29 May 1990, OJ C 157/3, 27 June 1990.

[28] Commission Recommendation of 27 November 1991 on the protection of the dignity of women and men at work, OJ C 27, 24 February 1992, p. 1.

[29] OJ L 348, 28 November 1992, p.1.

[30] The new Commission, which took over in mid-1999 and will serve until 2005, also includes five women.

[31] See chapter 3 for the British "opt out" from the Social Protocol.

[32] Council Directive 92/85/EEC of 19 October 1992 on the introduction of measures to encourage improvements in the safety and health at work of pregnant workers and workers who have recently given birth or are breastfeeding, Official Journal L 348, 28 November 1992, p. 1.

[33] *Proposal for a Council Directive on parental leave and leave for family reasons,* COM (83) 686 final, 22 November 1983.

[34] Union of Industrial and Employers Confederations of Europe (UNICE); European Center of Public Enterprises (CEEP); European Trade Union Confederation (ETUC).

[35] Official Journal C 176 of 5 July 1988, p. 5.

[36] Conclusions refer to guidelines issued by the European Council (http://ue.eu.int/en/Info/eurocouncil/).

[37] COM (98) 316 of 15 May 1998.

[38] Regardless of the subject discussed with interviewees in Brussels, mainstreaming came up repeatedly in all of my interviews and informal conversations with Commission officials.

[39] Commission Communication, COM (96) 67 final, 21 February 1996.

[40] United Nations CSW 42nd session, New York, March 12–3, 1998.

[41] EP hearing on gender mainstreaming, April 20, 1999.

[42] EP hearing on gender mainstreaming, April 20, 1999.

[43] An agreement in 1991 between the EC and the European Free Trade Association (EFTA) set up the EEA forming a free trade area in all domains except agriculture.

[44] Speech by Commissioner Flynn, Women's Rights Committee, EP, January 21, 1998.

Chapter 3
Unanticipated Consequences and Autonomous Supranational Institutions

T HIS CHAPTER EXPANDS FURTHER ON THE ARGUMENT THAT INTERGOV-
ernmentalism provides an inadequate theoretical approach for studying
European Union (EU) gender policy, and that historical institutionalism
offers a better framework for analysis. First, I review the major differences
between these theoretical approaches before using two cases to substantiate
the choice of approach. The first case examines the development of the concept of "pay;" the second examines the transfer of Article 119 from the
"Distortions to Competition" Section to the "Social Policy" Section of the
Treaty of Rome. Both cases emphasize that member-state preferences are not
the only determinants of EU gender policy and that unintended consequences falling outside of national control can play an important role in policy development. The impact of these consequences is cumulative and interactive, and this latter dynamic is transforming EU policymaking. National
control of EU policy is not only hampered by unanticipated consequences
but also by the autonomous behavior of supranational EU institutions. I
illustrate autonomous institutional action by concentrating on two
Commission functions: its ability to take advantage of rules in order to assure
institutional success and policy development, and its capacity to structure the
policy environment through the creation of an interest group constituency.

    Finding its roots in the (neo)-realist tradition of international relations
theory, intergovernmentalism emphasizes a state-centric model of European
governance (Marks *et al.* 1996, 343). Under this type of governance, states—
as represented by their national governments—are the primary actors in EU

policymaking, and their central concern lies with the preservation of sovereignty. EU policies are the result of calculated member state preferences. Supranational institutions, on the other hand, are "deliberate instruments to improve the efficiency of bargaining between states" (Moravcsik 1993, 507). In the case of the EU, supranational institutions do not pose a threat to member state autonomy; on the contrary, they have actually contributed to "rescuing" and strengthening the nation-state (Milward 1992; Moravcsik 1993). In Europe, the post-war nation-state was "rescued" insofar as it "could not have offered to its citizens the same measure of security and prosperity" without the EU (Milward 1992, 3). The West European nation-state was also strengthened because EU institutions increased "the efficiency of interstate bargaining" as well as the "autonomy of national political leaders *vis-à-vis* particularistic social groups within their domestic polity" (Moravcsik 1993, 507). The intergovernmentalist emphasis on the primacy of nation-states, their preoccupation with autonomy and sovereignty, and the "instrumentality" of institutions contrasts with a theoretical approach that presents supranational institutions as autonomous agents (Hoffmann 1966; Moravcsik 1993; Milward 1992).

Drawing from historical institutionalism, the history of EU gender policy cannot merely be construed as the combined result of individual member state preferences. EU supranational institutions, such as the Commission, have acquired a certain level of autonomy in affecting gender policy development. States certainly continue to enjoy an advantageous position in blocking policy, as was seen in the 1980s. However, institutional actors can influence issue definition, actor participation and the selective use of policymaking rules. Institutions have structured the policy environment by influencing the formation and goal identification of social group actors. Institutional rules such as qualified majority voting (QMV) and administrative routines organize the policy process. Past policies and institutional experience provide parameters within which future policy is negotiated.

A survey of the forty-year history of EU gender policy in the previous chapter revealed that the EU comprises not only an intergovernmental forum of governance but a policymaking arena where a variety of political actors interact to influence policy. The gender policy community included not only institutional actors such as the Commission's Equal Opportunities Unit and the European Parliament's (EP) Women's Rights Committee, but also individuals and organizations at the European and national levels. Individual women inside and outside formal structures, such as Nonon, Sullerot, Vogel-Polsky, and Roudy, are able to influence policy because of their experiences as women, independently policy positions of their home states.

EU policies are not the direct outcome of member state preferences insofar as the cumulative impact of past policies and the contributions of institutions intervene to alter the outcome. Past policies and definitions of equal pay developed by other international organizations, such as the ILO, have influenced EU policy. It thus becomes necessary to examine EU gender policy as a process "unfolding over time," and not just as a composite of the current preferences of the relevant actors. The history of Article 119 shows the importance of accounting for member state interests (France and Germany); but factors extending beyond national preferences (international conventions, institutional and individual expertise, interest group pressure) ultimately influenced both the definition and the scope of the Article. Although member states create supranational institutions, they cannot control their long-term development. Neither the Commission nor the European Court of Justice (ECJ) are merely the instruments of states; both have influenced policy development in ways that were unanticipated and even opposed by the member states.

UNANTICIPATED CONSEQUENCES

Circumstances shaping the origins and negotiation of Article 119 (described in chapter 2) had significant long-term effects on the development of EU gender policy, and *unanticipated consequences*, as posited by historical institutionalists and neo-functionalists. The resulting definition of pay and the transfer of Article 119 to a different section during the Treaty of Rome negotiations had long-term consequences that continue to affect current policy outcomes. Intergovernmentalist focuses on member states current interests to account for policies and thus ignores both the *historical* process and the *institutional* implications of the process. Historical institutionalists emphasize the *historical* dimension because they understand policy developments "as a process that unfolds over time" (Pierson 1996, 126). Concurrently they view institutions as *embedding* "many of the contemporary implications of these temporal processes" in the form of "rules, policy structures or norms" (Pierson 1996, 126).

THE CONCEPT OF PAY

Article 119 derives its expansive definition of the concept of pay in from an ILO Convention, and it might have been included to "compensate" for the exclusion of the phrase "work for equal value"[1] (Hoskyns 1996, 56). This definition of the concept of pay continues to guide contemporary policy at European and national levels through a significant amount of case law developed to interpret this concept. Hoskyns counts "more than sixty" cases in the area of women's rights (1994, 227). The Commission's 1996 Annual Report on Equal Opportunities (1997a, 109) does not offer a complete count of the legal cases but organizes the data according to the country, the legal basis (Article 119 or other Equality Directives), and the litigation mechanism (Article 169 or Article 177). An aggregation of the legal cases without differentiation by country of origin, legal bases, and litigation mechanism shows a total of 90 women's rights cases for the period 1971–1996. A little more than half of the cases (47) are based on Article 119 and a considerable number specifically concerns the concept of pay.

The EU relies on two litigation mechanisms: *direct effect* (Article 169) and *preliminary ruling* reference (Article 177). The principle of direct effect confers rights on individuals based on Community law, independent of national legislation (Dinan 1994, 297). Article 169 allows the Commission to bring a case against a member state before the ECJ for a failure to comply with Treaty obligations. Prior to filing a case, the Commission is required to give "the State concerned the opportunity to submit its observations" and then to "deliver a reasoned opinion on the matter." A "preliminary ruling reference" (Article 177) allows a national court to seek ECJ guidance on cases involving Community law and its relationship to national law. Given the supremacy of EU law, the preliminary ruling mechanism allows the ECJ to challenge national law.

The first of the three *Defrenne* cases, brought before the ECJ at the end of 1970, concerned the concept of pay. Drawing on the mechanism of preliminary ruling, the Belgian Administrative Court asked the ECJ to resolve two questions: first, whether pensions constitute pay and secondly, whether a pension scheme is to be viewed as a direct or indirect contribution from the employer to the employee.[2] The case was based on a 1969 Belgian pension scheme, which "gave any member of the air crew except air hostesses a special deal on pensions amounting to what was virtually full salary on retirement" (Hoskyns 1996, 70). The Sabena Airline airhostess Defrenne argued that pension constituted "deferred" pay, that is it constituted a payment received from the employer because the employer contributed into the scheme; it therefore fell within the scope of Article 119. The Court ruled that Article 119 covered pensions if the employer paid them, directly or indirectly, in return for employment. However, pensions paid through statutory social security schemes were judged to fall outside Article 119's scope. In the *Defrenne* case, the pension scheme was deemed to lie outside the scope of

Article 119 because there was no close link between the scheme in question and the employer's contribution.[3]

The question as to whether or not pensions constitute pay resurfaced in a 1981 case when the ECJ affirmed that an employer's contribution to a pension scheme on behalf of employees falls within Article 119.[4] The *Bilka* case involved a German department store that excluded part-time workers from occupational pension schemes.[5] The Court referred to the "contractual origin" of pension schemes and recognized these types of schemes as "pay." It stated further that the exclusion of part-time workers constituted indirect discrimination against women since it mainly affected female workers. The decision was significant in that it applied equal pay to part-time workers but also recognized the principle of indirect discrimination. National courts now use the "Bilka test" standard for deciding cases of indirect discrimination (Hoskyns 1994, 228).

The concept of pay was further expanded to include transport privileges in the 1982 case of *Garland v. British Rail Engineering Ltd.*[6] Retired male workers and their families benefited from transport privileges, but retired female workers did not enjoy the same privileges as their male counterparts. The Court defined these privileges "as an extension of the benefits conferred during the employment relationship" (EP 1998, 25). The exclusion of female workers from this form of payment deemed discriminatory and thus covered under Article 119. Between 1982–96, a series of EC cases defined a number of other benefits as constituting pay, e.g., supplementary allowances linked to unemployment pay[7] and maternity leave.[8]

Other benefits seen to constitute pay are redundancy benefits and pension benefits under a contracted-out scheme, as defined in the *Barber* case.[9] The 1990 *Barber* judgment "came like a bolt from the blue for employers" (EP 1998, 26) because Directive 86/378 on Equal Treatment in Occupational Social Security schemes gave member states until January 1993 to implement the provisions. The financial and social consequences would have been significant and the costs to employers' insurance schemes and pension funds would have been considerable if, following *Barber*, all benefits in occupational social security schemes had immediately been defined as remuneration under Article 119. Based on the *Barber* case, two other benefits defined as pay include survivors' pensions paid under contractual scheme[10] and supplementary pension schemes.[11]

The *Barber* case was filed and sponsored by the British Equal Opportunities Commission (EOC), an independent governmental agency established by the 1975 British Sex Discrimination Act (SDA). Created to monitor implementation of the SDA, this agency has the capacity to support individual applicants and fund court cases. Frustrated with unfavorable legal precedents and unsuccessful appeals in British courts, "the EOC turned to EC law" as a channel for overcoming national obstruction (Alter and Vargas 1997, 11). The EOC's success in the *Barber* case was a result of a long campaign to alter British pension inequalities that strategically used EU law to counteract unfavorable national law. The EOC had cooperated with the Commission in preparing a 1982 a case against the U.K. for failing to comply with its Treaty obligations regarding equal pay (Alter and Vargas 1997, 13). The resulting ECJ decision found the U.K. non-compliant with the Treaty, forcing the U.K. to amend its Equal Pay Act (Alter and Vargas 1997, 13).[12] The *Barber* decision contradicted both the British Equal Pay and Sex Discrimination Acts, which explicitly excluded pensions (Alter and Vargas 1997, 12).

The limit placed on the reach of Article 119 partly curtailed the consequences from the *Barber* decision. Paragraph 45 of the judgment stated:

> the direct effect of Article 119 of the Treaty may not be relied upon in order to claim entitlement to a pension with an effect from a date prior to that of this judgement [17 May 1990], except in the case of workers or those claiming under them who have before that date initiated legal proceedings.

The member states preempted a future ECJ judgment by confirming the retroactive limit in a Protocol on Article 119 annexed to the Maastricht Treaty: "benefits under occupational social security schemes shall not be considered as remuneration if, and in so far as they are attributable to periods of employment prior to 17 May 1990."

A "Post Barber Directive" eventually amended the 1986 Directive on equal treatment in occupational social security schemes, which became both contradictory and redundant in view of the Barber judgment.[13] Having defined pensions as pay, this judgment established the direct effect of Article 119, which protects equal pay for equal work. Article 119 "supersedes" any contradictory Directive provisions and renders them void (EP 1998, 29). The 1986 Directive provisions were contradictory because Article 9 allowed member states to "defer compulsory application of the principle of equal treatment" to survivors' pensions and retirement age in contractual old-age pensions. Article 9, as amended, still allows deferment but only in relation to self-employed workers (not covered by Article 119). Given the direct effect of Article 119, the Directive's deadline for applying the principle of equal treatment in occupational social security schemes (Article 8) was amended to apply only to schemes benefiting the self-employed. The deadline for complying with the amended Directive was July 1, 1997. None of the member states had communicated any implementation measures to the Commission by then. As a result, the Commission initiated infringement procedures against all the member states, with the procedure continuing only for France, Greece and Luxembourg (European Commission 1999, 26). [14]

The negotiators of the Treaty of Rome had embraced an expansive and abstract concept of pay promoted by the ILO without having calculated (or without even being able to foresee) the long-term consequences of this decision. The long-term effects became significant, especially after the *Barber* judgment. The byproducts were the Protocol on Article 119 annexed to the Maastricht Treaty, the 1996 Directive amending the 1986 Directive on occupational social security, the infringement procedures against the member states, and a considerable amount of case law. In defining and reconfirming what constitutes pay, the ECJ imposed significant costs on the member states by specifically disallowing unequal treatment in pension funds. Victoria Garcia Muñoz, editor of a Working Paper on Women's Rights published by the EP, characterized the *Barber* judgment as "severe" and "unexpected" (EP 1998, 30). It has created a "gap" (Pierson 1996) in member state control over EU institutions and policies.

The intergovernmentalist focus on the primacy of states' interests and the instrumentality of institutions does not explain the ECJ's role in expanding the definition of pay in ways clearly contrary to the desires and interests of the member states. In 1957, the Treaty of Rome negotiators borrowed the equal pay concept from the ILO and adopted it for short-term political reasons in order to appease the French. The member states did not fully comprehend the severity of the unanticipated consequences until the 1990s and the *Barber* judgment. At this time, the member states tried to decrease the emerging "gap" between their control of supranational institutions and EU policy development by adopting the Protocol annexed to the Maastricht Treaty that limited the retroactivity of *Barber*. Although the ECJ also placed limits on *Barber*'s retroactivity, the member states took the matter in their own hands because the ECJ's wording could have had different interpretations. At first, the member states' reaction seemed more in line with intergovernmentalism that expects states to assert their interests and control on supranational institutions. However, the member states attempted to decrease, rather than to eliminate the gap between their "interests" and EU supranational policy as defined by the ECJ. Although *Barber* does not apply to cases prior to 1990, the Protocol cannot reverse the judgment for all future cases. The ECJ not only set the parameters for future policy but also challenged and reversed past state preferences both at the supranational and national levels. At the national level, *Barber* directly challenged the British Equal Pay and Sex Discrimination Acts and, at the supranational level, the 1986 Directive. The ECJ's decision in the *Barber* case "forced" the states to alter their preferences (excluding pensions from equal pay provisions) in the form of the 1996 Directive.

THE TRANSFER OF ARTICLE 119 TO A DIFFERENT SECTION OF THE TREATY OF ROME

Much like the concept of pay, the transfer of Article 119 from the Distortions to Competition Section to the Social Policy Section of the Rome Treaty had long term effects and unanticipated consequences. This transfer must be understood as a historical process with many of the implications of this process "embedded" in institutional rules, routines and norms. Hoskyns holds that this transfer was "crucial" to gender policy development, because it imbued Article 119 with strong legal obligations originally associated with economic integration which were then transferred to the social policy section: "This transfer goes some way to explaining the unexpected force of Article 119 by comparison with the other social policy articles" (1996, 57). One of the legal obligations was the time limit for implementation. Given Article 119's original association with economic measures, it marked the "first stage" of the common market creation, planned to end in December 1961. This association with the "first stage" meant that Article 119's implementation could benefit from the momentum and interest in creating the common market.

Though the Council of Ministers decided in the mid-1960s to move even faster towards the second stage by reducing tariffs, there was no progress on the implementation of Article 119. A Commission Recommendation and the establishment of a special "Article 119 group" did not succeed in accelerating implementation. The "Article 119 group" was composed of representatives from the Commission and member states who had at their disposal a group of experts providing legal and statistical information. By the 1961 deadline, the Group observed that Article 119's provisions had not been implemented. The member states then adopted an intergovernmental Resolution on equal pay,[15] setting December 1964 as the new deadline for applying the equal pay principle and closing the gap between male and female salaries. During this period there were no significant implementation efforts despite Article 119's association with the "first stage."

Although "the Article 119 group" was not effective in facilitating Article 119's implementation, it set a precedent in allowing outside experts to influence the policy process. The Commission later consulted this same group in drafting the 1975 Equal Pay Directive. As regards the drafting of the Equal Treatment Directive, the Commission created a new Ad Hoc Group on Women's Work. These ad hoc institutional creations provided a forum for women activists such as Vogel-Polsky (Defrenne's lawyer) to influence European gender policy. In contrast to the negotiations for Article 119, these consultative structures provided the opportunity to incorporate women's interests directly in the drafting of legislation.

The association of Article 119 with the "first stage" eventually paid off in the second *Defrenne* case,[16] which dealt with income loss due to pay discrimination. The ECJ's verdict established the direct effect of Article 119, which as mentioned earlier, can be invoked against a state and against individuals. The compensation[17] for the income loss Defrenne suffered due to different pay scales for men and women covered the period 1962–66. The period of applicability began in January 1962, the same deadline noted in the Treaty of Rome (Article 8) for the completion of the "first stage." It ended in 1966 when Belgium adopted of Article 14 in order to translate Article 119 into national legislation, thus allowing women to "institute proceedings in the competent court for the application of the principle of equal pay."

Contrary to Hoskyns' view that the Article 119 transfer to a different section was beneficial, Agnès Hubert[18] infers that its association with the social chapter has actually weakened its effectiveness in the long term (1998, 54). Although the ostensible aim of the transfer was to strengthen the Social Policy chapter, subsequent developments might have led to the opposite effect. Institutional rules, such as the introduction of qualified majority voting (QMV), have organized the policy process (March and Olsen 1989) and affected policy outcomes. The SEA came into force on July 1, 1987[19] and introduced qualified majority voting (QMV) in the Council of Ministers for issues dealing with the creation of a single market. Had Article 119 remained as a measure to complete the single market, one can presume that policy developments concerning gender issues would have been different; those proposals that failed under unanimity could have benefited from qualified majority voting (QMV). The Parental Leave Directive, first proposed in 1984,[20] was rejected due to British opposition. The Directive regulating the burden of proof in cases of sex discrimination[21] also failed initially, owing to the opposition of a single country. Although the Directive on maternity leave was approved,[22] it was watered down from the original proposal that had included provisions for paid leave.

AUTONOMY OF SUPRANATIONAL INSTITUTIONS

The maternity leave directive is the first of a series of directives issued in the 1990s that reveal one of the two autonomous Commission functions presented in this section. The Commission function that reveals autonomous behavior is its ability to play the "treaty-base game" (Rhodes 1995), that is, the creative use of policy rules to overcome member state resistance and promote policy development.

THE COMMISSION'S FIRST AUTONOMOUS FUNCTION: PLAYING THE "TREATY-BASE GAME"

Martin Rhodes has described the Commission as playing a "treaty-base game" (1995, 99), referring to the attempt by the Delors Commission in mid-1990 to avoid the British veto in proposing labor regulations. Supported by European employers, the U.K. opposed any labor regulations at the EU level based on the argument of national sovereignty. Before the Maastricht summit in December 1991, the Commission, backed by some member states and labor groups, tried to find ways to avoid the Treaty's legal obstacles in social policy issues. "An entrepreneurial Commission," by playing the "treaty-base game," attempted to "push its legal competence to the limit by a skillful (and at times rather devious) interpretation of treaty provisions" (Rhodes 1995, 99–100).

Under the presidency of Jacques Delors, the Commission took advantage of new rules under the 1987 SEA and the 1993 Social Protocol to promote policies contrary to some member states' preferences. Although the U.K. was responsible for the rejection of many Commission proposals,[23] other member states also shared the British objections, e.g., Spain and Portugal (Rutheford 1989). In an effort to appear "more communautaire," these member states nonetheless used the predictable British position to hide their own opposition (Rhodes 1995, 103).

To circumvent British opposition, the Commission first attempted to base more draft directives on Articles 100a, and 118a which, under the SEA, allowed for qualified majority voting (QMV) instead of unanimity. Article 100a concerned measures for completing the single market; Article 118a dealt with legislation regarding and health and safety at work. The Commission's "entrepreneurial" strategy consisted of adopting an expansive definition of the type of issues that could be based on the above articles. It also consisted of packaging issues that could be unambiguously based on the Treaty Articles with other more contestable issues to form what Rhodes calls "hybrid" directives (1995, 100).

The Commission demonstrated its willingness to pursue an "entrepreneurial" strategy concerning women's rights in the Pregnancy Directive proposal of 1990 based on the new health and safety Article of the SEA. This "hybrid" proposal combined contractual and social security rights, such as maternity leave and pay, with more unambiguous health and safety provisions like those regulating toxin exposure (Rhodes 1995, 101). The protection of pregnant workers had already appeared on the public agenda in the early 1980s when the Women's Rights Committee and the Equal Opportunities Unit published separate reports on the subject (EP 1983; Coester-Waltjen 1984). However, the new voting rules offered an opportunity for the Commission to propose a draft directive. The British, predictably, challenged the issues packaged into one directive and abstained from the Common Position adopted in December 1991. The U.K. eventually gained some concessions, and the Directive was adopted in 1992. The Commission's strategy was characterized as "adventurous" (Hoskyns 1996, 157), "creative" and even "devious" (Rhodes 1995, 100). It was nonetheless effective in overcoming national obstruction to achieve goals perceived as benefiting Europe and the EU. The Pregnancy Directive follows the strategy adopted for other directives during this period. The Directive on working time sought to establish daily, weekly, night and shift work rest requirements based on Article 118a. The British challenged the legal base of this Directive, claiming that "it stretched the meaning of health and safety beyond recognition" (Rhodes 1995, 100). The Commission strategy of "packaging" different issues to take advantage of QMV under the SEA eventually paid off when the ECJ rejected the British position in a 1996 ruling (*Financial Times* 5 August 1996).

In addition to the SEA, new set of rules adopted under the Social Protocol gave the Commission a strategic opportunity to reintroduce Directives that had not been approved in the 1980s. Enacted as part of the Maastricht Treat negotiations, the Social Protocol, established a "code of practice" and extended qualified majority voting to issues dealing with living and working conditions, training and equal opportunities, gender equality, the needs of underprivileged groups, health and safety protection. The Social Protocol also formally introduced new actors into the policy arena. It allowed management and labor organizations to jointly conclude framework agreements, which the Commission could then submit to the Council as draft directives (Article 4.2). The Directives on parental leave, burden of proof, and part-time work were re-introduced, taking advantage of the absence of the U.K., which had blocked such proposals in the past (see chapter 2).

The rejection of Commission proposals at the Council of Ministers attests to the member states' disapproval of policy they perceive as contrary to their interests. Although member states might have altered their preferences over a decade, the reintroduction of proposals once rejected reveals the Commission's long-term goals and institutional persistence. Despite the clear indication that proposals were contrary to some member states' interests, the Commission did not discard the policy proposals; once the context for the development of EU social policy became more favorable, the Commission (re-) advanced its original agenda. The Social Protocol attests to the autonomy of the Commission and, at a theoretical level, it challenges the intergovernmentalist assumption of the centrality of sovereignty in European integration (Pierson 1996).

THE COMMISSION, THE U.K. AND THE SOCIAL PROTOCOL

Pierson has characterized the Social Protocol as a "hastily cobbled together agreement" that does not reflect the member states' interests but rather their "short-term domestic objectives" (1996, 154–5). The eleven member states expected the ambitious provisions in the draft version to weaken during the negotiations in an attempt to find a compromise with the anticipated British opposition (Pierson 1996, 154). However, the British did not agree on any version of the Protocol, a situation that left the remaining eleven member states with a document that was intended to offer a starting point to a bargain, not the final product. Facing a complete failure at the 1991 Maastricht conference, President Delors encouraged the eleven member states at the last minute to adopt a document that would not be binding on the U.K.. Had the Major government accepted a compromise, the value of the Protocol would have been more "symbolic" in nature. However, the very core of the "Thatcher ideology" was complete autonomy with regard to social policy vis-à-vis EU control. In an attempt to preserve unity in the Conservative Party and "perhaps also by conviction" (Lange 1992, 249), the British rejected any agreement. Based primarily on short-term domestic concerns, this decision posed a "long-term threat" to British autonomy (Pierson 1996, 155). The ephemeral position of the British "opt-out" was already questioned at an official level by 1994. In 1994, the Commissioner for Social Affairs, Padraig Flynn, declared during a press conference on the White Paper on Social Policy: "By 1997, I believe that the moment will have arrived to see whether a single framework should not be put in place, including the United Kingdom" (European Commission 1994, 38). Only a year after the Maastricht ratification, Flynn's public statement, expressed in precise language and providing a specific time framework, offered a striking example of the Commission's institutional confidence in its ability to reverse national policies. The position presented by Flynn shows that the British "opt out" was understood as a "short-lived" policy; given different political circumstances, the "double" social policy framework would be reversed in order to achieve efficiency in the supranational policy process.

In a 1996 article published before the change of government in Britain and prior to the negotiations for the Amsterdam Treaty, Pierson predicted that "a Labour government would probably reverse the choice" (Pierson 1996, 155). This scenario meant that the U.K. would come to accept a more "ambitious" document than would otherwise have been the case, had the Major government participated in the Maastricht negotiations. It also meant that the British would come to accept social policies made in their absence by the other member states during the post-Maastricht period and prior to the government's actual acceptance of the Social Protocol. Pierson's prediction proved quite accurate: Labour's victory in the 1997 U.K. elections enabled Prime Minister Blair to reverse Major's decision. The U.K. joined the other member states in accepting the Social Protocol now incorporated into the Amsterdam Treaty. Consequently, the U.K. was obliged to embrace all social policy directives that had been enacted under the Social Protocol during its absence. In 1997, the Council of Ministers adopted two directives, extending the Directives on Parental Leave [24] and on Informing and Consulting Workers to the U.K.. In 1998, two more Directives, on Part-time Work and on the Burden of Proof, were extended to the U.K.. These directives were adopted under the Social Protocol procedure allowing the social partners (associations representing employers and workers) to conclude framework agreements, which then the Commission submits to the Council as draft directives. The Parental Leave Directive was the first one agreed to by the social partners under the Social Protocol. The Commission had initiated the process by consulting with the social partners on the matter. The partners responded that they were interested in entering into negotiations that resulted in a framework agreement, consequently adopted by the Council as the Directive on Parental Leave.

THE COMMISSION'S SECOND AUTONOMOUS FUNCTION: STRUCTURING THE POLICY ENVIRONMENT

In addition to making "creative" use of rules, the Commission's second autonomous function involves its role in structuring the policy environment. As discussed earlier, the transfer of Article 119 to a different section of the

Treaty of Rome proved important not only for the second *Defrenne* case but also for the Commission. It allowed supranational action that both influenced policy and changed the policy environment. The original association of Article 119 with the competition section of the Treaty, along with a stricter implementation deadline, provided the ECJ with the applicability date in the second *Defrenne* case. This time frame for implementation was shorter than would have been the case, if Article 119 had not been associated with the first stage of the market completion. Yet the implementation date was not altered even after Article 119 was moved to the Social section. The "unintended" deadline gave the Commission the opportunity to create the "Article 119 group." This ad hoc consultative structure, formed in 1961 to examine the implementation of Article 119, was to become one of the many groups organized by the Commission initiated. These types of structures were important in enriching the "primeval soup" of policy ideas. They also fostered an interest group constituency (Mazey 1995, 607) around the Commission that strengthened its position and allowed autonomous action.

With the creation of the Article 119 group, the Commission started a tradition of establishing a policy community that would support and strengthen its action, and expand the scope of policy beyond the narrow equal pay provision of the original Treaty. Mark Pollack labels the Commission the "entrepreneurial ally of diffuse interests" (1997a, 579). The Commission attracts interest groups seeking to influence policy at the drafting stage. Beyond the natural interest it attracts because of its policymaking role, the Commission "has actively cultivated Euro-groups of all kinds," however (Pollack 1997a, 579). Sonia Mazey labels this Commission strategy "constituency mobilization" that would further support "bureaucratic expansion" (1995, 607). As noted in chapter 2, members of the Article 119 group, including Belgian Brunfaut and other trade unionists, were instrumental in incorporating "work of equal value" in the Equal Pay Directive, a concept, which had been explicitly rejected by the member-states during the Treaty of Rome negotiations. After the formation of the Article 119 group, the Commission invited outside experts like sociologist Evelyn Sullerot to write a report on women's employment in 1968 (see chapter 2). Sullerot's report (1970) proved influential in expanding the scope of EU women's policy beyond equal pay.

Sullerot's was one of the many experts who would gradually form an *epistemic community*, defined as "a network of professionals with recognized expertise and competence in a particular domain and an authoritative claim to policy-relevant knowledge within that domain or issue-area" (Haas 1992, 3). The Commission needed the "expertise and competence" of those professionals whose "authoritative" knowledge would legitimize the institution's policy initiatives. In comparison to the EU's intergovernmental structures, namely the Council of Ministers and the European Council, the Commission has developed an administrative capacity to promote and manage expertise in specific issue areas. The Commission's "leverage" depends, in part, on "the unique expertise it derives from its role as think-tank of the European Union" (Marks *et al.* 1996, 359).

Starting in 1982, the Commission organized expert networks in charge of monitoring existing policies, initiating research and gathering data to support further policy development (Mazey 1998, 142): "the Commission has virtually a free hand in creating new networks" (Marks *et al.* 1996, 359). These networks are composed of a coordinator and one or two independent experts from each member state. The Law Network monitors the application of equality directives and is staffed by both academics and practicing lawyers. Other networks focus on women's employment, vocational training, childcare, business creation, positive action and equal opportunities in education, broadcasting and decision-making (Hubert 1998, 73; Mazey 1998, 142). These experts bring national perspectives to the debate and establish a level of policymaking that bypasses national authorities. They share with the Commission a common goal that is the development or effective implementation of EU initiatives in a particular issue area. The Networks of Experts are a very structured form of epistemic communities as defined by Haas (1992). The Commission has actively sought the support of these epistemic communities and structured their participation through the Networks of Experts.

In addition to forging the Networks, the Commission has surrounded itself with a number of "technical assistance offices." These structures are either located in consulting companies already in operation or in new companies set up by free lance consultants to compete in securing work contracted out by the Commission. The "technical offices" are often temporary organizations, with the Commission being their sole client and source of funding. Lack of funding can abruptly result in their disappearance, but groups have also been known to reorganize under a different name to win another Commission contract. These consultants introduce a gender perspective independent of the member states and the Commission (interview with Seeland). These "feminist consultants" (Hoskyns 1996, 204) are very often social activists and experts in EU policies regarding women with long experience in Brussels and their home countries. Their continuous presence in a specific policy area contrasts with the turnover of Commission employees, a fact that renders the external assistance essential.

The Center for Research on European Women (CREW) was founded in 1980 with the purpose of providing consulting services and research and has significant experience in EU equal opportunities and women's vocational training. In 1988, CREW won the contract to coordinate the network for women's training (IRIS), which was part of the Second Action Programme (1988–1992); the Commission continued funding IRIS until 1995. When the Commission funding ended, IRIS became an association with membership paid by European vocational training centers, NGOs, employers, and trade unions. The association's brochure defines three objectives: promoting equal opportunities in vocational training, developing the quality of women's training, and creating links among European training organizations.

Similarly, the Commission contracted out work for the Fourth Action Programme for Equal Opportunities, not only creating a natural ally but also increasing the capability of the Equal Opportunities Unit with additional workforce. According to the Commission, this new structure (ANIMA) would "guarantee the coherence and visibility of all the Programme's [Fourth Action Programme] activities" (European Commission 1998, 2). The ability to create such structures was partly curtailed by a 1998 Court of Auditors report on the management and expenditures of technical assistance (TA) offices.[25] This rather critical report revealed that ANIMA's annual cost of 3,1 million ECU was "out of proportion to the funds being managed."[26] The Court of Auditor recommended that the Commission reexamine "the operation of the TA contract for the EO [Equal Opportunities]-Programme including a review of the selection procedures and the contractual terms." Consequently, the Commission did not renew ANIMA's contract. According to a consultant linked to another TA office, this event coincided with the adoption of stricter fraud standards and the result was "disastrous" not only for ANIMA but also for the Equal Opportunities Unit that had to deal with an increasing workload (interview with Seeland). Another TA office focused on women's policies, the European Office for Programme Support (EUROPS), was established to provide assistance for DG V's Community Initiatives, a strand of which is New Opportunities for Women (NOW). As a Program officer for NOW, Suzanne Seeland explained EUROPS' tasks: "we are working on the content level. Our responsibilities are, on one hand, project analysis from our database and, on the other hand, visiting the projects [in the member states]" (interview).

In addition to funding TA offices at the European level, the Commission has financed similar offices in each member state. National support structures are involved with the implementation and the financing of local projects. In most cases, these structures are newly established institutions and offices and they range from entirely governmental structures, to semi-independent agencies to independent companies. In Greece, the Ministry of Labor supervises the Labor Institute (*Ethniko Institouto Ergasias*) which has tripartite representation from government, labor and employers. Seeland described it as "a hub which helps the Greek administration to deal with all these European funding programs" (interview). In Italy, this structure (ISFOL) assumed the form of a limited company, while in Finland it has been integrated in the Ministry of Labor.

At the national level, another group "benefiting" from the Commission consists of the project promoters. These are national organizations that apply and compete for Community funding on behalf of the beneficiaries they represent—or plan to target. Supranational funding of local projects not only supports both "promoters" and beneficiaries but also structures their participation. In the case of the NOW program (see chapter 4), the Commission has actually promoted NGO participation in women's training policies. It encouraged national women's organizations to apply for Community funding with the potential of receiving funds and support unavailable to them at the national level. This allows small organizations to take an active part in not only developing alternative ideas for social policy but also in implementing them through their own pilot projects. For many NGOs, "it was the first time that they really had a large enough budget to do a good model project. One of the beauties of these initiatives—that in most cases member states have understood—is that this is an opportunity to really develop a test case even if it failed" (interview with Seeland). The funding opportunities provided by the Commission impelled these NGOs to restructure their organization in order to become competitive in attaining European funds. As Seeland observed, "small institutions over the years have become highly professional and specialized in this respect [Community funding for women's projects]. That was an enormous opportunity for these promoters to get another push and become more professional." Some of the smaller women's NGOs have also merged with each other "because for them it was difficult to apply for funding and they were not used to this kind of process" (interview).

Supranational institutions have not only influenced the organization and identity of national NGOs but also their agendas and activities. "Calls for proposals" issued by various DGs focus on specific issues and set particular requirements and criteria from applicants: "we encourage the participation from NGOs by inviting them to participate in projects and work closely with us on subjects that are *our* priorities" (interview with Pau, my emphasis). The "calls for proposals" issued by the Women's Information Service at

DG X have *inter alia* supported information campaigns on increasing women's turnout in elections and on the EURO. NGOs in the member states interested in securing these types of grants will channel their activity on issues announced and promoted by the Commission. A Commission-funded national campaign aiming to increase female voter turnout in national and European elections in 1999 had an impact on national electoral politics. The impact is not direct since the national NGOs play the intermediary role. Still, the Commission sets the priorities and enables NGO activity. "We encourage women's organizations to encourage women to vote. We can't ask them [female voters] to vote for women, therefore, we are supporting such an activity that is taking place in the states... we are partners with these organizations" (interview with Pau).

The "calls for proposals" not only channel NGO activity to European priorities, but also serve the purpose of changing organizational behavior and forms of participation. The eligibility criteria for applicants are intended to promote a specific European agenda. One of the criteria, *transnationality*, promotes a sharing of policy ideas and implementation across member-states. Transnationality is a "guiding principle" based on the idea that "the sharing of new ideas and approaches across national boundaries promotes further innovation and increases their impact, as they have the chance of being picked up and used in a number of different countries" (European Office for Programme Support (EUROPS) 1996, 3). Forming transnational partnerships is a requirement and applicants in need of funds must comply with it whether they support this principle or not. "We support a project that has a European dimension. We don't give subsidies directly to national projects because it is the nature of the function to develop a European dimension. If the partnership within the member states is achieved as required by the criteria, then an applicant can be part of the project" (interview with Pau). Through the mechanism of funding projects and NGOs, the Commission has at its disposal a tool for channeling national activity in accordance with institutional priorities. This mechanism enables the Commission to promote a European agenda and, at the same time, to gain national support for supranational institutions.

The Commission has also facilitated the establishment of the European Women's Lobby (EWL). In 1987, the two structures dedicated to women at DG V (Equal Opportunities Unit) and DG X (Women's Information Service) participated in assigning a group of forty individuals from European women's organizations the task of preparing the Lobby (Hoskyns 1991, 67). Commission funding of the preparatory work resulted in the establishment of the organization in 1990.

The same year, Vasso Papandreou became the first woman Commissioner responsible for Social Affairs and supported this effort (Hubert 1998, 70). The new Commissioner did not arrive in Brussels with a specific agenda regarding women's rights; her political connections, rather than her gender, were the primary reason for the appointment (interview with Papayiannakopoulou). However, the nomination of the first woman Commissioner was received in a climate of enthusiasm by the European media and the Brussels political scene; the French government soon followed the Greek lead with the nomination of Christiane Schrivener. As a result of this unexpected attention from her nomination as the first female Commissioner, Papandreou played up her role as a woman, thus her support for the EWL's creation must be understood within this context (interview with Papayiannakopoulou). The Commission continues to fund the EWL as it does other lobby organizations, such as the Migrant Forum (established in May 1991) and the Disabilities Forum (1996). The Commission likewise financed the creation of the European Network of Women (ENOW) with the aim of coordinating national networks to lobby at the EU level. These groups have become important policy actors in the Brussels arena: "the Commissioners opened themselves to pressures from different groups" (interview with Helfferich).

Barbara Helfferich, former General-Secretary of the EWL, observed that some groups were skeptical of this new alliance at the outset: "many women's organizations would say that it [the EU] does not help us at all, it is another men's club, another men's structure. Look at the European Commission personnel. We want to stay outside of it" (interview). Other national women's organizations realized that "the EU was developing very fast in the social field, and there was not an inclusion of a women's perspective in it. That presented a danger, if you have European integration without the active participation of women" (interview with Helfferich). These groups saw that "a lot of the legislation at the European level was actually more positive than the national level." There was a realization that women could "use" European integration to their benefit. As Helfferich stated: "this is an opportunity. It is certainly not easy but if we miss the boat now, we will never get on it. There was lot of awareness. Actually a lot more awareness than in other [policy] sectors, I would say" (interview).

The benefits emanating from a relationship between the Commission and women's groups were mutual. The relationship served the aims of an ambitious Commission seeking to legitimize its role in social policy, as well as those of women's groups demanding more policy changes than member states were offering. "They [women] realized that maybe by inserting themselves into the policy process, they could use the EU much more in order to pressure their governments to implement legislation in favor of women" (interview with Helfferich).

The establishment and maintenance of social policy interlocutors has therefore created direct links between supranational institutions and national constituencies. This funded constituency serves many Commission goals such as institutional legitimization, increasing support from skeptics (many women) and linking citizens with the EU arena. The Commission "needed to be seen as bringing the citizens on board. And who was the most skeptical sector of politics? It was women and to bring them they tried to bring them in the labor market and facilitate their participation" (interview with Helfferich). As a result, the Commission established a level of cooperation that in many ways bypasses national authorities. In preparing policy proposals, the Commission consults with the EWL on a systematic basis (Mazey 1995, 605; interview with Helfferich). The Lobby moreover enjoys an observer status within the more formal institutional structure at DG V, the Advisory Committee on Equal Opportunities. This Committee, composed of representatives from national equality agencies, was set up in 1981. It is consulted on EU women's policies and its objective is to channel information on EU equality policies from Brussels to European women through the national equality agencies (Hoskyns 1986, 307).

The Commission attempted to co-opt institutional critics such as women and to transform them into allies capable of supporting policy development against potential member state resistance. Two institutional actors have described the Commission's perception of its role in developing gender policies as targeting a "niche" issue area. Jacqueline Nonon, the first head of the Equal Opportunities Unit, portrayed the Commission's role in gender policies as "avant garde" seeking to demonstrate that "the integration process can be the driving power for real social progress" (Nonon 1998, 4). Ex-Commissioner for Social Affairs, Henk Vredeling, has commented:

> there is . . . one area of the Community's work responsibilities which we might describe as a *pioneering* one, and which gives a lead and generates enthusiasm—its efforts to banish from our society discrimination against women...In this area Community legislation represents more than merely deriving a common denominator of the laws applying in the member states. It is ahead of their legislation" (*The Times* 3 June 1980 quoted in Warner 1984, 160, my emphasis).

Women's groups in Brussels also understood that "European institutions wanted to be seen at the forefront of the social movement" (interview with Helfferich). The specific issue of equal pay had the potential to "touch European citizens directly" (Alter and Vargas 1997, 9), enabling both supranational institutions, the Commission and the ECJ, to exploit this issue to their benefit. Promotion of equal pay would benefit the institution by "giving more personal meaning to the somewhat abstract European Community and building a nationally based pro-ECJ and pro-Europe constituency within member states" (Alter and Vargas 1997, 9). Europe-wide polls show that in the majority of member states, women remain more skeptical about the EU than men (see chapter 2). Nonetheless, women in the 2,700 national organizations represented by the European Women's Lobby (EWL) have become active participants in the EU policy arena. These groups often lobby to alter their own government's position on EU primary and secondary legislation pertaining to gender issues. In one of their most recent and strongest campaigns, women's groups actively lobbied the member state negotiators during the intergovernmental conference for the Amsterdam Treaty.

CONCLUSION

This chapter has demonstrated that member state preferences are not the only determinants of EU gender policy. Historical "details" such as the expansive definition of the concept of pay and the last minute transfer of an article to a different section, have consequences that affect states' interests in the long term in ways that cannot be anticipated at the time of negotiation of policy instruments. The impact of these consequences has been cumulative and interactive, and this latter dynamic has transformed EU policymaking. Furthermore, the Commission's ability to "play the treaty-base game" and structure the policy environment by creating an interest group constituency hampers national control of EU gender policy.

The emergence of unanticipated consequences, heavily discounted by intergovernmentalists, not only creates a gap between member state control and supranational institutions but also allows the latter to develop autonomous action. The expansive definition of the concept of pay allowed the ECJ to further develop the concept and establish a considerable amount of case law at the same time that it was altering member state preferences through the *Barber* judgment and the subsequent amendment of the 1986 Directive.[27]

The transfer of Article 119 to the Social Chapter section late in the Treaty of Rome negotiations had long-term unanticipated consequences for gender policy development. On one hand, the transfer was beneficial because it strengthened social policy in ways envisioned only for economic policy.

Originally designed as an economic measure, Article 119 acquired a stronger wording than was the case with other social policy measures. Its economic origin explains its association with the "first stage" of the completion of the common market, a deadline formally recognized in the landmark second *Defrenne* case. On the other hand, the transfer to the social chapter might have been more detrimental to gender policy development, specifically, after the adoption of qualified majority voting (QMV) for issues relating to the completion of the single market. Had Article 119 remained as an economic measure, it could have benefited from QMV introduced with the 1987 Single European Act (SEA). This institutional rule has constrained the development of gender policy in the period following the adoption of the SEA.

However, an "entrepreneurial" Commission took advantage of some new rules under the 1987 SEA and the 1993 Social Protocol to promote policies contrary to the preferences of some member states. The Pregnancy Directive was adopted based on the health and safety Article 118a of the SEA, taking advantage of QMV to override British objections. New rules under the Social Protocol have also expanded QMV to gender equality issues and introduced new policy actors (social partners) into the EU policy process. Britain's initial rejection of the Social Protocol shows that short-term political reasons (reconciling the Tories) compromised the national interest, defined as autonomy in social policy. New institutional rules allowed policies such as the Parental Leave Directive to overcome the initial rejection and be reintroduced successfully. These new rules modified states' preferences as all new Directives agreed under the Social Protocol had experienced long periods of stalemate under the previous rules.

A policy once defined as contrary to national interests is now accepted even by the state that most vocally rejected it on grounds of preserving national autonomy. In principle, a future Conservative government in Britain may attempt to regain control over social policy and reverse Labour's decision in accepting the Social Protocol. However, as noted in chapter 1, treaty revision requires unanimity and ratification by national parliaments thus limiting Britain's exit option. New institutional rules in the Social Protocol introducing QMV in gender equality issues, and the participation of the social partners, do not preserve member state autonomy. The Social Protocol was not the result of careful intergovernmental negotiation. The implications for social policy development after the Protocol's incorporation in the 1997 Amsterdam Treaty remain to be evaluated.

Contrary to the intergovernmentalist view of supranational institutions as instrumental, the Commission's use of policymaking rules shows autonomy in achieving institutional goals and expanding policy. The Commission's other function in structuring the policy environment also challenges the intergovernmentalist view of institutional instrumentality. The Commission has actively created epistemic communities consisting of the Experts Network to legitimize and expand its scope of action. The Commission's role in establishing and funding national and European technical assistance offices, project promoters, calls for proposals and NGOs like the European Women's Lobby, has structured the policy environment and influenced the organization and agenda of national and supranational policy actors. Its voluntary and purposive activity in creating, organizing and mobilizing an interest group constituency reveals an autonomous institution and not an instrumental one. National control of EU policy is impeded not only by unintended consequences but also by the autonomous behavior of supranational institutions. EU policy outcomes are not the direct result of member state preferences defending their interests and sovereignty, as intergovernmentalists would predict.

NOTES

[1] The 1975 Equal Pay Directive (75/117) eventually expanded Article 119 to include equal pay for work of equal value.

[2] Gabrielle Defrenne v. Belgian State, CJEC 25 May 1971, Case 90/70, ECR 1971.

[3] The pension scheme in question was part of statutory social security scheme and although the employer (Sabena Airlines) contributed into it, it was managed by the state.

[4] Worringham & Humphreys v. Lloyds Bank Ltd., CJEC 11 March 1981, Case 12/81, ECR 1982.

[5] Bilka Kaufhaus GmbH v. Weber von Hertz, CJEC 13 May 1986, C 170/81, ECR 1986.

[6] CJEC 9 February 1982, Case 12/81, ECR 1982.

[7] Commission of the European Communities v. Kingdom of Belgium, CJEC 17 February 1983, Case 173/91, ECR 1981.

[8] Joan Gillespie and others v. Northern Health and Social Services Boards, Department of Health and Social Services, Eastern Health and Social Services Board and Southern Health and Social Services Board, CJEC Case 342/93 of 13 February 1996, ECR 1996.

[9] Douglas Harvey Barber v. Guardian Exchange Assurance Group, CJEC 17 May 1990, Case 262/88, ECR 1990.

[10] Ten Oever v. Stichting Bedrijfspensioenfonds, CJEC 6 October 1993, Case 109/91.

[11] Moroni v. Collo GmbH, CJEC 14 December 1993, ECR 1994.

[12] EC Commission v. United Kingdom (1982) ECR 2601.

13 Council Directive 96/97/EC of 20 December 1996.

14 OJ L 46 of 17 February 1997, p. 20.

15 *Bulletin of the ECs*, no.1, 1962, p. 8.

16 The second Defrenne case brought before the ECJ was actually initiated before the first Defrenne case in 1968. However, due to delays in the Belgian court system, it did not reach the ECJ until 1976.

17 The Belgian courts awarded Defrenne for all of her three cases the sum of 12,716 Belgian francs (approximately $240).

18 Hubert was head of the Commission's Equal Opportunities Unit from 1992–6. She is now adviser for gender dimension and information society at the Commission's Forward Studies Unit that directly reports to the Commission's President. The tasks of the Forward Studies Unit are "to monitor and evaluate European integration, to establish permanent relations with bodies involved in forecasting and to work on specific briefs."

19 The SEA provided that the Act "would come into force the month after the last country ratified it" (Dinan 1994, 148).

20 *Proposal for a Council Directive on parental leave and leave for family reasons*, COM (83) 686 final, 22 November 1983.

21 Official Journal C 176 of 5 July 1988, p. 5.

22 Council Directive 92/85/EEC of 19 October 1992 on the introduction of measures to encourage improvements in the safety and health at work of pregnant workers and workers who have recently given birth or are breastfeeding, Official Journal L 348, 28 November 1992, p. 1.

23 See chapter 2, for the influence of Thatcherism as a particularly obstructivist phenomenon in the 1980s.

24 Council Directive of 15 December 1997 amending and extending to the United Kingdom of Great Britain and Northern Ireland Directive 96/34/EEC on the framework agreement on parental leave concluded by UNICE, CEEP and the ETUC (97/75/EC).

25 Special Report No. 22/98 concerning the management by the Commission of the implementation of measures to promote equal opportunities for women and men accompanied by the replies of the Commission (Pursuant to Article 188c (4), second subparagraph, of the EC Treaty) Official Journal C 393, 16 December 1998, p. 0024 – 0046.

26 *Op. Cit.*

27 Equal Treatment in Occupational Social Security Directive 86/378.

Chapter 4

Supranational Institutions and Equal Opportunities Policy: The Role of the Structural Funds

I N THE LAST CHAPTER I ARGUED THAT MEMBER-STATE PREFERENCES ARE not the only determinants of EU gender policy, as unintended consequences and supranational institutions' autonomous behavior intervene to alter policy outcomes. In this chapter, I concentrate on equal opportunities policy in the Structural Funds demonstrating the influence of supranational institutions on national policies, in general, and the impact of specific European Union (EU) programs in particular.

The Structural Funds are the financial instruments enabling the EU to respond to regional disparities by aiming to achieve six EU Objectives (see table 2); one of the four Funds, the European Social Fund (ESF), provides the major source of funding for European social policy. The ESF co-finances specific programs to promote one of the EU-wide Objectives (Objective 3), which includes the promotion of equal opportunities in the member states. It also finances Community Initiatives defined as programs "whose guidelines are established by the Commission according to European priorities" (European Commission 1997, 6). These two type of programs, *Objective 3* and *Community Initiatives*, provide supranational funding for national projects in order to improve women's participation in the labor force, ameliorate the status of those already employed and reduce female unemployment. The Commission's role in financing, policy programming and implementation these two programs offer the opportunity to examine the influence of supranational institutions on national social policies and particularly in developing and improving employment opportunities for women.

91

First, I provide a brief statistical portrait with respect to women's position in the European labor market, defining the specific problems which the Structural Funds equal opportunity policies are attempting to address. Second, I situate Objective 3 and Community Initiatives within the context of the Structural Funds, in general, and the European Social Fund (ESF), in particular. I examine the ways in which the Commission has enhanced its autonomy through a number of reforms, using the Funds as an instrument for channeling and directing European social policy. The reforms have provided the Commission with two financial tools for promoting equal opportunities in the member states. I then examine the first financial tool, ESF funding of Objective 3 projects promoting equal opportunities. I analyze the case of the French Objective 3 Single Programming Document (SPD) for the period 1994–99, assessing the Commission's role in planning and implementing equal opportunity policy in France. I argue that EU influence on French policy has been procedural and ideological in nature, in spite of the latter's apparent non-compliance. Fourth, I examine the second financial instrument, the Community Initiatives, elaborating on the ways in which the Commission influences national employment policy through one such initiative that specifically targets women, the New Opportunities for Women (NOW) program. I contend that the Commission has managed to influence national policy and to promote the Europeanization of social policy through its enforcement of eligibility criteria for funding national projects in the NOW context.

As a prelude to discussing the Structural Funds, the French Single Programming (SPD) Document and the New Opportunities for Women (NOW) program, I will now review the situation of women in the European labor force which testifies to the need for European equal opportunity policy through the Structural Funds.

STATISTICAL PORTRAIT OF WOMEN IN THE LABOR MARKET

European women constitute 40% of those in paid employment (European Commission 1998a, 55), having benefited from much of the job growth in certain sectors over the last decade (European Commission 1997a, 29). Small and medium-sized enterprises (SMEs) accounted for most of the job growth in the EU member states and women created more than 25% of the new businesses (European Commission 1997, 4). Growth occurred mainly in the service sector, where 79% of women are already employed, compared to 52% among men (European Commission 1997a, 31). Service sector growth is nonetheless associated with an increase in atypical employment, characterized by temporary, night and weekend work.

The main trends of women's employment in the European labor market are occupational and vertical segregation, employment vulnerability, unequal pay, and atypical work. Occupational segregation refers to the "feminization" of certain economic sectors. In 1992, for example, women accounted for 90.4% of workers in domestic services, 71.8% of health professionals, and 65.4% of those in education; less than 10% of the labor force in building and civil engineering are women. Vertical segregation refers to the under-representation of women in management positions, as opposed to their over-representation in clerical posts. Although European women comprise 40% of the personnel in public administration, they hold only 10% of the managerial posts in that domain.

Another trend typical of women's employment is vulnerability to job loss. Unemployment in the EU member states is generally high, was forecasted at 10% for 1999. However, women face higher unemployment rates than men (13% for women, 10% for men). In 1992, the U.K. was the only country in which men had a higher unemployment rate than women, a trend partly explained by an increase in part-time work for women. Higher female unemployment rates remain constant; by 1996, only the U.K. and Sweden saw higher unemployment rates for men than for women (European Commission 1998, 57). Three countries, Ireland, Austria and Finland, had similar unemployment rates for men and women. In Spain, the gap between male and female unemployment rates remains substantial while it varies in the other member states. For the long-term unemployed (unemployed for more than one year), 52% of women versus 47% of men are unemployed in the "core age group" of 25–49 (European Commission 1998, 56).

Another trend regarding female employment is that women are paid less in all member states with differences ranging from 15–35% for manual workers and 30–40% for non-manual workers. Part-time jobs are generally considered "low paid, low-skilled, and have less favorable working conditions" (European Commission 1997, 4). While rates vary among member states, on average more than 30% of all employed women, compared to less than 5% for men, work part time (European Commission 1997, 4). The Netherlands evinces the highest percentage of part-timers among employed women with 64%, compared to 16% for men (European Commission 1995, 150). In the U.K., Denmark and Germany, part-time work accounted for more than 30% of female employment (European Commission 1995, 150).

The brief review of the main trends in women's employment shows that the EU member states share many of the same problems, which they have been unable to tackle at the national level. The severity and persistence of the problems, as well as the inability of national governments to find solutions, promotes and upgrades the EU's role as an alternative policy arena for employment policy. Structural policy attempts to address some of the gender-specific problems European women face in the labor force.

STRUCTURAL POLICY, THE EUROPEAN SOCIAL FUND (ESF) AND THE EVOLVING COMMISSION AUTONOMY

"Structural policy is the means by which the Community promotes cohesion" (Dinan 1994, 403). The Structural Funds are the "financial instruments" which the EU has at its disposal to respond to regional disparities in growth, per capita income, employment and investment. They are composed of four separate funds, the European Social Fund (ESF), established in 1958, the guidance section of the European Agricultural Guidance and Guarantee Fund (EAGGF), dating from 1962, the European Regional Development Fund (ERDF), begun in 1975, and the Financial Instrument for Fisheries Guidance (FIFG), which dates from 1993.

The preamble of the Treaty of Rome refers to the objective of reducing economic disparities among the regions and Article 2 to encouraging harmonization among the regions of the signatory countries. The European Social Fund (ESF), the oldest of the four Structural Funds, was established under Article 123 of the Rome Treaty "to improve job opportunities in the Community by promoting employment and increasing the geographical and occupational mobility of workers" (European Commission 1998b). Since its creation in 1958, the ESF has evolved into a structure very different from the one negotiators designed. Multiple ESF reforms were necessary to respond to the changing socioeconomic situation in Europe, the evolution of EU policy, the accession of new member states, and new needs identified by the periodic reviews assessing its operation, management and impact (European Commission 1998b).

During the early years of its operation, from 1958 until the first reform of 1971, the ESF focused on assisting geographical and occupational mobility. The Fund offered assistance in financing the resettlement and retraining of workers whose unemployment partly ensued from the common market. The majority of the funds financed the retraining of Italian workers to resettle in Germany, France and Belgium. Italy and Germany were the main beneficiaries of this period, both in terms of the number of workers involved and the amount of financial assistance received. Italians represented 65% of the assisted workers, while Germans accounted for 25% of the beneficiaries. The

ESF assistance for retraining and resettling workers covered 50% of the cost, subject to reimbursement only after the programs had been completed and the workers actually re-employed. Anderson suggests that "the ESF did little more than offer member states a way to partially offset the costs of their own labor market policies" (1995, 134). In its own publication, the ESF considers its operation during the period 1958–71 as problematic because "the system of retrospective grants precluded any *Community* influence on national labour market and vocational training policies" (European Commission 1998b, my emphasis). This self-evaluation illustrates the Commission's position, that supranational influence on national problems was the desired state of affairs and that such influence was required to provide effective policy solutions. To the extent that Community policies and structural factors were responsible for unemployment, the Commission's response was that European-level solutions were required for addressing the problem.

The 1969 Commission proposal for reforming the ESF marks the beginning of bureaucratic expansion and the promotion of European solutions for shared national problems. "The aim was to extend and strengthen the Fund as an instrument responding to Community rather than purely national objectives, while introducing greater efficiency and flexibility in its management" (European Commission 1998b, chapter 1). The proposal for reform was adopted in 1971 and became effective in May 1972. Following this reform, ESF resources available for Community action increased dramatically, with the budget of the first two years exceeding the budget of the previous twelve-year period (European Commission 1998b). Except for agriculture, the ESF received the largest share of the EC budget, and over the following four years, its budget increased by 500%. The Commission assumed what was to become a much larger role by setting the eligibility criteria, allowing aid to the private sector, and promoting pilot projects to encourage innovation. The new provisions in Articles 4 and 5 of the reformed ESF[1] went beyond the original concern with individual workers to cover groups of workers such as persons with disabilities.

The amendments of 1977–78 constitute the next major reform in ESF's history. The amendments expanded the ESF's role by allowing Community-level intervention in more policy sectors than the original Treaty had envisaged. The 1975 establishment of the European Regional Development Fund (ERDF) promoted the Commission's vision of regional rather than national development (European Commission 1998a). Categories of eligible beneficiaries were expanded to include migrant workers, women over 25, and young people under 25. The expansion of "policy clientele" also brought an expansion of policy to include issues of job creation. The Community assumed responsibility not only for employed or unemployed workers but also for future workers. Unemployed youth under 25 in need of employment could receive 30 ECU weekly for up to 12 months (European Commission 1998a).

The "years of reform" (Anderson 1995, 140), stretching from 1979 to 1994, resulted in an accentuated regional focus for the Funds and in increasing Commission involvement. Although final authority for approving reform rests with the Council of Ministers, the Commission—as the Fund's manager—has the information advantage to propose reforms. In light of the fact that 42% of the unemployed fell under the age of 25, the 1983 revision focused on the young people.[2] The new regime required that young people make up 75% of the total beneficiaries and allocated funds for vocational training projects and job premium schemes. The Commission's preference for the regionalization of ESF was developed through budget allocations. Greece, Greenland, the French Overseas departments, Ireland, Southern Italy and Northern Ireland were to receive 40% of the ESF budget. With the accession of Spain and Portugal, the regional allocations represented 44.5% of the ESF budget. The rest of the budget was distributed to regions characterized by long-term unemployment and industrial restructuring. The Commission became responsible for defining such areas according to its own formula based on unemployment and Gross Domestic Product (GDP). Its guidelines also prioritized funding for projects focusing on "aligning national practice and Community policy" (European Commission 1998b). The revision initiated a new "contractual" relationship between the Commission and the national recipients, a feature that became more important with subsequent reforms in 1988. The Commission aimed to replace the one-time project assistance with multi-year contracts involving subnational governments in a direct relationship (Anderson 1995, 143).

Greece's accession to the European Community (EC) required a special aid package to assist in the integration and the adaptation of national policy to EC standards. Greece received 120 million ECU over a period of five years, to be used for vocational training centers and rehabilitation centers for persons with mental disabilities. Since vocational training centers composed the majority of applicants and recipients of ESF aid, the Commission thus became directly involved in creating national structures for the channeling of supranational funds. The other important result of this aid was that EU funds contributed to a broader reform of Greek psychiatric care. Supranational funding of a sector not directly tied to economic issues illustrates, perhaps, the neofunctionalist prediction that activity in one functional area may "spill over" to activities in another.

The adoption of the 1987 SEA triggered the most comprehensive reforms in ESF's history: "the anticipated spatial effects of the single market initiative provided the main impetus for the sweeping reforms of the structural funds in 1988" (Anderson 1995, 142). Fearing that liberalization of the market would exacerbate regional disparities, the Commission allied itself with the poorer countries and supported an expanded structural policy (Dinan 1994, 405). Article 23 of the SEA addressed economic and social cohesion, specifically in "reducing regional disparities between the various regions."

The expenditures allocated to all Funds doubled during the period 1989–93, which coincided with the decline of spending for national regional policy (Anderson 1995, 144). Gary Marks considers this dramatic increase "a side payment or bribe paid by the wealthier members to the poorer peripheral members of the EC in return for their assent to the 1992 package of economic liberalization" (1992, 194). Marks also views the expansion of the Structural Funds as a "forced spillover in which the prospect of a breakthrough in one arena created intense pressure for innovation in others" (1992, 198). The 1988 structural policy reform was characterized as "radical" (Dinan 1994, 407; European Commission 1998b), "fundamental" (Marks 1992, 206) and "comprehensive" (Anderson 1995, 143). The reforms, "justified in terms of administrative efficiency and economic rationality," increased the Commission's autonomy "in allocating resources among individual programs and even among member states (Marks 1992, 211).

The "radical" 1988 reform moreover strengthened some concepts already introduced in previous reforms and presented a new approach based on four principles—*concentration, additionality, partnership,* and *programming.* Concentration refers to the need to channel the Funds according to a limited number of functional and geographic priorities in order to achieve greater efficiency. The Funds were to finance projects according to five objectives. These objectives, slightly modified in the 1993 review, will guide ESF operations until the end of the programming period 1994–99. The three funds— ESF, ERDF and EAGGF—can contribute to achieving certain objectives collectively to obtain a more integrated operation. ESF is a contributor in all five objectives, whereas it is the sole fund with regard to Objectives 3 and 4.

Under Objective 1, the poorest regions (with a per capita GDP of less than 75% of the EU average) can receive assistance from all three funds for development and structural adjustments. In the period 1994–99, Objective 1 regions, such as the overseas French departments, Corsica, and Greece, received 48% of the total 157 billion ECU allocated to Structural Funds. The second regional objective (Objective 2) targeted regions suffering from industrial decline. The last regional objective (Objective 5b) focuses on rural development. Objective 3, targeting long-term unemployment and Objective 4, increasing youth employment applied to the whole of the EU as a whole. The 1993 revision of the Funds modified the five Objectives, based on the Commissions' *White Paper on Growth, Competitiveness and Employment.* In December 1993, the Brussels European Council endorsed this White Paper which focused on increasing human capital investment and improving vocational training as a response to rising unemployment.

Table 2: Structural Fund Objectives for the Programming Period 1994–99

• **Objective 1**	Assisting the development of "less developed regions" (ERDF, ESF and EAGGF-Guidance Section)
• **Objective 2**	Restructuring regions affected by industrial decline (ERDF, ESF)
• **Objective 3**	Combating long term unemployment, facilitating the integration into working life of young people and those exposed to exclusion from the labor market, and promoting equal opportunities for men and women (ESF)
• **Objective 4**	Adapting the work force to industrial change and to changes in production systems (ESF)
• **Objective 5**	(a) restructuring of agriculture and fisheries (EAGGF-Guidance Section, FIFG);(b) development of rural areas (EAGGF-Guidance Section, ERDF, and ESF)
• **Objective 6**	Assisting the development of sparsely populated regions (ERDF, ESF and EAGGF-Guidance Section).

Source: European Commission. 1998b. The European Social Fund: an Overview of the Programming Period 1994–99.

The 1993 revision defined a new Objective 3 merging the old Objectives 3 and 4—long-term unemployment and youth employment. The new Objective 3 also addressed equal opportunities between men and women. The "policy clientele" was expanded to cover people "at risk" of long-term unemployment and those excluded from the labor force. The revised Objective 4 targeted workforce undergoing industrial change and change in production systems. Following the accession of Sweden, Finland and Austria in 1995, Objective 6 was added to assist "the development of sparsely populated regions" (European Commission 1998c, 7).

The most recent 1999 reform further modified the Objectives of the Structural Funds regime, regrouping the current six objectives into three.

The Council of Ministers formally adopted the new regulations on June 21, 1999, which took effect in the programming period 2000–2006 (European Commission 1999c).

The "regionalization" of EU funding under the concentration principle produced a new level of communication between supranational institutions, on the one hand, and local and regional authorities, on the other, bypassing national authorities. "In fact, the Commission *pursued* partnerships with vigor" (Anderson 1995, 145, my emphasis). Its officials visited regional authorities to encourage them to apply for EU funding. The Commission also required that national authorities cooperate with local and regional authorities in drafting applications. The Commission's actions had the effect of altering "sheltered relations" (Anderson 1995, 144) between national and regional authorities. By encouraging a demand for funding, the Commission stimulated an increase in the number of applicants and strengthened its position as the provider of assistance. The Structural Funds budget for 1994–99 was twice the size of that for the pervious programming period 1989–93.

The second principle introduced with the 1988 reforms was *additionality*, seeking to prevent member states from merely replacing national funds with EU funds. A combination of EU and national-level funds must be used to finance structural funds projects; additionality requires that increased EU aid be accompanied by an increase in the share contributed by the member state.

The *partnership* principle strengthened the Commission's role in structural policy by officially recognizing the evolving relationships among the Commission, national, regional and local authorities. The Commission has sought to institutionalize its separate relationship with local and regional authorities by way of the Consultative Council of Local and Regional Authorities (CCLRA) which is composed of 42 sub-national officeholders. Thus, the Commission not only intervenes in the relationship of states and their provinces but also structures and institutionalizes this relationship, thus strengthening links with the Funds' beneficiaries. Through Community Initiatives, for example, the Commission organizes its aid to the member states according to seventeen regional plans rather than fifteen national entities. Belgium is divided into French and Flemish parts, and Northern Ireland is separated from the U.K.; therefore, both the French and Flemish authorities of Belgium and the Northern Irish have independent relationships with the Commission that bypass the unitary state.

The partnership between the Commission, national and sub-national authorities has been strengthened by the *programming* principle. Programming concerns a series of documents that set priorities and specific implementation measures—the Plan, the Community Support Frameworks (CSFs), the Operational Programmes (OPs), and the Single Programming Document (SPD). During the programming phase, each member state submits a Plan with the national priorities for action according to the established Objectives. The Commission responds to the national Plans by submitting the Community Support Frameworks (CSFs). The CSF is a document that describes "the joint action undertaken by the Member State and the Union and sets out priorities for action, funding and forms of assistance" (European Commission 1998b). CSFs assist the Commission in targeting expenditures and in supervising or redirecting national-level priorities according to EU objectives.

Beyond the CSFs, the Operational Programmes (OPs) give the Commission a role not only in the programming phase but also in implementation and monitoring.[3] Each member state submits an Operational Programme listing specific multi-annual measures for implementing the priorities agreed upon in the CSFs and requesting financial assistance. Since 1993, member states have also had the option of submitting one document, the Single Programming Document (SPD), which combines the Plan and the financing request. The Commission makes a single decision in response to the Single Programming Document (SPD) and thereby speeding up the process.

The Structural Fund procedure, involving a number of cooperative documents such as CSFs and OPs, has established a contractual relationship between the Commission and member states. It has also accorded the Commission an increasing responsibility in national policies through its supervision of structural funding. An examination of the French Single Programming Document (SPD) for Objective 3 for the period 1994–99 demonstrates the increasing role of the Commission in the planning and implementation of French employment policy.

THE FRENCH SINGLE PROGRAMMING DOCUMENT (SPD) FOR 1994–99

France has proved eligible for Structural Fund assistance both under the functional Objectives 3 and 4, covering the entire country, and under the geographical Objectives 1, 2 and 5b covering only certain regions. Six regions qualify under Objective 1 for the period 1994–1999. The French regions identified under Objective 1 as "the least prosperous," with per capita GDP less than 75% of the EU average, are Corsica and the Overseas Departments (Guadeloupe, Guyana, Réunion, and Martinique). Due to their very low GDPs, Valenciennes, Douai and Avesnes in the Nord/Pas de Calais region also became eligible for the programming period 1994–99. These regions cover 17% of French territory and represent 4.4% of the French population (European Commission 1998b, chapter 8). All four Funds are operating in France with a total allocation of 13.5 billion ECU, 4.7 billion was an ESF contribution for the period 1994–99.

Subsequent to the 1989 and 1993 Structural Funds reforms, the procedure for allocating funds requires that the French authorities submit a Single Programming Document (SPD) to the Commission for financing approval. The SPD focuses specifically "in defining strategies, establishing priorities, and developing programmes and financial plans for actions co-financed by the Structural Funds" (European Commission 1998b). Structural Fund aid to France is organized in fifty-four SPDs covering the five Objectives. There are two horizontal SPDs concentrating on Objectives 3 and 4, 49 regional SPDs involving Objectives 1, 2, and 5b, and three horizontal SPDs addressing Objective 5a.

The horizontal SPD for Objective 3 has explicitly referred to equal opportunities since the 1993 Structural Funds reform. The latter introduced a new Regulation that required "actions funded by the Structural Funds...to respect the principle of equal opportunities between women and men."[4] The Regulation specifically required that Objective 3 projects, entirely financed by the ESF, promote equal opportunities. The priorities of Objective 3 are to facilitate "the vocational integration of people at risk of long-term unemployment," of young people, of those "exposed to exclusion from the labour market," and "to promote equal opportunities for men and women" (European Commission 1996, 15).

The preparatory phase for the SPDs includes a series of preliminary meetings, interdepartmental meetings and review of expert assessments of the French Plan (European Commission 1996, 6). The documents are prepared in a negotiating process between the Commission and the French authorities. One Commission official responsible for the implementation of Objective 3 in France described the procedure in the following terms: "at the starting point of the process we negotiate programming documents which are fairly general but set up what the member states are supposed to do in the context of this Objective [Objective 3] and how they are going to use the money" (interview with Levy).

Although the member states are responsible for the implementation and management of the Structural Funds, the Commission remains involved in supervising and communicating with the national structures. In the case of France, the Regional Planning Authority (DATAR), under the authority of the Ministry for Town Planning and Integration, is in charge of the Structural Funds' coordination and implementation. The ESF Mission in the Ministry of Employment is responsible for the management of the European Social Fund (ESF) in France. All member states have created ESF Missions generally situated within Employment Ministries that communicate directly with the Commission for the implementation of the ESF in each. For Objectives 3 programs, the national ESF Mission is responsible for the initiation, piloting, supervision, financing, control and support of programs (European Commission 1998b).

During the implementation phase, a Monitoring Committee examines whether "everything is going more or less according to plan" (interview with Levy). The National Monitoring Committee for Objective 3 meets at least bi-annually and is chaired by the French Employment Delegate (*Délégué de l'Emploi*). The other Committee members represent the Department of Employment and Vocational Training (DRTEFP), Regional Councils, social partners, the National Association of Regional Deputies (*Association Nationale des Elus Régionaux*), the Association of Mayors, the coordinating committees of the regional apprenticeship and vocational training programs, and the Commission (European Commission 1998b, chapter 8).

The Commission looks "at how the financial implementation is doing, if they [member states] spend the money, and if they spend it properly. We [the Commission] follow the evaluation, supervise major changes in the program so [we call this action] implementation but its is not exactly concrete implementation. It is more like a follow up of general tendencies" (interview with Levy). The Commission administrators responsible for the implementation and monitoring of ESF operations in France and Greece have all emphasized that the "concrete implementation" of ESF programs rests with the member states (interviews with Levy, Platsouka and Sigonis).

> Implementation itself is very decentralized, so a lot is actually done in the member states if only because of volume. Obviously, I could not do it on my own. It is for reasons of subsidiarity, political reasons, but also practical reasons. We are not able to implement the programs ourselves [Commission]. We are in relatively close relation with the national authorities who are responsible for implementation of the program" (interview with Levy).

A closer examination of the French SPD for Objective 3 for the period 1994–99 reveals strong interconnections between national and supranational policy and institutions and the role of the Commission in framing and supervising national policies. The first paragraph of the SPD states that the

French submission is "in accordance with Article 5 of Council Regulation (EEC) No 2082/93 of 20 July 1993" (European Commission 1996, 5). An EU regulation justifies the very existence of a Plan and an Operational Program that involves policy planning and budgeting for a specific issue (long-term unemployment, youth and equal opportunities). French authorities based their preparation of the SPD on work completed for the national "law on the five-year plan"[5] (*La Loi quinquennale*) concerning employment, labor, and vocational training (European Commission 1996, 5). The original French submission organized the document according to the following national priorities: access to employment, job creation, quality of training, adaptation to the labor market, and pre-training (European Commission 1996, 14). However, these priorities did not correspond to the ESF priorities. After discussion between France and the Commission, the priorities were reorganized to correspond to ESF policy, not to the national "law on the five-year plan" (European Commission 1996, 14). The Commission claimed that the different prioritization presented by the French "would present difficulties from the point of view of financial management, evaluation and visibility of the finalities of the policy pursued" (European Commission 1996, 14). From an administrative point of view, the Commission's claim is substantiated given the difficulties in managing and evaluating documents from fifteen member states.

In the case of the French prioritization for Objective 3, the Commission succeeded in channeling national programming documents in following EU regulations and priorities based on its supervisory role and administrative expertise. Nonetheless, the "Europeanization" of national programming documents varies according to the attitude of a member state towards European integration and the different national political traditions and context: "the fact is that if there is a very strong feeling in the member state, there is no way the Commission is going to transform that" (interview with Levy).

After the adaptation of French priorities to correspond with the EU priorities, the SPD revealed that one of the four basic EU priorities received less than 1% of the total budget. The French SPD allocated only 17.95 million ECU to specific measures promoting equal opportunities (one of the four basic Objective 3 priorities) out of a total of 2.6 billion ECU, representing a mere 0.7% of the Objective 3 budget (European Commission 1996, 16). In fact, even this small allocation to equal opportunities was only included following reviews and negotiations with the Commission (interview with Levy). France was not alone in allocating a very small budget for equal opportunities. As the ESF mid-term evaluation showed, Denmark, Finland,

Sweden, Ireland and the Netherlands also made very small allocations to equal opportunities (European Commission 1988d). The Scandinavian countries had integrated equal opportunities into their own employment policies long before the 1993 Structural Fund reform and therefore made no special provisions. Austria (14%), Germany (8%) and Italy (8%) were the only member states allocating "a relatively large proportion" to equal opportunities (European Commission 1998d, 154).

The French indifference to the ESF equal opportunities provision derives from a fundamental ideological disagreement between France and the EU on the merits of affirmative action or positive discrimination. The French consider positive discrimination an Anglo-Saxon influence on the Commission, a tradition they do not share: "In the Commission there is more of an Anglo-Saxon attitude... In policies, I think that the Commission took a little of what was being done in Anglo-Saxon countries and introduced it here" (interview with Levy). Fabienne Levy, a Commission administrator and French national attempted to explain the French view on affirmative action:

> In terms of equal opportunities, . . . there is a big fundamental and the-oretical conflict between the Commission's policy and the French poli-cy. In France, and this goes back to the Revolution, everybody is equal so we don't have positive discrimination. Why should we have positive discrimination, since everyone is equal? It's changing slowly. When this programming period was negotiated back in 1993, it was a very big issue. It was a conflictual era between the Commission and the French author-ities (interview).

France's apparent non-compliance with the EU equal opportunities provisions in the document coincided with the change of government during the same year that the SPD was prepared. After the March 1993 legislative elections, French president François Mitterrand appointed the conservative Eduard Balladur as Prime Minister. The preparation for the "law on the five-year plan" began in June 1993, prior to the publication of the EU Regulation (20 July 1993) reforming the EU Structural Funds, including equal opportu-nities in Objective 3. The French "five-year plan" law concerning employ-ment and vocational training did not include any measure explicitly referring to women. The new government opposed positive discrimination, favoring a policy of "neutrality" instead. The employment law was adopted on December 20, 1993; the following day the French authorities submitted their Objective 3 proposal to the Commission. Subsequent negotiations between

French authorities and the Commission lasted eight months (January-August 1994), at which time the Commission approved the document.

The French maintained that funding equal opportunity projects was not necessary since all national policies were already in accordance with the EU principle: "the French claimed that they did not need that [specific equal opportunity provisions] because they included equal opportunities everywhere. That was the main discussion" (interview with Levy). The French SPD stated: "the measures in favour of equal opportunities have a smaller appropriation, since France considers that this is a dimension extending across the board which applies to all the other measures and activities" (European Commission 1996, 14). The French position on equal opportunities triggered a conflict with the Commission during negotiations over the 1994–99 SPD. After reviews and revisions notwithstanding, the final SPD published by the Commission does not hide the disagreements between supranational and national authorities. Despite the fact that "programming documents are always stated in very neutral words," the SPD text for Objective 3 mentions "that the Commission was not satisfied with the French in terms of equal opportunities" (interview with Levy). According to the Commission, "the only aim where the proposal of the Member State remained below the expectations of the Community policy is that of equal opportunities for men and women, where the amounts applied for are too low. The balance between the priority aims is in this way reduced" (European Commission 1996, 17). Given the "vague and neutral language" typically used in Commission documents, "to have such a critical stand published means that the Commission was very unhappy indeed."[6]

In order to compensate for the dearth of equal opportunities stipulations in the French proposal, the Commission decided to co-finance the few equality measures submitted to the "exceptional maximum rate of 50%" (European Commission 1996, 27). The Structural Funds provide 50%-75% of the total cost of a project for Objective 1 and 6 regions; the rest comes from public or private funds in the member states. For Objective 3 regions, the ESF normally provides grants in the range of 25%-50%. Application of the maximum rate in the French case is "a sign of recognition of the importance attributed by the Commission to the implementation of an equal opportunities policy" (European Commission 1996, 27). Furthermore, the Commission requested that the French authorities make a new effort "to determine …other needs and new opportunities for assistance which may reinforce in a more significant fashion the effort currently made" (European Commission 1996, 27). These "new opportunities for assistance would be determined by "national, regional and local authorities and other bodies competent in the field" during the SPD implementation phase (European Commission 1996, 27). The Commission provided that the additional equal opportunities measures would be financed by an amount not lower than 20% of the "deflator" (European Commission 1996, 27). The "deflator" is an additional amount awarded annually to the Member States to compensate for inflation.[7] Far from determining "other opportunities for assistance," France has actually reduced even the small amount earmarked for equal opportunities in the SPD for the programming period 1994–99.

The Commission has the right to enforce compliance, should a member state fail to honor the financial provisions agreed to in the SPD. France cannot officially ignore or alter programming documents—but did so in this case by reducing the funds earmarked for equal opportunities, without any consequences. Rules and regulations may not deter a member state like France from non-compliance. However, a member state expecting to have a repeated and long-term relationship with the Commission may not want to "compromise" or abuse that relationship. "The SPD is an annex to a Commission Decision, so it is a legal document, and any change implies a new Commission Decision; this takes place about twice a year, when the financial plan is adapted. The use of ESF funds is the result of a negotiation between the member state and the Commission."[8]

To avoid long and counterproductive conflicts, the Commission seeks compromise through negotiation, a tactic also used in evoking member state compliance with Treaty Articles, regulations and directives. If a member state does not comply with Treaty obligations, Article 169 allows the Commission to bring a case before the ECJ. Yet the Commission is required to give "the State concerned the opportunity to submit its observations" prior to bringing such a case before the ECJ. After taking this step, the Commission delivers a "reasoned opinion on the matter" which may require no further action and therefore avoid litigation. Between 1971–96, only eleven equality cases brought before the ECJ rested on Article 169, constituting 12% of the cases (1997a, 109). National courts seeking preliminary ECJ rulings on cases involving Community law (Article 117) constitute the other 88% of all equality cases. The relatively low number of infringement cases, compared to a high number of preliminary ruling cases, shows that the Commission uses its "enforcement" authority sparingly, preferring to address non-compliance without initiating a litigation process. As regards SPD non-compliance, "in theory, the Commission could refuse a plan which did not comply with its priorities, but in practice, it would be difficult to adopt such a rigid stance. It would mean that the implementation of ESF would be blocked. Once again, the process is one of negotiation, not of coercion."[9]

The virtual disregard of equal opportunity provisions in the French SPD, the subsequent reduction of earmarked funds, and the lack of any concrete sanctions against French non-compliance indicate that the Commission's role is rather constrained. This case would suggest that supranational policy is only as "effective" as the member states allow it to be. The French case would reinforce intergovernmentalism's portrayal of states as primary actors and supranational institutions as instrumental. The Objective 3 episode might reintroduce ESF criticism of the period 1958–1971 when funds were used as a simple supplement to national funds. The French attitude might imply that "they [the member state] just take the money and use it for already existing measures" (interview with Levy).

However, French non-compliance in this particular case unveils a more complex relationship. Regardless as to whether or not France was fully compliant, the fact remains that the EU process of programming and implementation has altered the national policy-making process: "France…found itself increasingly constrained by Community rules, policies and the actions of EU institutions" (Kassim 1997, 178). Thus, the supranational process and the rules governing Structural Funds allocation has altered the way in which a state plans and implements policy for an important segment of the population, the labor force: "Certainly, for setting priorities, it [the EU] has an impact in addition to the time given for discussion and arguments during negotiation" (interview with Levy).

The co-financing rule of ESF projects further implies that the member state cannot simply "take advantage" of EU funds without contributing a large part itself. The Commission views co-financing as a key to "unlocking national funding" (European Commission 1998c, 10). "Co-financing is a very important point because it means that if member states don't want these measures, they are not going to do it, and they are not going to find national or regional co-financing sources. This is a very difficult issue but, in fact, if we look at a larger scope than just equal opportunities, the impact is slow for all the measures" (interview with Levy). ESF assistance constitutes a significant source of funding for the member state; for Objective 3 alone, France received 2.6 billion ECU.

One direct effect of ESF financial assistance has been an increase in the number of beneficiaries; it has moreover reinforced and facilitated policies tackling serious economic and social problems. French unemployment peaked at 12.6% in 1997, one of the highest rates in the EU, although it fell to 11.4% in April 1999. EU funding not only increases the resources to face such serious problems as unemployment but also introduces innovative solutions to national problems:

> The Social Fund sometimes allows for new projects to be set up which would not have existed without Social Fund money. Besides, they are so innovative that it was very difficult to find national support...In Objective 3, we have a measure [entitled] 'local plans for economic integration' (*plans locaux d'insertion économique*). This would not have existed without Social Fund money. This measure tries to reinforce coordination between different measures to make them a passage to integration. This is one example of the positive impact of the ESF (interview with Levy).

The EU offers policy solutions to member states so that the latter can address chronic problems such as unemployment. The Structural Funds not only co-finance these policies but also provide an administrative expertise with a unique comparative perspective. Based on its institutionalized relationship with fifteen national administrations, the Commission can provide policy ideas to address EU-wide problems.

The supranational process has also increased the type and number of policy actors involved in French policy. The Monitoring Committee for Objective 3 engages not only national, regional and local actors but also the social partners, in the spirit of "partnership" favored by the 1989 Structural Fund reform: "in terms of partnerships money has been given not only to the national level but also to regional authorities" (interview with Levy). In France, decentralization was already an official policy since the early 1980s but the EU has reinforced the existing process and has given an international voice to actors normally confined within regional structures. "It [decentralization] was not initiated at Community level but certainly the Community has reinforced this tendency" (interview with Levy). Kassim suggests that "the role of the French government has been eroded as societal interests make direct contact with EU institutions. French regional authorities, companies and labour are all increasingly represented in Brussels" (1997, 177).

The impact of the EU on French policymaking regarding equality issues is not only procedural but also ideological and attitudinal: "things change slowly from the attitude where it was thought that they [French authorities] had nothing to learn from countries in the EU. People come to the Committees and meet people from other countries. It is a slow integration process. I think it does have an impact but it is diffused over a long period of time" (interview with Levy).

The legislative proposal for an amendment of Articles 3 and 4 of the 1958 Constitution in December 1998 illustrates the ideological shift taking place in France. Article 3 refers to national sovereignty, suffrage and definition of voters. The amendment adds that the "law favors the equal access of women and men to electoral mandates and public office." Article 4 regarding political parties attaches the phrase "political parties contribute to the implementation of equality" (*Le Monde* March 6, 1999). Levy observed:

> There is also a big change in course now because there is going to be a change of the Constitution to introduce a positive action for women in politics. They [the French] realized that together with Greece, they were last in the EU in the number of women in parliament. It has not moved much since 1945. This is very controversial and very new and it will require a change in the Constitution because the Constitution states that everybody is equal and that we cannot favor specific groups (interview).

Both Conservative President Jacques Chirac and Socialist Prime Minister Lionel Jospin supported the amendment. The amendment to promote equal access for women in politics marks a significant departure from the French tradition of "republican universalism" (*l'universalisme républicain*). In a speech before the National Assembly addressing the Constitutional amendment, former Justice Minister Elizabeth Guigou declared:

> The idea of parity would endanger the traditional equality among citizens, abstractly conceived without consideration of race, religion, or opinion ... But I do not agree...In order to defend an abstract universalism, we end up erasing history and reality. If women have been excluded for a longtime from citizenship, it is certainly because they were women (quoted in *Le Monde* December 17, 1998).

Women like Elizabeth Guigou, France's first female Justice Minister, and former Minister of Employment Martine Aubry have experienced the difficulties for women in decision-making first-hand and also supported the amendment.

> What is changing is the women in politics who used to say that they did not want positive discrimination and that they just wanted to succeed because they were just as good as men. But now there is a change, and a lot of them are saying that they used to be against positive discrimination but after being in politics for many years and seeing no changes, they feel that this is the only way (interview with Levy).

The proposal for a Constitutional amendment passed the Lower House, but as occurred in the case for women's suffrage,[10] the Senate, dominated by the Conservatives, rejected the proposal (*Le Monde* January 26, 1999). The Lower House re-approved the text almost unanimously (two votes against), and sent it back to the Senate, which finally approved it on March 4, 1999 (*Le Monde* March 6, 1999). After approval from both Houses, the final text was submitted by President Chirac to the Parliament that met in Congress, adopting the Constitutional amendment on June 28, 1999.

The undertaking of a lengthy and arduous procedure to amend the French Constitution demonstrates the commitment of both the government and the National Assembly to encouraging a greater participation of women in politics. This commitment indicates that at least for women in politics the idea of non-discrimination was no longer sufficient. Although the Constitutional amendment is only indirectly tied to EU developments, the ideological transformation it signifies cannot be viewed in isolation from European developments. The acceptance of positive discrimination was not gradual but abrupt, as only five years earlier the Conservative Balladur government defended "universalism" and "policies of neutrality" against EU provisions of equal opportunities.

The French claim that specific equal opportunity provisions were not needed in the 1994–99 SPD because "they included equal opportunities everywhere" (interview with Levy), can be viewed as an early application of mainstreaming in French policy.[11] The French case may confirm the fears of women's activists that mainstreaming will be used as a "backlash" instrument to cut budgets for women's programs. The French reassurance that men and women "have" equal access to all ESF programs does not take into account women's different position in the labor market and specific training needs. The evaluation of the application of mainstreaming in French policy will be possible after the completion of the next ESF programming period (2000–2006). "It will be different for the next programming period, we are changing slowly to what we call mainstreaming. Instead of having separate actions for women, equal opportunity is to be looked at in every single thing we support. It's quite a change" (interview with Levy).

THE COMMUNITY INITIATIVES: THE NEW OPPORTUNITIES FOR WOMEN (NOW) PROGRAM

Objective 3 funding is considered "mainstream" structural funding, "designed essentially to support Member State policies in the drive towards economic and social cohesion" (European Commission 1998b). Although the Commission is involved in programming, setting priorities and supervision of national implementation, each member state is responsible for the specific policy definition and implementation. As the French case initially showed, the national policy on equal opportunities can, in effect, neutralize EU priorities. Although there were other EU effects on France (procedural, attitudinal, ideological), the direct EU impact of equal opportunity provisions in Objective 3 was minimal. France's allocation of a mere 0.7% for equal opportunity projects under Objective 3 for the period 1994–99 seemed to show a total disregard for the ESF priorities and the 1993 Structural Fund reform (which had redefined Objective 3). The subsequent reduction of an already small equal opportunities budget suggests a disregard of supranational policy in general and Commission procedures in particular.

However, since the 1988 Structural Funds reform, the Commission possesses a second financial instrument for implementing EU policy in the member states. The 1988 reform has introduced the Community Initiative (CI) concept, defined as a "special financial instrument of EU structural policy which the Commission proposes to the Member States on its own initiative" (European Commission 1998b). During the 1988–93 programming period, mainstream funding received 85% of the total Structural Funds, with the remainder reserved for the Initiatives. The 1993 Regulations for the period 1994–99 reserved 9% of the Funds for the Initiatives. The Community Initiatives' budget accords the Commission a significant source for financing projects in line with its own priorities. Community Initiatives, in contrast to other mainstream Structural Fund aid such as Objective 3, established three eligibility criteria for projects financed under this heading. The Commission requires that projects funded under the Community Initiatives be transnational, innovative in terms of new methodologies and practices, and evince a multiplier effect (European Commission 1998c, 9). In 1997, there were thirteen Community Initiatives funded by one or more Structural Funds: "In each of these programs [Initiatives] there are 'measures,' as we call them, funded by several Structural Funds, normally only two, the Regional Fund and the Social Fund" (interview with Livingstone). There are Initiatives focusing on industrial conversion, on cross-border economic development for small firms, urban pilot projects, the information society; there is also special Peace and Reconciliation Initiative for Northern Ireland.

The Community Initiative LEADER funds, for example, programs for local projects of agricultural development. Three contributing Funds finance this Initiative, with the Agricultural Fund (EAGGF) being the primary one in terms of investment. The ESF also contributes to the LEADER Initiative,

funding the training aspect of the project. Ian Livingstone, responsible for
the Community Initiatives at DG V, noted: "the parts that are contributed by
the Social Fund are designed to fund training measures. Therefore, there is
an issue of equal opportunities. For the part that we [ESF] contribute, we
want to make sure that there are equal opportunities enshrined in the projects. For each of these programs, there is an equal opportunity dimension"
(interview). LEADER funded women's cooperatives in Greece involved in
agricultural tourism, small and medium enterprises, traditional handicraft
and environmental protection (European Commission 1997a, 25). The 1988
reforms promoted co-funding by the different Structural Funds in order to
increase integration and coordination among them. The involvement of two
or more funds in some ways complicates the management of Initiatives. In
reality, the "lead Structural Fund," the fund with the most significant contribution, normally takes over the management of the Initiative: "for
LEADER, that would be the Agricultural Fund, for INTEREG [Initiative]
is the Regional Fund" (interview with Livingstone).

The ESF almost exclusively finances two Community Initiatives, the
Employment and Adapt human resources initiatives. "They [Employment
and Adapt] deal only with training so we [ESF] have almost no contribution
from the other Funds. The Regional Fund contributes a very small amount
in some member states, normally the ones that are headed for cohesion,[12]
Greece, Spain, Portugal, Italy and Ireland. In those states, the Regional Fund
makes small contributions" (interview with Livingstone). For the period
1994–99, the ESF allocated 9% of its 47 billion ECU budget to Community
Initiatives (European Commission 1998c). The 9% allocated to Community
Initiatives compares unfavorably with the 27.4% allocated to Objective 3 for
1994–99 though it is higher than the amount allocated to Objectives 2, 4, 5b
and 6.

As observed by Livingstone, the Adapt Initiative "is designed primarily for workers within the workforce who have a possibility to be laid off
because their industry is changing because of competition" (interview). The
Employment Initiative "targets groups which face specific difficulties in the
employment market" (European Commission 1997, 18). The groups facing
specific difficulties are "very much like Objective 3 target groups, people
with disabilities, young people, women and migrants who currently are
unemployed because they have trouble finding jobs" (interview with
Livingstone).

The Employment initiative was introduced for the programming period 1994–99, and it consists of four different strands each targeting a specific
group: women in NOW, young people in Youthstart, migrants in Integra,

and disabled people in Horizon (European Commission 1997, 18). According to Suzanne Seeland, a consultant involved with the Employment Initiative, the combination of different programs under one Initiative was the result of a compromise between those who supported mainstreaming and those who favored special treatment for target groups:

> When they created the second generation of Community Initiatives [at the end of 1993 and early 1994], the Commission was very much in favor of doing away with what they called target group programs. They [the Commission] were all in favor of just two Initiatives under the ESF. . . . They were quite opposed to creating something for women, something for people with disabilities, something for youth (interview). [13]

Different interest groups that the Commission had originally helped to establish were opposed to this early mainstreaming effort and defended the earmarking of funds for specific target groups (interview with Seeland). Seeland remembered that "there was a lot of pressure from different lobbies like the European Women's Lobby (EWL) and the Disability Forum. All the different target groups have their lobby but also the European Parliament (EP) put pressure (sic). The EP insisted that there should be programs targeting disadvantaged groups" (interview). The interest group and EP pressure seem to have been successful. "The kind of compromise they achieved is to label it Employment but to have four different strands" (interview with Seeland).

Prior to the programming period 1994–99, when NOW became one of the four strands of the Employment Initiative, NOW used to be a separate Initiative. During the previous programming period 1989–93, the first NOW, subsequently known as NOW I, "was an integral part of the Third Action Programme for Equal Opportunities"[14] (interview with Seeland). The new NOW II (1994–99) is no longer part of the current Fourth Action Programme for Equal Opportunities but a strand of the Employment Initiative. "This means that NOW II belongs entirely in the strategic concept and the implementation procedures of the ESF" (interview with Seeland). The definition of NOW as an Action Programme or as a Community Initiative means a change of venue within the Commission. Although NOW I was co-financed by the ESF, "the Equal Opportunities Unit was involved in the whole discussion on how to implement and evaluate it because it was part of the [Third] Action Programme" (interview with Seeland). The Community Initiatives Unit responsible for NOW II is organizationally situated within ESF Operations. Although both units are in DG

V, the change of venue was important because it reveals strategic action on the part of institutional actors and autonomous behavior.

The change of venue for NOW II, from the Equal Opportunities Unit to the ESF department, can be construed as a conscious effort to institutionalize equal opportunities and to open to women the biggest funding source for EU social policy. Since its origins, ESF funding was theoretically available to women as members of the labor force. It was not until the 1970s, however, that special attention was given to promote equal opportunities and to earmark funds specifically for women. As of 1978, the ESF began funding specific training schemes for women. Women returning to the labor force after a long absence to raise a family required different types of training. As my initial statistical profile illustrated, European women face particular employment problems, e.g., segregation into specific sectors of the economy and concentration in low-paid, part-time positions. The 1988 ESF Regulation "introduced a specific reference to women as being among those encountering special difficulties in the labour market" (European Commission 1997a, 21). Under Objectives 3 and 4, 5% of the budget amounting to 380 million ECU was reserved for programs for women. After the 1988 reforms introduced the Community Initiatives, NOW I was allocated 156 million ECU for the period 1991–94, but it remained under the management of the Equal Opportunities Unit. By 1993, promoting equal opportunities was explicitly defined as an Objective 3 priority and as a task involving all the Structural Funds. NOW II received 500 million ECU from the Structural Funds covering the period 1994–99. The available funds almost doubled with the contributions required from national public and private sources. The one billion ECU-budget, combining EU and national sources "is by far the largest programme in Europe for conceiving, testing and implementing new ideas for women's training and employment" (European Commission 1998e, 1).

The budget increase for women's employment projects, the gradual integration of equal opportunity provisions in all Structural Funds, and the venue change for NOW II are related to two other factors: the persistently disadvantaged position of women in the labor market through the 1990s and the strategic actions of institutional actors.

Advocates of equal opportunities in the Commission realized that they needed "a permanent infrastructure" (interview with Seeland) and that they needed to take a share of "the big money," that is the Structural Funds (interview with Helfferich). The women who formerly headed the Equal Opportunities Unit, Nonon (1976–81), Quintin (1982–90) and Hubert (1992–96), were indeed dedicated women's rights advocates:

> People like Jacqueline [Nonon] and people who came after her were really fighting. They were pushing for the directives for many years in the Equal Opportunities Unit. Odile [Quintin], who is now the Director,[15] was the successor of Jacqueline Nonon. They [Nonon and Quintin] fought hard like a lioness. And she [Nonon] can really fight (interview with Seeland).

Nonon and Quintin can be characterized as state feminists, defined as "both feminists employed as administrators and bureaucrats in positions of power and politicians advocating gender equality policies" (Siim 1991, 189 quoted in Stetson and Mazur 1995, 10). Beyond the feminist administrators in the Equal Opportunities Unit, Seeland noted that women in other DGs and politicians in the European Parliament also advocated and pressed for policy change (interview). "The idea, to take a certain percentage of the huge Structural Fund budget and develop pioneer pilot programs which could help fight unemployment, took them years and years to understand that there is no recipe for mass unemployment. They [EU] did it eventually and 9% of that is huge" (interview with Seeland). Seeland also suggested that administrators in the Equal Opportunities Unit and other members of the policy community realized that in order to expand policy, they would have to compete for funding outside the narrow confines of the Unit: "As far as I understand it, I think it was easier to argue the case in the context of pilot programs within the Structural Funds and new Community Initiatives and require equal opportunities or women's programs among those Initiatives, than to increase the budget of the Equal Opportunities Unit" (interview).

Other members of the policy community, such as the European Women's Lobby (EWL), also understood the importance of acting strategically to place women's issues in the most advantageous venue. On two occasions the EWL supported a venue change, away from the Equal Opportunities Unit to DG V, its closest ally with which it has an institutionalized relationship. First there was the venue change for NOW II and then for the Daphne program which addresses violence against women.

The EWL did not yet exist at the time NOW I was designed, but it was involved in NOW II and its placement under ESF management. Barbara Helfferich, former general-secretary of the EWL, considers the Structural Funds as "the most important issue" on women's agenda, given its significance as a source of funding. The EWL's privileged relation with the Commission's Equal Opportunities Unit did not prevent the Lobby from supporting a NOW II under ESF management. The EWL cooperates closely with the Equal Opportunities Unit which it considers as the "center" of gender policy; it moreover supports individuals in the Equal Opportunities Unit. Helfferich described the EWL's role in EU policymaking:

> At the Commission, we [EWL] sit in two advisory committees, can speak, we have the status of permanent interlocutor. We are important for the Commission because we are easy to consult. Somebody from the Unit calls me and asks me 'what does the Lobby think about the National Action Plans (NAPs) and the Commission proposals (interview).

Despite the privileged relationship with the Equal Opportunities Unit, the EWL offered strategic support to the NOW II transfer of authority from the Unit to the ESF department because the new venue would serve to integrate women's policies into the important funding sources.

On another occasion, the EWL favored the option of locating the Daphne program in the Secretariat General of the Commission over the DG V's Equal Opportunities Unit.[16] The Lobby is aware of the jurisdictional conflicts within the Commission but tends to support the most beneficial venue, not its closest allies.

> Obviously, DG V does not like it very much that any women's issues are now in the Secretariat General. The Commissioner [of DG V], Padraig Flynn, has been known to try to keep everything concerning women in the Equal Opportunities Unit in his DG. And it's like fighting for turf. We would like the Secretariat General to take the issue of violence against women because more power rests with the Secretariat General (interview with Helfferich).

Although the Equal Opportunities Unit and the EWL acted strategically to enter into the ESF context, it is uncertain whether its leading figures understood the costs of the venue change at the time. The Equal Opportunities Unit might have not realized its loss of power over a significant policy issue concerning women. NOW I was still managed by the Equal Opportunities Unit; it was not until NOW II that the ESF took over the management of the program change.

The loss of managerial control over NOW II resulted in a change of personnel that brought new administrative perspectives. Many women working at the Equal Opportunities Unit identify themselves as feminists and examine issues from a gender perspective (interview with Stratigaki). ESF administrators are not necessarily involved in gender issues and have different priorities. "The ESF and the Structural Funds have always been a very specific world with their own kind of programming and financing exercise and its own rational. Their first concern is to make sure that the money gets out. I always thought that they were more concerned to get rid of all the money and see that it flows smoothly. That had to change drastically with the arrival of the Community Initiatives" (interview with Seeland). ESF administrators confirmed the view that they are preoccupied with the absorption of funds by the member states, although they do not necessarily admit that this issue takes precedence over substantive policy issues (interviews with Platsouka and Sigonis).

As regards financial resources, the venue change has dramatically increased the budget available for women-specific training programs. In the past, such programs were financed through the various Equal Opportunities Action Programmes initiated as of the early 1980s. The Fourth Action Programme that funds projects covering a variety of issues has a budget of 30 million ECU, while NOW II has on its own an one billion ECU budget under ESF management. The resources available for the Action Programmes managed by the Equal Opportunities Unit are minimal in comparison to programs under ESF management (interview with Seeland). "It was clear that if there was (sic) funding to feed a larger women's program, the budget would only come from the Structural Funds" (interview with Seeland).

The determination of NOW II as Community Initiative also means that the Commission is responsible for determining the design and priorities, the eligibility criteria, and the calls for proposals. Since the 1998 reforms, the Commission has acquired the legal framework to propose on its "own initiative" programs "of significant interest to the Community."[17] The NOW Initiative offers the opportunity to examine the Commission's supranational autonomy through the process of negotiating, implementing, supervising and applying the programs' eligibility criteria.

The Commission is responsible for preparing proposals for specific policy areas, the texts of which are sometimes presented in documents called Green and White Papers. Green Papers present ideas for discussion and debate; they are followed by White Papers containing a more official set of proposals on a specific issue. For example, the Employment Initiative's targeting of specific groups in the labor market was presented in a White Paper (European Commission 1994, 150). Throughout the process, from the formation of a policy proposal to its actual implementation in the member state, the Commission is closely involved in all phases. The following description of the NOW II's evolving stages is based largely on the account of a Community Initiatives administrator in DG V.

Based on a Council Regulation that allows the Community to use its "own initiative," the Commission published a Communication in 1994 setting up the NOW II program. In this document, "the Commission lays down the objectives, the priorities, and the eligible 'measures.' The Commission decides what can be done in quite some detail" (interview with Livingstone). The process continues with the preparation of Operational Programs by the member states which are similar to the type of documents submitted for Objective 3. The Operational Program is "a specific plan on how it will implement this initiative in the member state" (interview with Livingstone). As was the case with the Single Programming Documents (SPDs) for Objective 3, the Commission discusses the Operational Program with each member state, a process which takes several months, proving that the Commission will not accept Operational Programs without serious examination of the proposal: "We look at their Operational Program, we get documents, and we arrive at the situation where they are obliged to describe what they intend to do and why they intend to do it" (interview with Livingstone). During the negotiation process, the Commission might not agree with the Operational Program and can give its own suggestions. "It will go on for several months until we [Commission and member state] arrive at the situation that we are both happy with the program... and then what we both agreed becomes formal, a Commission Decision" (interview with Livingstone). The last phase of the negotiating process is the "formal procedure where the Commissioner officially agrees with the program and it becomes a formal legal document" (interview with Livingstone).

Although each member state is responsible for the concrete implementation of the program, the Commission continues to supervise and to evaluate the general application of the agreed operational program. "Once the key objectives, the goals, the types of national obligations are agreed, the operational program is signed, then it is the member states who deal concretely with everything that is application and the actual projects' approval" (interview with Seeland).

As noted earlier, three characteristics and eligibility criteria that define Community Initiatives are that projects must be transnational, innovative in character, and have a multiplier effect (European Commission 1997, 6). These criteria have been determined at the supranational level, and member states eager for funding need to comply with these rules. Transnationality[18] requires evidence of cooperation among projects across member states. For example, a training organization seeking funding would need to show in its application that it plans to cooperate with a similar institution in one or more member states. The logic behind this requirement is to induce members to share policy ideas, exchange information and expertise in order to develop transnational policies throughout the EU countries (EUROPS 1996). "There is a wave of experiences, opportunities, choice, product development, in transnational projects and is really special" (interview with Seeland).

Although Commission administrators insist that the process is one of cooperation with the member states, eligibility criteria such as transnationality are imposed whether the latter are in agreement or not. National programs would not have complied with these criteria, if the Commission had not defined them as requirements for funding. In fact, transnationality was mentioned in ESF mainstream regulations prior to the creation of the Community Initiatives, but it was never taken seriously. Transnationality "hardly ever happened. I think that there are few exceptions when it comes to the border region of Belgium and Luxembourg, Germany and France that have done it for years, but they did not wait for ESF to do a transnational project. But for the rest, they never took this opportunity. They only use it when they are *obliged*" (interview with Seeland, my emphasis).

Many member states were reluctant to comply with this requirement: "they [member states] complained that it was so complicated, it froze up all the money available and that it wasted money" (interview with Seeland). A large segment of a transnational project's budget is dedicated to transportation, and some member states complained, for example, that "unemployed women have to travel from Denmark to Spain. Member states were gritting their teeth because they felt that it was extremely difficult getting it on the way and implementing it, the whole financial procedure and because of the transnational dimension" (interview with Seeland). However, despite the considerable commitment that member states made as a co-financing partner, they complied with the transnationality requirement. "They knew if they were not complying, they could forget about the money, so they eventually did it. I think that increasingly they became aware of the benefits of transnational cooperation" (interview with Seeland).

The second Community Initiative requirement, innovation, has also influenced policy in the member states. By requiring innovation as a criterion for funding, the Commission has stimulated interest in new policy ideas and solutions. NOW promotes projects that would have otherwise been considered risky for funding at the same time that it "unlocks" national funds for such projects. For example, DATAWEB, a NOW project in Greece, assisted women in creating small firms through a variety of activities, such as information and communication technologies training (European Commission 1998e). Another Greek project, SAPFO, trained women in to organize conventions in smaller municipalities, a market they consider to be a niche (1997, 12).

The third Community Initiative requirement, that projects produce a multiplier effect, aims to encourage member states and NOW projects to disseminate the lessons learned by each. Since NOW finances pilot projects on a small scale, it is hoped that "best practices" from various projects will be integrated into national and European training and employment policy: "A very important point is that member-states are responsible for mainstreaming the results of the projects in . . . national policy" (interview with Livingstone).

The Commission encourages and coordinates the mainstreaming effort through its participation in the national Monitoring Committees. These Committees have functions and memberships similar to the Objective 3 national Committees. The Committee's task is to manage NOW at the national level. With the exception of one Commission representative, the members are all national actors, governmental administrators, the social partners, employers, employees, and Equal Opportunities Commissions (interviews with Livingstone and Seeland). The Committee meets at least twice a year "to discuss issues and to make certain that the program is progressing correctly" (interview with Livingstone).

Ian Livingstone participates in the meetings of some of the national Monitoring Committees as the Commission representative. He observed that the Commission's role in these Committees is mainly to supervise and promote the integration of policy lessons from NOW projects into national policy. Although the Commission is not primarily responsible for the implementation of these programs, it remains an important actor in the process through its monitoring role. The emphasis on integrating project ideas into national policies creates a direct link between the Commission and national policy development:

> One of the main responsibilities of the Committee is to push the concept of mainstreaming. So each Committee is supposed to produce a mainstream plan, to take the results of the project and make certain that they are pushed into national policy and development. One of the things we [the Commission] are very interested in seeing is how the mainstream plan is developing and what actions have been carried out (interview with Livingstone).

The Commission does not take legal action if the member state does not make sufficient efforts to mainstream the NOW results, but it does assume an advising role and assists the state throughout the process. The effectiveness of mainstreaming NOW "lessons" into national policy depends on the type of project promoter. Project promoters are the intermediaries between the EU and the national authorities and the individual beneficiaries. Since individuals cannot directly apply for ESF funding, project promoters representing various organizations, universities, NGOs, local authorities and training institutions become the direct applicants. If the promoter is already a "mainstream" institution (for example, a public training agency), integrating the results into national policy may be easier than if the promoter is a small women's NGO:

> If you have a huge mainstream promoter, this institution in itself already is a first stage in a mainstreaming process. This institution, if it is serious about it, has a completely different standing when it comes to the process of decision-making and pushing towards changing the legislation, changing the vocational training system and the whole structure . (interview with Seeland).

Even small women's organizations have been successful in mainstreaming ideas developed in NOW projects, given a favorable political climate. Suzanne Seeland, who evaluated some of these projects, described one NOW project arising from a women's organization in Austria.[19] The NOW project *Cinderella*[20] managed to develop vocational training for family-based caregivers and to have the curriculum recognized and accepted nationally. The organization focused on family rather than on institutionalized care; but without funding "they struggled for years. The NOW initiative gave them the opportunity to have a fresh start" (interview with Seeland). The training was presented as an "access module" for women without the educational backgrounds of nurses or social worker. "Given the visibility of the European program and the Austrian Presidency [during the second half of 1998], they [project promoters] fought and…got a hearing in the Austrian Parliament" (interview with Seeland).

The Austrian Parliament put pressure on the government to prepare legislation to integrate the vocational profile developed in the NOW program. The vocational profile "would be recognized in the long educational training as the official entrance module for care professionals in Austria, and at the same time, they set quality standards for the service as such" (interview with Seeland). The NOW project was also included in the 1998 Austrian National Action Plan (NAP) submitted to the EU in the framework of the European Employment Strategy.[21] The Plan referred to the need for 140,000 additional childcare places and the creation of 3,000 jobs for family-based caregivers by the end of 1998.[22] Furthermore, the Austrian Trade Union

Federation and the promoters for the *Cinderella* project are currently negotiating a collective agreement covering these caregivers. The Austrian project offers a successful illustration of how mainstreaming a pilot project in
national policy can assist in creating employment opportunities for women.

CONCLUSION

This chapter examined the role of supranational institutions in promoting
equal opportunity policy and the impact of the latter on national policy
through the use of the Structural Funds. The Commission has increased its
own autonomy vis-à-vis member states through a series of reforms regulating the Structural Funds, in general, and reshaping the European Social
Fund, in particular. These reforms have allowed the Commission to promote
the regionalization of EU funding and the Europeanization of policy. The
programming principle introduced in conjunction with the "radical" reforms
of 1988 fostered a contractual relationship between the Commission and the
member states. This contractual relationship is expressed through a series of
documents, i.e., the Single Programming Documents and Operational
Programs that give the Commission an increasing role in national planning,
programming and implementation. The Commission has at its disposal two
critical financial tools for promoting equal opportunities among and within
the member states. The first financial tool is ESF funding of Objective 3
projects that includes equal opportunities among its objectives. An examination of the French Objective 3 Single Programming Document for the period 1994–99 revealed the increasing role of the Commission in planning and
implementing structural policy. French policy during the period 1994–99
failed to comply with the EU-defined Objective 3 prioritization of equal
opportunities. However, supranational processes of programming and
implementation have altered the national policy-making process. The co-
financing rule unlocks national funds that, combined with EU funds,
increase the number of beneficiaries and fund programs that would have otherwise lacked the resources. The EU policymaking process also changes and
increases the number and type of policy actors by encouraging regional
authorities and the social partners. In the case of France, the impact was not
only procedural but also ideological, as the Constitutional amendment
revealed.

Community Initiatives are the second financial instrument allowing
the Commission to promote equal opportunity policy in the member states.
Strategic institutional action allowed a specific program dedicated to creating employment opportunities for women to change its institutional venue

from the Equal Opportunities Unit to the ESF in order to capitalize on the EU funds. The designation of NOW II as Community Initiative also allowed the Commission to define the priorities and the eligibility criteria of the program. The Commission was directly involved throughout the planning, negotiation and implementation processes. Three of the eligibility criteria, transnationality, innovation, and the mainstreaming of program practices have had a direct impact on equal opportunity policy in the member states. Both financial instruments, Objective 3 and Community Initiatives, enable the Commission to promote equal opportunities as a component of national policies. The next chapter will focus on the role of the EU in countries applying for EU membership.

NOTES

[1] Council Decision 71/66/EEC.

[2] Council Decision 83/516/EEC.

[3] See Bache (1998) for an account on the politics of implementation in EU regional policy.

[4] Regulation 2081/93 of 20 July 1993, OJ L 193 of 31 July 1993.

[5] Law No. 93-1313 of 20 December 1993.

[6] Personal Communication with Fabienne Levy who used to be responsible for the implementation of Objective 3 in France, September 22, 1999.

[7] Personal Communication with Fabienne Levy, September 22, 1999. The deflator for the next programming period is a 2% annual rate. The amount will be included from the beginning of the programming period and will be revised at mid-term.

[8] Personal Communication with Fabienne Levy, September 23, 1999.

[9] Personal Communication with Fabienne Levy, September 23, 1999.

[10] See chapter 2.

[11] For definition of mainstreaming, see chapter 2.

[12] After the 1987 SEA, the term *cohesion policy* was used to describe "a range of Community measures, including the structural funds, aimed at reducing economic and social disparities in Europe" (Bache 1998, 14).

[13] The first generation of Community Initiatives was introduced during the programming period 1989-93.

[14] See chapter 2 for the definition and development of Action Programmes.

[15] Quintin was the Deputy Director-General in DG V.

[16] The Secretariat General is accountable to the President of the Commission and coordinates the work of all the Directorate-Generals.

[17] Regulation No. 4255/88.

[18] For a definition, see chapter 3.

[19] The Austrian promoter is *Verein Initiative Pflegefamilien (VIP)* and coordinates the activities of organizations in three federal states (Bundesländer Vienna, Niederösterreich and Steiermark).

[20] See EUROPS website (http://www.europs.be/) for a description of the project under "Success Stories."

[21] See chapter 2.

[22] EUROPS, http://www.europs.be.

Chapter 5
The Influence of International Institutions on National Gender Policy: The Case of Cyprus

W HILE CHAPTER 4 EXAMINED THE INFLUENCE OF SUPRANATIONAL institutions on the equality policy of member states, chapter 5 concentrates on the influence of the EU and other international institutions on countries aspiring to join the European Union (EU). I will focus on the case of Cyprus, which applied for EU membership on July 4, 1990 and, together with five other countries from Eastern and Central Europe, commenced its accession negotiations on March 31, 1998.[1] Cyprus is the only country among the six "first-wave" applicants that did not belong to the ex-Communist bloc and whose market economy is more closely aligned with those of the EU member states. Given its British colonial past, its Greek heritage and close relationship with Greece, conditions in Cyprus also closely resemble the legal and social conditions found in at least two of the EU member states. However, in terms of *de jure* and *de facto* gender equality policy, Cyprus lags far behind EU policy. I will argue that the prospect of EU accession can act as a strong catalyst for modifying social policies, in general, and gender equality policies, in particular, even in candidate countries that are resistant to change. I demonstrate that supranational institutions can become external agents of change and play a progressive role in reshaping social policy in countries applying for membership.

Intergovernmentalist assumptions regarding the primacy of the state and the instrumentality of institutions are problematic in the case of candidate countries accepting supranational policy developed without their participation: "When you are in the EU, you obviously take part in the framing of that policy whereas when you apply, you have to take the whole package" (interview with Levy). The first section of this chapter examines the "empirical paradox" of an increasing number of candidates applying for EU membership in hopes of strengthening themselves despite the organization's increasing supranational authority. I explain the reasons behind Cyprus's "paradoxical" application and the expanding role of the EU throughout the history of the Cyprus-EU relationship. I argue that the domination of the "Cyprus problem" as the major policy concern for both state and society, and the subsequent "negligence" of gender equality issues have, until recently, left a vacuum with regard to the development of policy in that area. This has allowed external actors (international institutions) to play a significant role in national policy formation.

The second section analyzes the impact of three further international institutions on national policy regarding women in Cyprus. I focus on the United Nations (UN), the Commonwealth of Nations, and the Council of Europe and their respective influences on national policy through conventions, declarations and court cases that have altered national preferences with respect to certain social issues. The value Cyprus assigns to its membership in international institutions has facilitated the latter's influence on domestic politics. The country's prospective EU membership is likely to have the most significant and extensive influence on national policy by way of the accession procedure and the Commission's role in "preparing" a country for membership.

The previous chapter examined the ability of supranational institutions to promote equal opportunity policy, as well as their impact on national policy through the use of the Structural Funds. The financial instruments utilized by the Funds, i.e., Objective 3 and Community Initiatives, have increasingly enabled the Commission to promote specific equal opportunities vis-à-vis national policies. A series of Structural Funds reforms allowed the Commission to exercise ever more autonomy in the programming and implementation of national policies. The Commission has influenced national policies by unlocking national and EU funds for programs, by increasing the number of beneficiaries and the type of policy actors involved in the process, by introducing new policy ideas and by defining the programs' priorities and the eligibility criteria. The EU, in general, and the Commission, in particular, has developed an equal opportunity agenda independent of—and sometimes contrary to—those of the member states. For example, EU equal opportunity policy (as defined in the Structural Funds) contravened French equality policy. Although the analysis of the 1994–99 Single Programming Document for Objective 3 showed that France initially failed to comply with the EU-defined policies, the eventual impact on French policy was both procedural and ideological. The Community Initiative New Opportunities for Women (NOW) had a more direct impact, as the Commission defined both the priorities and the eligibility criteria of the program by way of *transnationality, innovation,* and *mainstreaming.* The intergovernmentalist argument that supranational institutions are the instruments of member states is not confirmed by the relationship, for example, between France and the Commission. French non-compliance at first seemed to support the intergovernmentalist assumption that states determine policy outcomes and defend their national preferences. However, the fact remains that the Commission developed policy contrary to the perceived interests of one of the EU's most important member states. With 16% of the EU population, France controls ten votes in the Council of Ministers,[2] 87 of the 626 seats in the European Parliament, and appoints two of the twenty Commissioners. If EU equality policy can succeed in overturning the national policy of one of its most powerful members, then supranational institutions are far from instruments merely expressing member state preferences. Insofar as the Commission's role in the Structural Funds developed gradually, founding member states such as France could not have anticipated the expanded role of supranational institutions and policy.

THE "EMPIRICAL PARADOX"

A growing number of countries are seeking EU membership despite the organization's expanding supranational authority. Gerda Falkner characterizes this increasing drive for EU membership as an "empirical paradox" (1996, 235). The author wonders "why is it that more and more states are willing to give up much of their otherwise cherished national sovereignty by joining the Union, knowing that even more sovereignty will be eroded over time" (Falkner 1996, 235). The prospect of doubling EU membership over the next decade would moreover require institutional reforms to accommodate an enlarged Union. The reforms necessary for the smooth functioning of an enlarged Union implies that "individual governments' powers will obviously have to be further diminished in the interest of the efficiency of the Union's policy-making process" (Falkner 1996, 235).

The prospective benefits of membership must outweigh the potential loss of sovereignty required in an enlarged Union. Cyprus values membership in international organizations for reasons that go beyond the specific benefits other states enjoy as members of various organizations. The nature of Cyprus "political problem" and its small size have increased the importance the country assigns to its international position secured through membership in international organizations. Turkey invaded and occupied the Northern part of the island in 1974, following a short-lived military coup prepared by the Greek military junta which overthrew the Cypriot government. The invasion divided Cyprus into two parts and resulted in the *de facto* segregation of the Greek and Turkish Cypriot communities. In 1983, the northern part was unilaterally declared the "Turkish Republic of Northern Cyprus" and was recognized only by Turkey. The Republic of Cyprus, by contrast, is the only internationally recognized legal entity. The 1983 Turkish Cypriot secessionist attempt effectively reduced any chances of settling the political problem and restoring a unitary state. Greek Cypriots immediately appealed to international organizations not to recognize the unilateral declaration of the Turkish Cypriots and to support the sovereignty and territorial integrity of Cyprus. The UN Security Council, the Council of Europe, the EC, and the Commonwealth condemned the "Turkish Republic of Northern Cyprus." Thus, the Republic of Cyprus' membership in international organizations entails more benefits than would be the case for other states. The very survival and legitimacy of the state are at stake, given the internal conflict, the *de facto* division of the country and the importance of international recognition for the Turkish Cypriots.

Historically, the reasons motivating Cyprus' interest in the EU were economic. Subsequently, security reasons were added. Acquiring social policy benefits was never considered an important reason for seeking EU membership. The Cyprus and EU Accession Negotiations web page enumerates in great detail and at length the economic and political advantages to be derived from accession.[3] The social benefits are summarized in one sentence, grouped with environmental and quality of life benefits in a paragraph entitled "other benefits anticipated from EU membership." However, the implications for social policy and, specifically, the ramifications for gender equality are significant.

The beginning of Cyprus-EU relationship coincided with Britain's initial application for membership in 1962. After securing its independence from Britain in 1960, Cyprus enjoyed the advantages of a preferential Commonwealth tariff, and the British market remained the most important recipient of Cypriot exports. Because British EEC membership would have meant the end of preferential treatment, Cyprus sought to institutionalize its relationship with the European Economic Community (EEC) by becoming an associate member (Joseph 1997, 116). When Britain withdrew its application in 1963, Cyprus did not proceed with associate membership; Britain resubmitted its application, signed an accession treaty in January 1972, and joined the EEC in 1973, impelling Cyprus to take action on its own behalf.

Cyprus signed an association agreement with the EEC in December 1972 that provided for the elimination of customs for industrial and agricultural products. The elimination of trade obstacles between Cyprus and the EEC was to occur over a ten-year transitional period, ultimately resulting in a customs union. The transitional period was divided into two phases, one ending in 1977 and a second reaching completion in 1982. Turkey's 1974 invasion of Cyprus and the occupation of 37% of its territory had catastrophic effects on the latter's economy, which delayed implementation of the association agreement; the deadline for ending the first transitional phase was thus extended to 1987. A 1987 Protocol was signed for the implementation of the second phase leading to a customs union divided in two phases. During the first phase, 1987–1997, the Protocol obliged Cyprus to reduce customs duties, impose quantitative restrictions on industrial and agricultural products, to adopt the EU's Common Customs Tariff, and to harmonize policies and laws on state aid and competition. The second phase, starting in 1997, was expected to lead to a customs union by 2002 or 2003.[4]

Cyprus applied for EC membership in 1990, and the Commission's Opinion on the application, delivered in 1993, deemed the country eligible for membership. Following the Opinion, the Commission initiated "substantive discussions" with Cyprus to prepare the country for accession negotiations. The Corfu European Council[5] of June 1994 concluded that Cyprus and Malta would be included in the next EU enlargement. The decision to include Cyprus in the enlargement was repeated in subsequent European Councils at Essen in December 1994, Cannes and Madrid in 1995, and Florence in 1996.

Following a report submitted by the European Union Observer for Cyprus of March 1995, the Council of Ministers decided to start accession negotiations six months after the conclusion of the 1996 Intergovernmental Conference. The Intergovernmental Conference ended in June 1997; in December 1997, the Luxembourg European Council decided to begin the enlargement process with ten applicant countries from Central Eastern Europe and Cyprus. The applicant countries were divided into two groups. A first group consisting of six countries—comprised of Cyprus, Hungary, Poland, Estonia, the Czech Republic and Slovenia—commenced their accession negotiations on March 30, 1998. A second group—consisting of Romania, Slovakia, Latvia, Lithuania and Bulgaria—continued and accelerated the process of preparing for negotiations. Having applied for membership in 1990, and been judged eligible for membership in 1993, Malta suspended its application in 1996. However, Malta reactivated its interest in

September 1998, and in February 1999, the Commission recommended that accession negotiations begin at the end of 1999.

Initial Cypriot interest in joining Europe in the early 1960s, coinciding with the first British application, was based primarily on economic concerns. It was also motivated by secondary political and security concerns. Had political factors been as important as economic factors, Cyprus would not have delayed its associate membership until Britain's re-application and entry in the early 1970s. As long as Britain did not become a member of the EEC, Cyprus could expect to enjoy the preferential Commonwealth tariff. However, as early as 1963 and only three years after gaining independence, Cyprus faced inter-communal strife between Greek Cypriots and Turkish Cypriots; this, in turn, posed the risk of an unworkable Constitution, impeding the functioning of the young Republic (Joseph 1997, 25).[6] A relationship with the EC, even at the associate level, would have served to upgrade the country's international and European position, thus lending an external legitimacy that would maintain the stability and independence of Cyprus. Security concerns were not the primary driving force behind the country's European orientation in the 1960s, at least not until the 1974 Turkish invasion that resulted in the occupation of 37% of the Cypriot territory. The solution of what came to be known as the "Cyprus problem" or the "Cyprus question" was not connected with the EU because conflict resolution was defined within the United Nations (UN) framework. It was not until Cyprus officially applied for membership in 1990 that finding a solution to the political problem came to be seen as a major benefit of accession.

The EC/EU was indirectly involved in the political problem insofar as it promoted and financed bi-communal projects through the four Financial Protocols covering the period 1979–98. For example, the first two Financial Protocols financed infrastructure development benefiting both communities, for example, the Nicosia sewage system and the pedestrianization of streets in both parts of the divided capital of Nicosia. The Fourth Financial Protocol, covering the period 1995–98, earmarked 12 of a total of 24 million ECU "for initiatives aiming to promote a comprehensive settlement of the Cyprus question." The EU has gradually adopted a more active role in addressing the Cyprus political problem while simultaneously proceeding with preparing the country for accession. The European Councils in Dublin (June1990) and Lisbon (June 1992) expressed their opposition to the continuation of the *status quo*. During intercommunal talks sponsored by the UN in February 1994, the EU appointed an Observer to compose reports on the political developments and the implications for adopting the *acquis communautaire*. Since 1996, the EU has also intensified its involvement in the political problem by appointing a Special Representative for the Cyprus problem. Both Cyprus and the EU view accession as a "conducive framework" (Joseph 1996, 126) for settling the political problem.

The Cypriot government openly links EU accession with political developments on the Cyprus issue: "this process and the prospect of EU membership which will benefit the population of Cyprus in its entirety, will act as a catalyst, inducing all sides to work for an early solution."[7] The EU echoes the national government's position in viewing accession negotiations as a "catalyst" for solution to the Cyprus problem. The Presidency Conclusions of the 1997 Luxembourg European Council stated: "thé accession negotiations will contribute positively to the search for a political solution to the Cyprus problem through the talks under the aegis of the United Nations, which must continue, with a view to creating a bizonal, bicommunal federation."[8] The Luxembourg European Council also encouraged the inclusion of Turkish-Cypriot representatives in the delegation negotiating EU accession. As a result, the President of Cyprus, Glafkos Clerides, invited the Turkish-Cypriots to participate in the process, an offer that was rejected in March 1998.

The Cyprus-EU relationship, originally based on specific economic concerns, has therefore already expanded to include political and security considerations. The EU is now expected to play the role of peace negotiator and community reconciliator in a conflict that numerous UN mediators have failed to resolve over a quarter of a century.[9] The EU efforts to find a political solution to the "Cyprus question" have ranged from promoting the rapprochement of the communities through funding of common projects to specifically requiring bicommunal representation in the Cypriot accession delegation.

The "Cyprus question" has dominated Cypriot politics for the last twenty-five years and has consequently influenced its participation in international institutions. As the Cypriot National Report to the 1995 Fourth World Conference on Women in Beijing stated, "no study of contemporary Cyprus can ignore the major political upheaval of 1974 which has had such profound effect upon the lives of all people in Cyprus" (Republic of Cyprus 1994, 5). In the period following the 1974 invasion, the primary concern was the political and security problem. All other policies—including social policies—were assigned secondary importance: "the issue of the divided island hangs over every aspect of life in Cyprus. It pushes other issues down any agenda" (Abdela 1997, 12). The government's Beijing Report (1994) enumerated its national priorities by defining the Cypriot context within which the advancement of women had taken place since the first UN Women's

Conference in 1975. Between 1975 and 1995, Cypriot policy on the gender equality issues was subservient to the issues of "survival from an invading military force" and "economic recovery from the destruction of the 1974 military invasion" (Republic of Cyprus 1994, 5).

The "Cyprus question" has also dominated the development and the actions of the Cypriot women's movement. One of the first mobilizations of women's organizations was to support peace and reconciliation in Cyprus. Starting in 1987, women's groups organized the "Women Walk Home" marches; women attempted to walk across the dividing line separating the two communities, in an effort to return to the homes that 200,000 refugees had been forced to leave behind in 1974. The domination of the political issue as the major policy concern for both state and society, and the subsequent "negligence" of gender equality issues left a vacuum in the development of policy in that area; this has allowed external actors, that is, international institutions to play a role in national policy.

INTERNATIONAL INSTITUTIONS AND NATIONAL POLICY

In this section I examine the role of three international institutions—the United Nations (UN), the Council of Europe and the Commonwealth—in influencing and promoting policy developments in gender and social issues in Cyprus. Then I focus on the role of the EU and elaborate on the process of harmonization by which candidate countries adopt EU legislation.

All ten domestic laws and one Constitutional amendment relating to gender equality were passed after 1987, except for Article 28 of the 1960 Constitution establishing the principle of legal equality between men and women. Eight of its ten laws were adopted in the relatively short period between 1987–1991. This spate of activity followed the 1985 ratification by Cyprus of the UN Convention on the Elimination of All Forms of Discrimination against Women (CEDAW).

Maro Varnavidou, secretary-general of the Machinery for the Advancement of Women (see below), observed that organized women's groups have been active in pressuring the government to respond to their concerns; one of their demands was the creation of an institutional structure for women's rights. However, most national women's groups are sections of political parties and have not generally developed an independent agenda from party policy. Nor have political parties included any gender equality issues on their agendas. Only recently have some political parties adopted quotas for the appointment of women in party structures. The Constitution of the Democratic Rally Party (DISY) requires that in District Committees, "the proportion of female party officers has to reflect the proportion of female members in that region often around 25%" (Abdela 1997, 13). The Socialist Party (EDEK) requires a 15% quota for women in its General Committee. The United Democrats established a 20% quota for women in all party organs. These quotas have not yet produced an increase in women's representation either in party leadership positions or in the parliament.

In the absence of national efforts to promote gender equality, the influence of international institutions has been significant. The government's Beijing Report characterized the CEDAW as a "landmark" which has had a "tremendous impact" on Cyprus (Republic of Cyprus 1994, 63). The Cypriot Report clearly recognizes the UN Convention's contribution in altering discriminatory national legislation:

> Legislation for the advancement of women has moved forward at great speed since 1985 [the year of CEDAW's ratification]. This reform was mainly based on the provisions of the UN Convention on the Elimination of all Forms of Discrimination against Women, on the Forward Looking Strategies of the UN Nairobi World Conference on Women,[10] as well as on the Conventions and Recommendations of the Council of Europe and other international organizations (Republic of Cyprus 1994, 63).

This Report openly declared and recognized the role of international institutions on national policy. The results of this international influence have been significant because of the rapid pace of the reforms. These reforms were successful even when opposing the entrenched interests of the Orthodox Church, one of the most powerful institutions in Cypriot politics, especially in a field like family law.

In 1989, the first Constitutional amendment in Cypriot history made possible the reform of family law. Law 21/90 introduced civil marriage as an alternative to ecclesiastical marriages. Law 23/90 established independent Family Courts to deal with family relations issues, thereby taking power away from the ecclesiastically dominated Family Courts. The review of women's advancement since CEDAW's ratification in the government's Beijing Report links the Family Law reforms to the UN Convention's provisions. The Constitutional amendment "was introduced to facilitate the reform and modernization of Cyprus Family Law *bringing the existing legislation in line with the provisions* of this [CEDAW] Convention" (Republic of Cyprus 1994, 16, my emphasis).

Following CEDAW's ratification, other national legislation was introduced in order to eliminate discriminatory provisions against women. The

1987 Protection of Maternity provided for a twelve-week paid maternity leave which was increased to fourteen weeks by way of a 1994 amendment.[11] Other reforms granted women equal rights in income tax (Law 26/88), pay (Law 158/89), parental care (Law 216/90) and property rights and alimony (Law 232/91). The 1989 Equal Pay Law was specifically introduced in order to "give effect to the provisions" of the ILO Convention 100[12] which Cyprus had ratified in 1987 (Law 213/87). In the area of social security, the state provided unmarried rural women with insurance (Law 199/87), and accorded persons over the age of 68 without pensions a state-financed social pension. The provision of a social pension benefits mainly housewives and women farmers. In 1994, legislation was introduced on preventing violence in the family (Law 479(1)/94), a taboo issue long kept in the private realm. In keeping with the secularization of laws affecting family relations, a bill on adoptions was moreover introduced in preparation for signing onto the European Convention on the Adoption of Children (Republic of Cyprus 1994, 17).

Ratification of the CEDAW moved Cyprus to establish a permanent governmental structure for women's rights to accompany the intensification of legislative activity. The Permanent Central Agency for Women was created in 1988, reformed, and renamed the National Machinery for the Advancement of Women in 1994. Since its establishment, this structure has been situated within the Ministry of Justice, yet it has only a consultative status and no executive power. The Machinery is composed of four structures—the Council for Women's Rights, the National Committee, the Interministerial Committee and the General-Secretariat. The Minister of Justice chairs the Council of Women's Rights, which consists of ten members of women's organizations and trade unions. The Justice Minister also chairs the National Committee, which represents both NGOs and various government departments. The Interministerial Committee is composed of Women's Rights Officers representing every Ministry. The Secretary-General is the only person staffing the Secretariat and, in fact, lacks the resources, the personnel and the authority to respond to the increasing needs for addressing gender discrimination and implementing existing women's rights legislation.

The location of the National Machinery in the Justice Ministry is unusual in comparison to other countries that have often created a separate ministry or have placed such structures in the Ministries of Employment and Social Affairs. The Cypriot Secretary-General has defended this administrative arrangement by pointing out that having the Justice Minister as chairperson ensures the Machinery direct access to the Council of Ministers, government funding and a supportive infrastructure (interview with

Varnavidou). These advantages, relevant when comparing independent versus governmental status, are not sufficient to justify the choice of a specific ministry.

Although some domestic women's organizations had supported the idea of this structure, the creation of this Machinery one year after Cyprus' ratification of CEDAW was not coincidental. The establishment of women-specific institutional structures has been "central to the implementation" of the UN women's rights agenda (Stetson and Mazur 1995, 4). The UN effort intensified during the Women's Decade 1975–85 and was elaborated in the Nairobi Forward Looking Strategies (Stetson and Mazur 1995, 4). The ratification of CEDAW required that signatory countries submit periodic reports to the UN describing the "legislative, judicial, administrative, or other measures" (Article 18) for implementing the Convention's provisions. Stetson and Mazur suggest that domestic groups, combined with "monitoring by international agencies, have encouraged political leaders in many countries to establish and retain some sort of institution to treat women's issues" (1995, 4). In fact, the UN Commission on the Status of Women (CSW) invented the term "national policy machinery for the advancement of women" which is almost identical to the term adopted for the Cypriot structure (Stetson and Mazur 1995, 3). In some countries, such structures are more symbolic than effective. However, the UN Oversight Committee requires periodic follow-up reports which forces national governments to account for measures taken to improve women's position according to UN criteria and guidelines. The establishment of the National Machinery in Cyprus was an integral part of these global trends and cannot be examined in isolation from the UN policy developments.

Women in decision-making, another item on the UN agenda, has influenced national policy beyond the establishment of national policy machineries. One of the recommendations agreed to at the 1995 Beijing Conference, and included in the resulting UN Global Platform for Action, was to increase the share of women in leading and representative positions to a level of at least 30%. The Commonwealth of Nations began implementing the Platform for Action recommendations by adopting the 1995 Commonwealth Plan of Action on Gender and Development. The Commonwealth of Nations is a "voluntary association of independent sovereign states." The organization incorporates fifty-four developed and developing countries that accept Queen Elizabeth II of England as the Head of the Commonwealth. Cyprus became a member in 1961, after attaining its independence from Britain in 1960. The organization's activities include cooperation in economic development, agriculture and food production, industry, law, education, health, youth, women's affairs, science and public management.

The Commonwealth's 1995 Plan focuses on increasing the number of women in decision-making at all levels of governance—local, national, regional and international. The Plan also provides member governments with technical assistance needed to achieve this target. The Oakland Declaration from the 1995 Heads of Government meeting in New Zealand set a target of 30% female representation by the year 2005. The Meeting of Commonwealth Ministers Responsible for Women's Affairs reconfirmed this target in its November 1996 meeting held in Trinidad and Tobago. In mid-1998, one of only three female members of the Cypriot parliament (MP) and former first lady, Androula Vassiliou, nonetheless criticized the government for its failure to implement the Commonwealth Plan (*Fileleftheros* May 31, 1998).[13]

Vassiliou's critique rested solely on Cypriot non-enforcement of its international obligations under the Commonwealth Plan and the UN Action Plan. She admonished the government for not taking any measures to achieve the 30% target agreed to by the President and by the Justice Minister in the Oakland and Trinidad and Tobago respectively. Despite the Oakland Commonwealth Declaration, the President did not appoint any women ministers after the 1998 presidential elections or at the Public Service Commission, the independent agency responsible for hiring and promoting all public sector employees. A declaration adopted at the international level (Commonwealth Plan) has provided domestic actors a useful tool to hold the government accountable for implementing its obligations.

Although the impact of the Commonwealth with regard to women in decisionmaking did not seem significant at the time of Vassiliou's criticism, the National Machinery was already making some preparations for achieving the 30% target. British consultant and women's rights activist Lesley Abdela was invited to prepare a report with the aim of developing "an effective training programme to increase the participation of women in politics" (Abdela 1997, 4). Her 1997 Report included sixteen "recommended actions" to increase the number of women in Cypriot politics. As stipulated in the Commonwealth's 1995 Plan, the organization's Secretariat provided the technical assistance necessary for carrying out the investigation for this report. Abdela's first recommendation was to "launch the training programme with a high profile event." Accordingly, the National Machinery, in cooperation with the Commonwealth Secretariat, organized the seminar "Women and men in partnership in Cyprus for the politics of the future" in October 1998. President Glafkos Clerides addressed the opening ceremony together with the Justice Minister, the British High Commissioner, party leaders, women MPs and prominent British equality activists (*Cyprus News Agency* (CNA) October 7, 1998). In his opening speech, the President "promised that by the year 2005 Cyprus will have approached the 30 percent women's participation in all political fora, as foreseen by the Commonwealth" (CNA October 9, 1998). As in Vassiliou's case, international-level agreements furnished the terms of reference in discussing national policy.

A month after the seminar, the President announced the appointment of Chrystalla Yiorkatzi as the first female Auditor General to head the Independent Audit Office of the Republic (CNA November 18, 1998).[14] The President announced this appointment in the context "of the government's intention to promote more women in decision-making" as required by the Commonwealth Plan. The government defended and justified this appointment in relation to the country's obligations to meet the 2005 deadline set by the 1995 Commonwealth Declaration and Plan. This was another sign that the international level provided the terms of reference for domestic policy. The appointment of a female Auditor General was soon followed by the naming of another woman at to an important government position, viz., Iliana Nicolaou, as Cyprus' second Ombudsman (CNA December 11, 1998). Again, the justification offered by the government was the long-term Commonwealth goal of increasing the number of women in decision-making.

Beyond the pressures exerted by the UN and the Commonwealth, the Council of Europe has likewise shaped Cypriot national policy, while providing domestic actors with an important external ally. The self-defined role of the Council of Europe is to "strengthen democracy, human rights and the rule of law throughout its member states." Since its foundation in 1949, the Council of Europe has produced international treaties, such as the European Convention on Human Rights, "to protect individuals' fundamental rights and freedoms." The Convention was opened for signatures in 1950 and entered into force in September 1953, as a vehicle for implementing the 1948 UN Universal Declaration of Human Rights. The Council of Europe's key enforcement mechanism rests in allowing individuals to bring actions against governments for violations of rights protected under the Convention. The European Court of Human Rights was set up in 1959 and reformed in 1994 in response to a mounting number of cases;[15] its membership expanded after the accession of new states from Eastern Europe after 1990. States or individuals may apply directly to the Court, located in Strasbourg, to remedy violations of rights protected under the Convention.

Gay rights activist Alecos Modinos fought to decriminalize homosexuality in Cyprus by taking his own case before the European Court of Human Rights. The Orthodox Church and the country's overridingly conservative social values left no other forum for gay activists but the international arena. In 1993, the European Court of Human Rights ruled that Cypriot law violated human rights accords and required Cyprus to decriminalize homosexuality or face expulsion from the organization. The Parliament delayed revision on the law for five years, under great pressure from the Church and some public opposition from religious groups. On May 21, 1998, just eight days before the Council of Europe deadline, the Parliament finally adopted a law decriminalizing homosexuality. Gay activists and international human rights organizations have criticized the vague wording of the new law which still leaves open the possibility of jail terms (*Cyprus Mail* May 28, 1998). Parliament's half-hearted attempt at reform reflected a compromise between domestic and international forces. On one hand, the new law's vagueness was an effort to appease the Church and the anti-gay lobby. On the other hand, the law passed only after the government itself had pressured the Parliament, emphasizing the consequences of non-compliance for the international and European position of Cyprus. The administration's arguments in support of the law focused consistently on the importance of Council of Europe membership rather than on the merits of the issue *per se*.

The threat of expulsion from the Council of Europe, had Cyprus not complied with the European Court ruling in the gay rights case, carried certain implications for the standing of other cases brought by the country. Cyprus has appealed to the Council of Europe regarding human rights violations by Turkey in the occupied territory. Council reports have found Turkey, likewise a signatory to the European Convention on Human Rights, responsible for violations of the Convention.

Non-compliance would hold implications not only for human rights cases prepared by the state but also for lawsuits submitted to the Council of Europe by individuals. One of the most prominent, the case of *Loizidou v. Turkey*, was initiated in 1989. Titina Loizidou's case against the Turkish government was based on the violation of her right to enjoy her property peacefully in the occupied northern part of Cyprus. A 1996 ruling found that Loizidou's rights had been violated and required Turkey to pay compensation for her loss of control over her property. The Republic of Cyprus considered this ruling a great diplomatic victory not only for human rights but also for the international position of the state. The ruling confirmed that Turkey exercises effective control over the Northern part by relying on a large number of military personnel; the "Turkish Republic of Northern

Cyprus" does not qualify as a state under international law; thus the Republic of Cyprus remains the only legitimate Government. The stakes for Cyprus in the Council of Europe membership are important. Therefore, it would have been untenable to accuse Turkey of non-compliance, if Cyprus itself had failed to comply with the Court's ruling in the gay rights case.

The gay rights case also bore important implications for EU accession. The European Parliament (EP) denounced anti-gay laws in a September 1998 Resolution. The EP denounced discrimination against gays in one member state (Austria) and four candidate counties (Bulgaria, Cyprus, Hungary, Lithuania and Romania). It proclaimed further that it would refuse to consent to the accession of candidate countries, which continue to tolerate violations of gay rights. Given the importance of EU accession for all candidate countries, it is likely that these countries will be forced to reform discriminatory national laws despite substantial domestic opposition.

The UN, the Commonwealth, and the Council of Europe have influenced national policy through conventions, declarations and court cases and have altered national preferences on issues involving women in decision-making and gay rights. The value Cyprus assigns to its membership in international institutions has facilitated the influence of the latter on domestic politics. Although the United States can afford to withdraw from organizations like UNESCO, a small country like Cyprus, seeking external support to settle its conflict, depends on these institutions for its own legitimacy and survival. Given the primacy of "Cyprus question," national preferences in all other issue areas are altered in the interest of international membership. This was the case with decriminalizing homosexuality, given the importance of Council of Europe membership for Cyprus and the implications of non-compliance. Although human rights and gay activists criticized the wording of the new law, the fact that the issue entered the public agenda and was debated in Parliament was entirely due to international pressure.

EU membership will have the most significant and extensive influence on domestic policy in Cyprus. The EU begins to influence national policy of candidate countries well before they are accepted for membership, that is, during the negotiation procedure. In the case of Cyprus, eight years passed between the date of application for EU membership and the beginning of accession negotiations in March 1998. The Commission examined Cypriot "eligibility" before issuing an Opinion to be considered by the Council of Ministers. The 1993 Copenhagen European Council defined the criteria for accession for all states applying for EU membership. An applicant must be able to meet three conditions. The first condition centers on the presence of stable democratic institutions ensuring human rights, the rule of law and protection of minority rights. Secondly, the applicant must possess a functioning market economy. The third criterion is the ability to adhere to the political, economic and monetary obligations set by the EU.

The Commission's favorable Opinion (1993) on its eligibility, along with the Council of Ministers endorsement, was followed by a 1995 resolution establishing a "structured dialogue" between the EU and Cyprus. This dialogue has consisted of a series of meetings among heads of state, ministers and experts familiarizing Cypriot officials with the *acquis communautaire* and the review of harmonization efforts prior to accession. The acquis communautaire is composed of all the Treaties, legislation and case law that have come into being since the EC founding of 1957. It also includes the Common Foreign and Security Policy (CFSP) as expressed in common positions, declarations and conclusions, justice and home affairs acts, e.g., joint positions, resolutions and statements and EU-related international agreements. This unique collection of diverse laws and policies covers 80,000 pages and is constantly expanding as European integration progresses. Every new member state is obligated not only to accept the acquis in its entirety but also to implement it effectively within specified time frames.

The procedure for accession negotiations is divided into two stages, the "acquis screening" and the substantive negotiations. During the "acquis screening," the Commission explains the acquis that has been organized into thirty-one issue areas, such as energy, environment, social policy etc. After the presentation and explanation of the acquis by the Commission, the candidate country presents its own laws and policies and assesses the degree of harmonization its must undertake to meet the terms of the acquis. It then proposes time schedules for completing the harmonization.

Following completion of the "acquis screening," the EU and the candidate country begin substantive negotiations on the "screened" chapters.[16] During this stage, candidate countries can negotiate transitional periods in sectors in which they expect to face great difficulties in harmonizing immediately with the acquis. During the substantive negotiations on the first seven screened chapters, Cyprus requested only one transitional period in relation to the chapter on telecommunications and information technologies.

Efforts to harmonize Cypriot laws with the community acquis on gender equality will have a significant impact on national policy. During the stage of "acquis screening," several issues were identified that must be addressed in order to conform to the EU legal framework.[17] Despite some existing legislation on equal pay (presented above), Cyprus is not in line with all EU provisions pertaining to that issue. The Equal Pay Law 158/89 applies only to "work of equal value of like nature" and not to "work of equal value of unlike kind," for example. The Equal Pay Law is only complementary to the system of collective agreements that govern labor relations and determine the workers' terms and conditions of employment in Cyprus. Although collective agreements include equal pay for work of "unlike kind," they do not include provisions for access to justice and "effective remedies and sanctions" (Republic of Cyprus 1998, 25). Thus Cyprus would need to amend its national law further in order to adopt and implement the EU Equal Pay Directive (EPD) and in order to incorporate the access to justice provision (Article 2) and ECJ rulings on "effective remedies and sanctions."

None of the existing non-discrimination provisions in the Cypriot Constitution (Articles 25, 28), Equal Pay Law 158/89, and other laws ratifying ILO Conventions (ILO No. 11 and 142) are sufficient for incorporating and implementing the 1976 Equal Treatment Directive (ETD). The main shortcoming of the current national legislation rests with the lack of enforcement mechanisms for victims of discrimination in employment, vocational training, promotion and working conditions. The government has presented a plan for establishing such an enforcement body, thus effectively implementing the Equal Treatment Directive.

Nor are certain national provisions in social security and occupational social security in line with the relevant EU Directives (Directives 1979 and 1986). The marriage grants, the payment of widows' pensions and special credits for childrearing are only available to women and not to men. Provident Funds (occupational pension schemes) are established by way of collective bargaining and concern private sector employees. The operation of these Funds include "discriminatory provisions related mainly to the entitlement of benefits" (Republic of Cyprus 1998, 28). In 1998, Cyprus has declared its intention to make the necessary amendments to the Provident Funds legislation.

The only gap between national law and the Directive on the Equal Treatment of the Self-Employed (86/613) lies in the issue of social insurance for married women who are assisting spouses in agriculture but are not insured. The national law needs to be amended to include specific provisions in regard to the 1992 Directive (92/85/EEC) on the protection of pregnancy and maternity. Article 9 of the 1992 Directive allows pre-natal examinations during working hours without loss of pay. Cyprus would also have to issue regulations protecting the health and safety of pregnant workers and those who have recently given birth or who are breastfeeding (Republic of Cyprus 1998, 32). At the time of the "acquis screening," there was no national legislation regarding parental leave. The Ministry of Labour and Social insurance is preparing legislation for the adoption and implementation of the

Parental Leave Directive (95/34). The Burden of Proof Directive 97/800/EC also needs to be incorporated by legislative measures. The Termination of Employment Law, which states that the burden of proof lies with the employer, does not in and of itself effectively integrate the terms of the Directive. Cyprus plans to introduce "a clause regarding the burden of proof... in the existing equal pay legislation and in the new legislation that will be enacted with respect to equal treatment (Dir. 76/207) and parental leave (Dir. 94/34)" (Republic of Cyprus 1998, 33).

The Cyprus Report moreover identified measures that must be adopted to ensure the harmonization of national law with the EU acquis in the field of gender equality. The Ministry of Labor and Social Insurance prepared the Report and identified a number of new measures and amendments needed by remarking that legislation is "under consideration." The government's report to the Commission presents the translation of the EU acquis into national law as a simple identification of problems and a direct adoption of corrective measures. The government reports tend to ignore likely or real opposition from domestic forces, e.g., political parties and trade unions, in an effort to present unproblematic reports to the Commission. EU membership is one of the government's primary policy priorities, and therefore it is assumed that all measures necessary for accession will be taken to speed up the process.

Gisela Lange, responsible for enlargement in the Commission's Equal Opportunity Unit, observed regarding the gap between applicant governments and domestic actors: "The problem is that the candidate's delegation does not know whether the Parliament will be willing to act. Some countries come to the screening and have beautiful reports, but they are rejected in their parliaments" (interview with Lange). The Council of Europe gay rights case showed that the Cypriot government could not count on automatic parliamentary cooperation. When new legislation endangers the interests of powerful political actors, the Parliament may stall the adoption of new proposals or compromise its contents. The Parliament took five years to find a compromise solution and comply with the Court's decision. However, the gay rights episode showed that, ultimately, the stakes of membership in international organizations could override the domestic resistance. The external actor's role (the Council of Europe) in "imposing" the unpopular reform also allowed domestic political actors (that is, government and political parties) to avoid some of the political costs associated with the new legislation. The broad support of EU membership by all political parties suggests that Parliament will accept the acquis by assigning the "blame" to external forces (EU). As long as all political parties favor EU accession, there would be little risk of shifting political alliances. The gay rights case suggests that parliamentary cooperation cannot be assumed at the outset. As regards the acquis, it is unlikely that the Parliament presently realizes the extent and the cost of reforms that will be necessary in order to integrate the vast body of EU law into national legislation.

Even if the Parliament integrates the EU acquis by legislative acts, the Commission is not satisfied with a symbolic adoption of laws: "We always point out and emphasize in our talks with the candidate countries that what is on paper is not good enough unless you have enforcement. I always make a very strong point that laws are fine, but what we need is enforcement" (interview with Lange). The Commission takes an active part in the enlargement process and assists candidate countries in understanding, incorporating and effectively implementing supranational policy.

With the emphasis on enforcement, the Commission has also encouraged candidate countries to adopt the acquis through the judicial process. In the first gender discrimination case stemming from Eastern and Central Europe, the Hungarian Monor City Court ruled that a job advertisement requiring a young man was unlawful (European Commission 1999, 29).[18] This case involved a woman who was not considered for a position because of gender-based advertisement. It was prepared as a test case by lawyers in the Hungarian Ministry of Employment: "There were very active women in the Hungarian Ministry who took our [the Commission's] word [on enforcement] seriously" (interview with Lange).

The Commission's involvement in domestic policy developments goes beyond merely encouraging the implementation of equality legislation through test cases. The Commission has realized that it is important not only to encourage individuals to bring cases to court but also to train lawyers in equal opportunity legislation.

> Our strategy now is to start training lawyers in equality law because you cannot expect citizens to take something to court; we also need attorneys who know about equality law to start bringing cases. It is a really big problem, and we are really focusing all the time on lawyers and people from NGOs and ministries, with a particular attention to lawyers, in order to make them aware (interview with Lange).

The first equality cases to be brought before the European Court of Justice (ECJ) in the 1970s, e.g., the *Defrenne* cases, played an important role in the development of EU gender equality.[19] The *Defrenne* cases were presented to the ECJ because lawyer Vogel-Polsky actively searched for a test case. The Commission now appears to have adopted a role similar to the external-actor role played by Vogel-Polsky in compelling the enforcement of supranational policy. An examination of the equality cases brought before the ECJ shows that the majority of cases come from Germany. Among the German cases, most have derived from the Northern region where the Commission organized a seminar for equal opportunity lawyers and where there is a University program specializing in equal opportunities (interview with Lange).

The Commission's role as an advocate shows that it is not only interested in the symbolic implementation of supranational policy but also in the effective restructuring of the norms and values the policy entails:

> I do believe in the training of lawyers. For me, it is much more important than programs, action plans and projects. It is more important than doing the best project with a charitable organization, which is brilliant but local. We do need to target women who want to change the world by starting a test case; because a test case can really cause changes in the whole country (interview with Lange).

The training of lawyers specializing in equal opportunity law indicates that the Commission is capable of bypassing the states and forming direct alliances with domestic actors who share its supranational agenda. The EU's impact on candidate countries consists not only requiring the incorporation of 80, 000 pages of laws, procedures and institutional arrangements; it also lies in the ability to impel the re-organization of domestic forces: "You have to use the momentum [of accession]. Now it is there. Once they [candidate countries] become members, they will sit back. Now women can ask for their rights" (interview with Lange).

The "EU accession tool" is important not only for women but also for other groups traditionally subject to discrimination whose interests seem to be better represented at the supranational than at the national level. Environmentalists have found an important ally in the EU against national policy. A conflict arose between the Cypriot government and environmentalists over the protection of the pristine peninsula of Akamas, its designation as a national park, and the limits on tourist development in the area. During one protest against the government's unwillingness to protect the area, Greenpeace director Mario Damato declared: "We know that Cyprus is aiming to join the EU, and I am certain European countries would not condone such behaviour. So we will concentrate on informing Europeans, mainly, about the Cyprus government's behaviour" (*Cyprus Mail* May 19, 1999). On another issue, the importation of dolphins for entertainment purposes, environmentalists accused the government of "irresponsibility and provocative selective harmonization with European demands" (*Cyprus Mail* May 19, 1999). The violation of due process in a series of corruption scandals involving public officials was also linked to EU accession insofar as malfunctioning institutions would negatively impact Cyprus accession negotiations (*Simerini* October 23, 1999).

Small states like Cyprus, seeking EU membership for security and other reasons, are perhaps more eager to adopt the EU acquis even if that implies domestic political costs. Lange has compared a small state like Lithuania with Poland in terms of their attitude towards adopting gender equality legislation:

> A country like Lithuania, not a very prosperous country, has a huge government program on mainstreaming and equal opportunities in every single sector. Even if they do not enforce it immediately, I think that the fact alone that a twenty-page paper is presented by the Prime Minister has to be honored. They want to do it because we wrote in our report that there is a patriarchal society in Lithuania. They want to please us and that is fine (interview).

On the other hand, Poland has shown no interest in equal opportunities: "If the country is (sic) interested, they would at least ask about the Fourth Action Programme [for Equal Opportunities]. The Poles have never ever inquired about the Program and what it is all about." The Polish Parliament has also rejected a bill that included provisions against gender-based advertising. "They [Polish Parliament] said that it [the bill] was not necessary because they have non-discrimination in the Constitution. But everybody has that in their Constitution" (interview with Lange).

Poland's "constitutional excuse" for rejecting new legislation was also used by Germany back in 1957. Hoskyns suggests that the German delegation accepted the French demand of including Article 119 during the Treaty of Rome negotiations "presumably on the understanding that the Articles in the Treaty were not likely to be directly applicable and that equal pay was in any case covered by the German Constitution" (1988, 38). The German understanding was based on a 1955 Federal Labor Court ruling which established that collective bargaining agreements were bound by the equality provisions in the Constitution; thus different rates for men and women were in breach of the Constitution (Hoskyns 1988, 38). After the passage of the first three equality Directives in the 1970s, which were not incorporated in national legislation in Germany, "the Commission wrote officially to the German government requesting information" on the national measures taken to implement the Directives (Hoskyns 1988, 42). Consequently,

Germany adopted the 1980 "Labour Law to Comply with European Community Provisions" which it inserted into its Civil Code. The two 1983 cases referred to the ECJ by two local courts in Hamm and Hamburg[20] also indicated the failure of German law to fully implement the equality Directives. These cases involved discrimination relative to hiring and the denial of damage awards awarded by the German courts. In 1984, the ECJ ruled that the lack of damage payments under German law did not constitute "real and effective legal protection" which would act as a "deterrent" on the employer.

This case showed that Germany initially (1957–1980) believed that national legislation effectively met the conditions of EU law. However, the adoption of subsequent EU directives eventually forced Germany to alter its original position both through new legislation and case law. Polish failure to adopt a law prohibiting gender-based advertisement might weaken the case supporting the strong EU influence on candidate countries. Potential infringement proceedings by the Commission against non-compliant states and ECJ rulings may eventually ensure that the EU acquis will be effectively implemented. The Commission's role in funding, organizing and encouraging training for lawyers in candidate countries will not only affect current but also future national policy developments. Once candidate countries become EU members, these trained lawyers will be able to make most effective use of the supremacy of EU law.

However, as Lange noted, the "momentum" during accession negotiations can provide the strongest impetus for national policy development. Given the persistence of member state non-compliance with EU law (Mendrinou 1996), the Commission can have the strongest policy impact before these countries accede. The Commission's DG V considers the harmonization of social policies an integral part of the accession process. While defending its jurisdiction, DG V becomes an advocate for "upgrading" the social dimension in accession negotiations. DG V's task is not only to convince the candidate countries but also other EU institutions, e.g., the Council of Ministers: "this is our on-going work to convince them [candidate countries and the Council] of the importance of the social sector" (interview with Lange). Lange observed further that the DG V's ability to hold strong negotiating positions on social issues also depends on the commitment to social policy of DG V's leadership (interview). The new Commissioner for Social Affairs, Anna Diamantopolou, is known to be committed to the EU social agenda and has appointed three women to her six-member private office (*cabinet*). One of these female *cabinet* members is Barbara Helfferich, former general-secretary of the European Women's Lobby (EWL). With the participation of a women's rights advocate in such a position, it is likely that gender policy will remain high on the Commissioner's agenda, and that the social dimension will gain visibility in the accession negotiations.

CONCLUSION

This chapter has argued that the intergovernmentalist assumptions regarding the primacy of the state and the instrumentality of institutions are problematic in the case of candidate countries accepting supranational policy which had been developed without their participation. A state-centric theory cannot explain the "empirical paradox" of increasing candidacy for EU membership despite the organization's expanding supranational authority. For a small country like Cyprus, whose international membership has been closely linked with national survival, the loss of sovereignty over certain issues is of secondary importance relative to the political and economic benefits. The domination of the "Cyprus problem" as the major policy concern for both state and society and the subsequent "negligence" of gender equality issues, until recently, left a vacuum in the development of policy in that area. This has allowed external actors, especially international institutions, to play a decisive role in shaping national policy.

Three international institutions—the UN, the Commonwealth, and the Council of Europe—have influenced national policy through a series of Conventions, Declarations and court cases that have altered national preferences on social issues. International policy has provided domestic actors with the tools necessary to hold their own government accountable for implementing policy. The value Cyprus assigns to its membership in international institutions has facilitated their influence on domestic politics. Its prospective EU membership will have the most significant and extensive influence on national policy through the accession procedure and given the role of the Commission in preparing a country for membership. Except for negotiating temporary transitional periods, candidate countries seeking EU admission cannot be selective in the adoption of the EU acquis. Supranational institutions can effectively use the "EU accession tool" for achieving policy change in candidate countries whose primary goal is EU membership. The accession of candidate countries is conditional upon meeting certain criteria in a variety of national issue areas. The Commission's conditional clauses concern the reform of children institutions in Romania, the closure of nuclear plants in Bulgaria, the protection of minority linguistic rights in Estonia, and the reform of public administration and the judiciary in Latvia. Supranational institutions have become external agents of change and this can play a progressive role in the national politics of countries seeking EU membership.

NOTES

¹ The other five countries are Hungary, Poland, Estonia, the Czech Republic and Slovenia. The December 1999 Helsinki European Council added seven other countries to the "first-wave" group: Bulgaria, Latvia, Lithuania, Malta, Romania, and Slovakia. Turkey was given a "candidate status."

² The large states, Germany, Britain, France and Italy, each hold 10 votes of the total 87 votes in the Council of Ministers. Qualified majority requires 62 votes.

³ The web page is maintained by the office of George Vassilliou, the Chief Negotiator and Coordinator for the Harmonization Process in Cyprus (http://www.cyprus-eu.org.cy).

⁴ Completion of the customs union was subsequently postponed as a result of the decision to begin accession negotiations in March 1998.

⁵ The European Council is the term used to describe the biannual meetings of the EU heads of state or government.

⁶ For accounts on the Constitutional difficulties, see Kyriacides, Stanley. 1968. *Cyprus Constitutionalism and Crisis Government.* Philadelphia: University of Pennsylvania Press; Adams, Thomas and Alvin Cotrell. 1968. *Cyprus Between East and West.* Baltimore: Johns Hopkins Press.

⁷ Comments of Cypriot Foreign Minister Kasoulides on the opening ceremony for the enlargement process March 30, 1998 quoted on the official Cyprus government's web site (http://www.pio.gov.cy).

⁸ For extracts from the Presidency Conclusions, December 13, 1997, see the Cyprus and EU Accession Negotiations web page (http://www.cypruseu.org.cy/eng/07_documents).

⁹ For more on the role of the EU as a "diplomatic broker" in peace negotiations, see Theophylactou, Demetrios. 1994. *Security, Identity and Nation Building in a Mini- and a Super-state: Cyprus and the European Union in Comparative Perspective.* Ph.D. Dissertation. Washington State University.

¹⁰ The 1985 UN Nairobi Conference was the third Women's World Conference after the Conferences in Mexico in 1975 and Copenhagen in 1980. The Nairobi Conference adopted Forward Looking Strategies, "a blueprint for women's future in all realms of life and another milestone on the path to equality" (UN 1995, 6).

¹¹ It is not clear whether the 1994 amendment to the Protection of Maternity Law that increased maternity leave from 12 to 14 weeks is connected with the passage of the 1992 EU Pregnancy Directive (92/85/EEC) which required a minimum maternity leave of 14 weeks.

¹² For more on the ILO Convention, see chapter 2.

¹³ Interview with Androula Vassiliou in the Cypriot daily newspaper *Fileleftheros.*

¹⁴ The Independent Offices are not under the authority of ministries. The seven Independent Offices are: the Attorney-General, the Public Service Commission, the Educational Service Commission, the Planning Commission, the Planning Bureau,

the Auditor-General and the Ombudsman.

[15] The number of applications increased from 404 in 1981 to 4,750 in 1997.

[16] For the Report on the substantive negotiations, see the Cyprus and EU Accession web page (http://www.cyprus-eu.org.cy./eng/04_negotiation_procedure/substantive_negotiations.html).

[17] The analysis that follows draws largely from the 1998 Cypriot Report assessing existing national legislation and the degree of harmonization with the EU acquis (Republic of Cyprus. 1998).

[18] Case Kadar, Monor City Court, No. 3p21321/1997/13, Hungary.

[19] See chapter 2.

[20] ECJ Case 14/83 Von Colson and Kamann v. Land Nordrheim-Westfalen; ECJ Case 79/83 Harz v. Deutscher Tradex.

Conclusions

PUBLIC POLICY INCREASINGLY TAKES SHAPE IN FORA BEYOND THE confines of the nation state. This dissertation examined the impact of international institutions on states by focusing on the EU's gender policy. I tested three main propositions: that states are no longer the primary actors in EU policymaking, that institutions are not solely the instruments of nation-states, and that policies are not inevitably the direct outcome of member-state preferences. I argued that the state has lost some of its traditional attributes, above all, its absolute sovereignty and autonomy as a policymaker in a number of issue areas. The choice of gender policy for testing the above propositions was important insofar as it represents an arena where the role of the state has long been considered dominant and the role of supranational institutions moderate to weak.

I examined the long-term development of EU gender policy as the outcome of three independent policy streams. I considered the origins of Article 119, the formulation of policy ideas, and the political context. The joining of the streams in the 1970s produced policy change in the form of strong directives, landmark court decisions and the creation of new institutions. These new structures inaugurated an extended period of incrementalism (end of the 1970s–beginning of the 1990s), followed by a mid-1990s punctuation facilitated by new institutional rules within the EU *per se*. The introduction of gender mainstreaming during this last period now has the potential to modify the policy system even more radically.

Drawing from historical institutionalism, I identified the factors that intervene between member states' preferences and policy outcomes: institutional autonomy vis-à-vis states, the institutional ability to structure the policy process, the influence of past policies, the development of unintended consequences and the possibility of policy "spillover."

Influence of Past Policies and Multiple Relationships. My efforts to trace Article 119's origins revealed the existence of multiple relationships among international institutions. These relationships involved the ILO and the EU during the Treaty of Rome negotiations, the ILO and the UN Committee on the Status of Women (CSW) in preparing the Equal Remuneration Convention, and the UN Women's Conferences influence on national and EU policy development. The ILO became a venue for equal pay policy proposals, internationalizing and legitimizing the issue as early as 1919. It provided the parameters, the policy definitions and the institutional expertise within which Article 119 was negotiated in 1957.

"Spillover." As neofunctionalists would have predicted, policy did "spillover" into issue areas lying outside the original Treaty definition and included, for example, parental leave and sexual harassment. Article 119 provided the basis for the future development of policies in support of women's equality and the transfer of competency from the nation-state to the EU. Based on Article 119, the EU developed nine Directives on gender equality, four Action Programs and several ECJ court cases. The expansion of policy competence beyond the equal pay provision of Article 119 was "unanticipated."

Unanticipated Consequences. Historical "details," such as the expansive definition of the concept of pay and the last-minute transfer of Article 119 to a different section of the Rome Treaty, can have consequences that affect states' interests in the long term in ways that cannot be anticipated at the time of negotiation of policy instruments. The impact of these consequences has been cumulative and interactive, and this latter dynamic has transformed EU policymaking, creating a gap between member state control and supranational institutions. The expansive definition of the concept of pay allowed the ECJ to develop the concept further and to establish a considerable amount of case law at the same time it was altering member state preferences after the *Barber* decision and the subsequent amendment of the 1986 Directive.

The transfer of Article 119 to the Social Chapter Section late in the Treaty of Rome negotiations also held long-term, unanticipated consequences for gender policy development. The transfer was beneficial because it strengthened social policy in ways envisioned only for economic policy. Its economic origin explains its association with the "first stage" of the completion of the common market, a deadline formally recognized in the landmark second *Defrenne* case. On the other hand, the transfer to the Social Chapter could have been more detrimental to gender policy development, specifically, after the adoption of qualified majority voting (QMV) for issues relating to the completion of the single market. Had Article 119 remained as an economic measure, it could have benefited from QMV introduced with the 1987 Single European Act (SEA). This institutional rule has constrained the development of gender policy in the period following the adoption of the SEA and before the 1993 adoption of the Maastricht Treaty.

Institutional Autonomy. The Commission's use of policymaking rules demonstrates the critical importance of autonomy in achieving institutional goals and expanding policy. An "entrepreneurial" Commission took advantage of new rules under the 1987 SEA and the 1993 Social Protocol to promote policies contrary to the preferences of some member states. New rules under the Social Protocol have also expanded QMV to gender equality issues and introduced new policy actors (social partners) into the EU policy process. Britain's initial rejection of the Social Protocol showed that short-term political reasons compromised the national interest. New institutional rules allowed policies to overcome the initial rejection and be reintroduced successfully (Parental Leave Directive). These new rules modified states' preferences as all new Directives agreed under the Social Protocol had experienced long periods of stalemate under the previous rules.

The Commission enhances its own autonomy by way of its ability to structure the policy environment by actively creating epistemic communities (Experts Networks) to legitimize and expand its scope of action. The Commission's role in establishing and funding both national and European technical assistance offices, project promoters, grant proposals and NGOs, has structured the policy environment and significantly influenced the organization and agenda of national and supranational policy actors. Its voluntary and purposive activity in creating, organizing and mobilizing an interest group constituency shows it to be an autonomous institution, not an instrumental one.

Institutions Promoting Supranational Policy and their Impact on States. I provided further evidence for the proposition that institutions are not merely instruments of states by demonstrating the impact of supranational institutions on national policy through the use of EU financial instruments. The EU's capacity for financing national programs allowed the Commission to promote an agenda independent of that of some of the member states. The financial instruments utilized by the Funds, such as Objective 3 and Community Initiatives, have increasingly enabled the Commission to promote specific equal opportunities vis-à-vis national policies. A series of Structural Funds reforms allowed the Commission to exercise ever more autonomy in the programming and implementation of national policies. The Commission has influenced national policies by unlocking national and EU funds for programs, by increasing the number of beneficiaries and the type of policy actors involved in the process, by introducing new policy ideas and defining the programs' priorities and the eligibility criteria. The EU, in general, and the Commission, in particular, has developed an equal opportunity agenda independent of —and sometimes contrary to—those of the member states.

Although the analysis of the 1994–99 Single Programming Document for Objective 3 showed that France initially failed to comply with the EU-defined policies, the eventual impact on French policy was both procedural and ideological. The Community Initiative New Opportunities for Women (NOW) had a more direct impact, as the Commission defined both the priorities and the eligibility criteria of the program, namely, *transnationality*, *innovation*, and *mainstreaming*. The intergovernmentalist argument that supranational institutions are the instruments of member states is not confirmed by the relationship, for example, between France and the Commission. French non-compliance, at first, seemed to support intergovernmentalism. However, the fact remains that the Commission developed policy contrary to the perceived interests of one of the most powerful EU member states.

Institutions as External Agents for Change. Examining the influence of supranational institutions on candidate countries further enhanced the evidence supporting the independent role of these institutions on national gender policies. Although these countries have full knowledge of the increased supranational autonomy, they voluntarily surrender their sovereignty to allow external influence on national policy in exchange for security and economic benefits.

A state-centric theory cannot explain the "empirical paradox" of increasing candidacy for EU membership despite the organization's expanding supranational authority. In the case of Cyprus, international membership has been closely linked with national survival and therefore the loss of sovereignty over certain issues is of secondary importance relative to the anticipated political and economic benefits. The domination of the "Cyprus question" as the major policy concern for both state and society and the subsequent "negligence" of gender equality issues left a vacuum in the development of domestic policy in that area. This allowed external actors to play a decisive role in reshaping national policy.

Three international institutions—the UN, the Commonwealth, and the Council of Europe—have influenced national policy through multiple Conventions, Declarations and European Court of Human Rights court cases that have altered national preferences in regard to social issues. International policy has provided domestic actors with the tools necessary for holding their own government accountable for policy implementation. The value Cyprus assigns to its membership in international institutions has facilitated their influence on domestic politics. Cyprus' prospective EU membership will have the most significant and extensive influence on national policy through the accession procedure and the control of the Commission in preparing a country for membership.

Supranational institutions can effectively use the "EU accession tool" for achieving policy change in candidate countries whose primary goal is EU membership. The accession of candidate countries is conditional on meeting certain criteria in a variety of national policy domains. Supranational institutions have become external agents of change and thus can and do play a progressive role in the national policies of countries seeking EU membership.

Policymaking increasingly takes place not only at national but also at international and supranational levels. The EU's role in gender policy development is significant and reflects the changing position of supranational institutions vis-à-vis states, as well as their growing influence on national policymaking. This supranational influence is moreover important because it is touching policy areas traditionally reserved to nation states. Supranational policy not only affects EU member states but also a mounting number of candidate countries from Central/Eastern Europe and the Mediterranean who seemingly are prepared to knowingly surrender critical parts of their policymaking capacity. The case of EU gender policy demonstrates that EU policy outcomes are not the direct result of member state preferences, and that beyond states, supranational institutions have acquired a unique policy-making role.

Appendix A
Interviews

Havnoer, Ann, Detached National Expert, Equal Opportunities Unit-Mainstreaming, DG V - Employment, Industrial Relations and Social Affairs, Brussels, January 19, 1999.

Helfferich, Barabara, (Former) General-secretary, European Women's Lobby (EWL), Brussels, January 18, 1999.

Laissy, Ana-Paula, Head of Unit, Equal Opportunities, DG IX - Personnel and Administration, Brussels, January 20, 1999.

Lange, Gisela, Equal Opportunities Unit- Enlargement, DG V/D5, Brussels, January 21, 1999.

Levy, Fabienne, National Employment Monitoring & ESF Operations I, Unit B/3, France, Denmark, Sweden, Finland, DG V- Employment, Industrial Relations and Social Affairs, Brussels, January 21, 1999.

Livingstone, Ian, Community Initiatives, DG V/B/4, Brussels, January 21, 1999.

Papayannakopoulou, Olympia, Personnal Assistant of the Director-General of DG X- Information, Communication, Culture and Audiovisual Media, Brussels, January 18, 1999.

Pau, Giancarlo, Women's Information Section, DG X - Information, Communication, Culture and Audiovisual Media, Brussels, January 20, 1999

Platsouka, Elisavet, National Employment Monitoring & ESF Operations II- Italy and Greece, DG V/C/1, Brussels, January 21, 1999.

Seeland, Suzanne, Program Officer for New Opportunities for Women (NOW), EUROPS, Brussels, January 20, 1999.

Shlinke, Jutta, Equal opportunities for men and women in vocational training, DG XXII - Education, Training and Youth, Brussels, January 22, 1999.

Sigonis, Panayiotis, National Employment Monitoring & ESF Operations II- Italy and Greece, DG V/C/1, Brussels, January 20, 1999.

Stratigaki, Maria, Detached National Expert, Equal Opportunities Unit, DG V/D5, Brussels, January 18, 1999.

Varnavidou, Maro, Secretary-General, National Machinery for Women's Rights, Ministry of Justice and Public Order, Nicosia, Cyprus, May 8, 1998.

Appendix B
Chronological Table of EU Gender Policy Development

DIRECTIVES

Year	Policy
1975	Equal Pay Directive (EPD) 75/117/EEC.
1976	Equal Treatment Directive (ETD) 76/207/EEC.
1986	Equal Treatment in Occupational Social Security Directive 86/378.
1986	Equal Treatment of the Self-employed (including agriculture) 86/613/EEC.
1992	Directive on safety and health at work of pregnant workers and workers who have recently given birth or are breastfeeding 92/95/EEC.
1996	Directive on parental leave 96/34/EC.
1997	Directive regulating the burden of proof in cases of sex discrimination 97/80/EC.
1997	Directive on part-time work 97/81/EC.

RESOLUTIONS, RECOMMENDATIONS, PROPOSALS, AND ACTION PROGRAMMES

1981	Commission Proposal for a Council Directive on part-time work COM (81) 775, 22 December.
1982	Council Resolution on the promotion of equal opportunities (approval of Action Programme 1).

1983	Commission Proposal on parental leave and leave for family reasons, COM (83) 686, 22 November.
1984	Council Recommendation on the promotion of positive action for women 84/635/EEC.
1984	Council Resolution on action to combat unemployment among women OJ C 161, 21 June.
1985	Council Resolution on equal opportunities for girls and boys in education OJ C 166, 5 July.
1986	Council Resolution on the promotion of equal opportunities (approval of Action Programme 2).
1986	Commission Recommendation 87/567/EEC on vocational training for women
1987	Commission Proposal on completing the implementation of equal treatment in statutory and occupational social security schemes COM (87) 494 final, 23 October.
1988	Council Resolution on the reintegration and late integration of women into working life OJ C 333, 28 December.
1988	Commission Proposal on the burden of proof COM (88) 269 final, 27 May.
1990	Third Medium-term Action Programme on Equal Opportunities 1991–1995 COM (90) 449 final.
1992	Commission Recommendation on the protection of the dignity of women and men at work OJ C 27, 24 February.
1992	Council Recommendation on childcare 92/241/EEC.
1995	Fourth Medium-term Action Programme on Equal Opportunities 1996–2000. Adopted by Council Decision of 22 December, OJ L 335 of 30 December.

References

Abdela, Lesley. 1997. Consultancy Report prepared for the Commonwealth Secretariat and the Cyprus National Machinery for the Advancement of Women, May/June 1997.

Alter, Karen and Jeanette Vargas. 1997. "Shifting the Domestic Balance of Power in Europe: European Law and UK Gender Equality Policy." Paper presented at the 93rd American Political Science Association (APSA) Conference, Washington D. C., August 28–31, 1997.

Anderson, Jeffrey. 1995. "Structural Funds and the Social Dimension of EU Policy: Springboard or Stumbling Block?" In Stephan Leibfried and Paul Pierson (Eds.). *European Social Policy: Between Fragmentation and Integration*. Washington, D. C.: The Brookings Institution.

Arthur, W. 1988. "Self-reinforcing Mechanisms in Economics." In P. Anderson, K. Arrow and D. Pines (Eds.). *The Economy as an Evolving Complex System*. Reading, MA: Addison Wesley.

Axelrod, Regina and Norman Vig. 1999. "The European Union as an Environmental Governance System." In Norman Vig and Regina Axelrod (Eds.). *The Global Environment: Institutions, Law and Policy*. Washington D.C.: CQ Press.

Bache, Ian. 1998. *The Politics of European Union Regional Policy: Multi-Level Governance or Flexible Gatekeeping?*. Sheffield: Sheffield Academic Press.

Baldez, Lisa. 1997. "Democratic Institutions and Feminist Outcomes: Chilean Policy Toward Women in the 1990s." Working Paper #340. Department of Political Science, Washington University.

Baumgartner, Frank and Bryan Jones. 1993. *Agendas and Instability in American Politics.* Chicago: University of Chicago Press.

Burley, A. and W. Mattli 1993. "Europe Before the Court: A Political Theory of Legal Integration." *International Organization*, 47: 41–77.

Cameron, David. 1992. "The 1992 Initiative: Causes and Consequences." In Alberta Sbragia (Ed.). *Institutions and Policymaking in the "New" European Community.* Washington, D. C.: The Brookings Institution.

Clark, Ian. 1989. *The Hierarchy of States: Reform and Resistance in the International Order.* Cambridge: Cambridge University Press.

Coester-Waltjen, Dagmar. 1984. *Protection of Working Women during Pregnancy and Motherhood in the Member States of the EC.* CEC, V/1829/84.

Cohen, Michael, James March, and Johan Olsen. 1972. "A Garbage Can Model of Organizational Choice." *Administrative Science Quarterly*, 17: 1–25.

Collins, Evelyn. 1996. "European Union Sexual Harassment Policy." In Amy Elman (Ed.). *Sexual Politics and the European Union: The New Feminist Challenge.* Providence and Oxford: Bergham.

Cowles, Maria Green. 1994. *The Politics of Big Business in the European Community: Setting the Agenda for a New Europe.* Ph.D. Dissertation. The American University.

Cowles, Maria Green. 1995. "Multinational, Two-Levels Games and the European Community." Paper presented at the International Studies Association conference, Chicago, Illinois, 21–25 February 1995.

Deshormes, Fausta. 1992. "Women of Europe." *Women's Studies International Forum*, 15, 1:51–52.

Dinan, Desmond. 1994. *Ever Closer Union?: An Introduction to the European Community.* Boulder, CO: L. Rienner.

Edelman, Murray Jacob. 1988. *Constructing the Political Spectacle.* Chicago: University of Chicago Press.

Eurobarometer (EB). 1997. 44.3, Brussels 1997: 15.

European Commission. 1990. *Equal Opportunities for Men and Women-the Third Medium-term Action Programme 1991–1995*, COM (90) 449 final.

European Commission. 1994. *Law Network: An Internal Document of the Network of Experts on the Implementation of Equality Directives.* Newsletter 3, No.11, Autumn 1994.

European Commission. 1994a. *Growth, Competitiveness, Employment: The Challenges and Ways Forward into the 21st Century-White Paper.* Luxembourg: EUR-OP.

European Commission. 1995. *Les femmes et les hommes dans l'Union européenne: portrait statistique.* Luxembourg: EUR-OP.

European Commission. 1996. *France: Single Programming Document 1994–99.* Luxembourg: EUR-OP.

European Commission. 1997. *Employment-NOW: New Employment Opportunities for Women.* Special Report, February 1997.

European Commission. 1997a. *Equal Opportunities for Women and Men in the European Union: Annual Report from the Commission: 1996.* Luxembourg: EUR-OP.

European Commission. 1998. *Equal Opportunities Magazine: Selected Articles 1996–1998.* Brussels: Anima.

European Commission. 1998a. *Equal Opportunities for Women and Men in the European Union: Annual Report from the Commission: Annual Report 1997.* Luxembourg: EUR-OP.

European Commission. 1998b. *The European Social Fund: An Overview of the Programming Period 1994–99.* Luxembourg: EUR-OP.

European Commission. 1998c. *Promoting Equal Opportunities for Men and Women: ESF Project Examples.* Luxembourg: EUR-OP.

European Commission. 1998d. *Conclusions of the ESF Mid-term Evaluations.* Luxembourg: EUR-OP.

European Commission. 1998e. *Employment-NOW: Business Creation by Women.* Luxembourg: EUR-OP.

European Commission. 1998f. Progress report on the follow-up of the Communication "Incorporating equal opportunities for women and men into all Community policies and activities" COM (98) 122 final.

European Commission. 1999. *Equal Opportunities for Women and Men in the European Union: Annual Report from the Commission: 1998.* Luxembourg: EUR-OP.

European Commission. 1999a. *The European Employment Strategy.* Luxembourg: EUR-OP.

European Commission. 1999b. Communication from the Commission to the member states establishing the guidelines for Community Initiatives. Brussels, 13 October 1999 COM (1999) 476 Final.

European Office for Programme Support (EUROPS). 1996. *Guide to Transnationality for ADAPT and EMPLOYMENT Projects.* Brussels: EUROPS.

European Paliament (EP). 1983. *Maternity, Parental Leave and Pre-School Facilities.* (Le Roux Report) PE 83.064.

European Parliament. 1997. Report on the Communication of the Commission entitled "Integrate equality of opportunities between women and men into all Community policies and activities"-

Mainstreaming. Reporter: Angela Kokkola, Strasbourg, 18 July, 1997.

European Parliament (EP). 1998. *Women's Rights and the Treaty of Amsterdam.* Luxembourg: European Parliament.

European Women's Lobby (EWL). 1998. *EWL News.* No. 10, October 1998.

European Women's Lobby (EWL). 1998a. *EWL News.* No. 11–12, November-December 1998.

Evans, Peter, Dietrich Rueschemeyer and Theda Skocpol (Eds.). 1985. *Bringing the State Back In.* Cambridge, New York: Cambridge University Press.

Falkner, Gerda. 1996. "Enlarging the European Union." In Jeremy Richardson (Ed.). *European Union: Power and Policy-making.* London and New York: Routledge.

Garrett, Geoffrey. 1992. "International Cooperation and Institutional Choice: the European Community's Internal Market." *International Organization,* 46: 533–60.

Garrett, Geoffrey and George Tsebelis. 1996. "An Institutional Critique of Intergovernmentalism." *International Organization,* 50, 2: 269–99.

Garrett, Geoffrey and Barry Weingast. 1993. "Ideas, Interests and Institutions: Constructing the European Community's Internal Market. In Judith Goldstein and Robert O. Keohane. *Ideas and Foreign Policy.* Ithaca: Cornell University Press.

Gelb, Joyce. 1989. *Feminism and Politics: A Comparative Perspective.* Berkeley: University of California Press.

Grieco, Joseph. 1988. "Anarchy and the Limits of Cooperation: A Realist Critique of the Newest Liberal Institutionalism." *International Organization,* 42, 3: 486–507.

Haas, Ernst. 1958. *The Uniting of Europe: Political, Social, and Economic Forces.* Stanford: Stanford University Press.

Haas. Ernst. 1970. "The Study of Regional Integration: Reflections on the Joy and Anguish of Pretheorizing." *International Organization,* 24: 607–46.

Haas, Ernst. 1975. "The Obsolescence of Regional Integration Theory." *Research Studies,* 25. Berkeley: Institute of International Studies.

Haas, Peter. 1992. "Introduction: Epistemic Communities and International Policy Co-ordination." *International Organization,* 46, 1: 1–35.

Heclo, Hugh 1978. "Issue Networks and the Executive Establishment." In Anthony King (Ed.). *The New American Political System.* Washington D. C.: American Enterprise Institute.

Hoffmann, Stanley. 1966. "Obstinate or Obsolete? The Fate of the Nation-State and the Case of Western Europe." *Daedalus,* 95: 862–915.

Hoskyns, Catherine. 1986. "Women, European Law and Transnational Politics." *International Journal of the Sociology of Law*, 14: 229–315.

Hoskyns, Catherine. 1988. "'Give Us Equal Pay and We'll Open Our Own Doors' — A Study of the Impact in the Federal Republic of Germany and the Republic of Ireland of the European Community's Policy on Women Rights." In Mary Buckley and Malcolm Anderson. *Women, Equality and Europe*. London: Macmillan Press.

Hoskyns, Catherine. 1991. "The European Women's Lobby." *Feminist Review*, 38: 67–70.

Hoskyns, Catherine. 1994. "Gender Issues in International Relations: The Case of the European Community." *Review of International Studies*, 20: 225–239.

Hoskyns, Catherine. 1996. *Integrating Gender: Women, Law and Politics in the European Union*. London, New York: Verso.

Hoskyns, Catherine. 1996a. "The European Union and the Women Within: An Overview of Women's Rights Policy." In Amy Elman (Ed.). *Sexual Politics and the European Union: The New Feminist Challenge*. Providence and Oxford: Bergham.

Hubert, Agnès. 1998. *L' Europe et les femmes: identités en mouvement*. Paris: Éditions Apogée.

Joseph, Joseph. 1997. *Cyprus: Ethnic Conflict and International Politics*. New York: St. Martin's Press.

Kassim, Hussein. 1997. "French Autonomy and the European Union." *Modern & Contemporary France*, 5, 2: 167–180.

Kegley, Charles (Ed.). 1995. *Controversies in International Relations Theory: Realism and the Neoliberal Challenge*. New York: St. Martin's Press.

Keohane, Robert 1983. "The Demand for International Regimes." In Stephen Krasner (Ed.). *International Regimes*. Ithaca: Cornell University Press.

Keohane, Robert. 1984. *After Hegemony: Cooperation and Discord in the World Political Economy*. Princeton: Princeton University Press.

Kiewiet, R. and M. MacCubbins. 1991. *The Logic of Delegation: Congressional Parties and the Appropriations Process*. Chicago: Chicago University Press.

Kingdon, John W. 1984. *Agendas, Alternatives, and Public Policies*. Boston: Little, Brown.

Klein, Viola. 1965. *Women Workers-Working Hours and Services*. Paris: OECD.

Kok, G.H.S. 1967. *Report on the Political and Civic Position of Women in Europe*. Strasbourg: Council of Europe.

Krasner, Stephen (Ed.). 1983. *International Regimes*. Ithaca: Cornell University Press.

Krasner, Stephen. 1989. "Sovereignty: An Institutional Perspective." In J. Caporaso (Ed.). *The Elusive State: International and Comparative Perspectives*. Newbury Park, CA: Sage.

Kreppel, Amie. 1997. "The European Parliament's Influence over EU Policy Outcomes: Fantasy, Fallacy or Fact?" Paper presented at the 1997 APSA meeting, Washington DC.

Lange, Peter. 1992. "The Politics of the Social Dimension." In Alberta Sbragia (Ed.). *Institutions and Policymaking in the "New" European Community*. Washington, D. C.: The Brookings Institution.

Lange, Peter. 1993. "The Maastricht Social Protocol: Why Did They Do It?" *Politics and Society*, 21: 5–36.

Leibfried, Stephan and Paul Pierson (Eds.). 1995. *European Social Policy: Between Fragmentation and Integration*. Washington, D. C.: The Brookings Institution.

Liebert, Ulrike. 1997. "The Gendering of Euro-skepticism: Public Discourses and Support to the EU in a Cross-national Comparison. Institute for European Studies Working Paper no. 97.2, Cornell University.

Lindberg, L. 1963. *The Political Dynamics of European Economic Integration*. Stanford: Stanford University Press.

Lubin, Carol Riegelman and Anne Winslow. 1991. *Social Justice for Women: the International Labor Organization and Women*. Durham: Duke University Press.

Maghroori, Ray. 1982. "Major Debates in International Relations." In Ray Maghroori and Bennett Ramberg (Eds.). *Globalism Versus Realism: International Relations' Third Debate*. Boulder, Colo.: Westview Press.

March, James and Johan Olsen. 1989. *Rediscovering Institutions: The Organizational Basis of Politics*. Free Press.

Marjorin, Robert. 1986. *Le travail d'une vie*. Paris: Robert Laffont.

Marks, Gary. 1992. "Structural Policy in the European Community." In Alberta Sbragia (Ed.). *Institutions and Policymaking in the "New" European Community*. Washington, D. C.: The Brookings Institution.

Marks, Gary, Liesbet Hooghe and Kermit Blank. 1996. "European Integration from the 1980s: State Centric v. Multi-level Governance." *Journal of Common Market Studies*, 34, 3: 341–378.

Mazey, Sonia. 1995. "The Development of EU Equality Policies: Bureaucratic Expansion on Behalf of Women?" *Public Administration*, 73: 651–609.

Mazey, Sonia. 1996. "The Development of the European Idea: From Sectoral Integration to Political Union." In Jeremy Richardson (Ed.). *European Union: Power and Policy-making*. London and New York: Routledge.

Mazey, Sonia. 1998. "The European Union and Women's Rights: from the Europeanization of National Agenda to the Nationalization of a European Agenda." *Journal of European Public Policy*, 5,1: 131–152.

Mazur, Amy. 1995. "Strong State and Symbolic Reform: The *Ministère des Droits de la Femme* in France." In Dorothy McBride Stetson and Amy Mazur (Eds.). *Comparative State Feminism*. Thousand Oaks: Sage.

Mendrinou, Maria. 1996. "Non-Compliance and the European Commission's Role in Integration." *Journal of European Public Policy*, 3, 1: 1–22.

Milward, A. 1992. *The European Rescue of the Nation-State*. Berkeley: University of California Press.

Moravcsik, Andrew. 1992. "Negotiating the Single European Act: National Interests and Conventional Statecraft in the European Community." *International Organization*, 45: 19–56.

Moravcsik, Andrew. 1993. "Preferences and Power in the European Community: A Liberal Intergovernmentalist Approach." *Journal of Common Market Studies*, 31: 473–524.

Moravcsik, Andrew. 1995. "Liberal Intergovernmentalism and Integration: A Rejoinder." *Journal of Common Market Studies*, 33, 4: 611–63.

Morgenthau, Hans Joachim. 1948. *Politics Among Nations: The Struggle for Power and Peace*. New York: Knopf.

Moss, Peter. 1988. *Childcare and Equality of Opportunity: Consolidated Report to the European Commission*, CEC V/746/88.

Mushaben, Joyce Marie. 1994. *A Forum for Gender Equality?: The European Community Discovers the Other Democratic Deficit*. St. Louis: University of Missouri-St. Louis, Center for International Studies.

Mushaben, Joyce. 1998. "The Politics of *Critical Acts*: Women, Leadership and Democratic Deficits in the European Union" *The European Studies Journal*, XV, 2: 51–91.

North, Douglass. 1990. *Institutions, Institutional Change, and Economic Performance*. Cambridge: Cambridge University Press.

Nonon, Jacqueline. 1998. *L'Europe, un atout pour les femmes?* Paris: La documentation Française.

Nye, Joseph. 1971. *Peace in Parts: Integration and Conflict in Regional Organizations*. Boston: Little, Brown.

OECD. 1970. *Employment of Women*. Paris: OECD.

Offen, Karen. 1994. "Women, Citizenship and Suffrage with a French Twist, 1789–1993." In Caroline Daley and Melanie Nolan. *Suffrage and Beyond: International Feminist Perspectives.* New York: New York University Press.

Ostner, Ilona and Jane Lewis. 1995. "Gender and the Evolution of Social Policies." In Stephan Leibfried and Paul Pierson (Eds.). *European Social Policy: Between Fragmentation and Integration.* Washington, D. C.: The Brookings Institution.

Peters, Guy. 1992. "Bureaucratic Politics and the Institutions of the European Community." In Alberta Sbragia (Ed.). *Institutions and Policymaking in the "New" European Community.* Washington, D. C.: The Brookings Institution.

Pierson, Paul and Stephan Leibfried. 1995. "Multitiered Institutions and the Making of Social Policy." In Stephan Leibfried and Paul Pierson (Eds.). *European Social Policy: Between Fragmentation and Integration.* Washington, D. C.: The Brookings Institution.

Pierson, Paul. 1996. "The Path to European Integration: A Historical Institutionalist Analysis." *Comparative Political Studies*, 29, 2: 123–163.

Pollack, Mark. 1997. "Delegation, Agency, and Agenda Setting in the European Community." *International Organization*, 51, 1: 99–134.

Pollack, Mark. 1997a. "Representing Diffuse Interests in EC Policy-making." *Journal of European Public Policy*, 4, 4: 572–90.

Puchala, Donald and Raymond Hopkins. 1983. "International Regimes: Lessons from Inductive Analysis." In Stephen Krasner (Ed.). *International Regimes.* Ithaca: Cornell University Press.

Republic of Cyprus. 1994. Cyprus National Report to the Fourth World Conference on Women, Beijing 1995. Nicosia: Printing Office of the Republic of Cyprus.

Republic of Cyprus. 1998. *Equality between Men and Women in Cyprus.* Report on the existing situation with the Community Acquis and the measures necessary to achieve full harmonization, prepared by the Ministry of Labour and Social Insurance, Nicosia, September 1998.

Rhodes, Martin. 1995. "A Regulatory Conundrum: Industrial Relations and the Social Dimension." In Stephan Leibfried and Paul Pierson (Eds.). *European Social Policy: Between Fragmentation and Integration.* Washington, D. C.: The Brookings Institution.

Richardson, Jeremy. 1996. "Policy-making in the EU: Interests, Ideas and Garbage Cans of Primeval Soup." In Jeremy Richardson (Ed.). *European Union: Power and Policy-making.* London and New York: Routledge.

Richardson, Jeremy and Grant Jordan. 1979. *Governing Under Pressure: The Policy Process in a Post-Parliamentary Democracy*. Oxford: Martin Robertson.

Robertson, David. 1993. "The Return to History and the New Institutionalism in American Political Science." *Social Science History*, 17, 1.

Rochester, Martin J. 1986. "The Rise and the Fall of International Organization as Field of Study." *International Organization*, 40, 4: 778–813.

Rosenau, James. 1982. "Order and Disorder in the Study of World Politics: Ten Essays in Search of Perspective." In Ray Maghroori and Bennett Ramberg (Eds.). *Globalism Versus Realism: International Relations' Third Debate*. Boulder, Colo.: Westview Press.

Rutheford, Françoise. 1989. "The Proposal for a European Directive on Parental Leave: Some Reasons why it Failed." *Policy and Politics*, 17, 4: 301–10.

Sbragia, Alberta (Ed.). 1992. *Institutions and Policymaking in the "New" European Community*. Washington, D. C.: The Brookings Institution.

Sbragia, Alberta. 1999. "Politics in the European Union." In Gabriel Almond, Russell Dalton and G. Bingham Powell (Eds.). *European Politics Today*. New York: Longman.

Scott, Joan Wallach. 1996. *Only Paradoxes to Offer: French Feminists and the Rights of Man*. Cambridge, Mass.: Harvard University Press.

Spaak, Paul-Henri. 1969. *Combats inachevés*. Paris:Fayard.

Stein, Arthur. 1983. "Coordination and Collaboration: Regimes in an Anarchic World." In Stephen Krasner (Ed.). *International Regimes*. Ithaca: Cornell University Press.

Steinmo, Sven, Kathleen Thelen and Frank Longstreth (Eds.). 1992. *Structuring Politics: Historical Institutionalism in Comparative Analysis*. Cambridge: Cambridge University Press.

Stetson, Dorothy McBride. 1987. *Women's Rights in France*. New York: Greenwood Press.

Stetson, Dorothy McBride and Amy Mazur (Eds.). 1995. *Comparative State Feminism*. Newbury Park: Sage.

Strange, Susan. 1987. "The Persistent Myth of Lost Hegemony." *International Organization*, 41, 4: 55–574.

Stuenenberg, Bernard. 1994. "Decision-making under Different Institutional Arrangements-Legislation by the European Community." *Journal of Institutional and Theoretical Economics*, 150: 642–69.

Sullerot, Evelyn. 1968. *Histoire et sociologie du travail féminin*. Paris: Editions

Gonthier.

Sullerot, Evelyn. 1970. *L'emploi des femmes et ses problèmes dans les états membres de la CE.* Brussels: CEC.

Sullerot, Evelyn. 1975. "Equality of Remuneration for Men and Women in the Member States of the EEC." *International Labour Review*, 112, 2–3: 87–108.

Tinker, Irene and Jane Jacquette. 1987. "UN Decade for Women: Its Impact and Legacy." *World Development*, 15, 3: 419–427.

Tsebelis, George. 1994 "The Power of the European Parliament as a Conditional Agenda Setter." *American Political Science Review*, 88, 1: 128–42.

Tsebelis, George and Anastasios Kalandrakis. 1997. "Europarliament and Environmental Legislation: The Case of Chemicals." Paper presented at the 1997 APSA meeting, Washington D. C.

United Nations. 1995. *The United Nations and the Advancement of Women, 1945–1995.* New York: Department of Public Information, United Nations.

Waltz, Kenneth Neal. 1979. *Theory of International Politics.* Reading, Mass.: Addison-Wesley.

Warner, Harriet. 1984. "EC Social Policy in Practice: Community Action on Behalf of Women and its Impact in the Member States." *Journal of Common Market Studies*, XXIII, 2: 141–167.

Whitworth, Sandra. 1994. *Feminism and International Relations: Towards a Political Economy of Gender in Interstate and Non-governmental Institutions.* New York: St. Martin's Press.

Wiener, Antje. 1999. "Citizenship Policy in a Global Framework: The Case of the European Union." In Kenneth Thomas and Mary Ann Tétreault (Eds.). *Racing to Regionalize: Democracy, Capitalism and Regional Political Economy.* Boulder: Lynne Rienner.

Young, Oran. 1983. "Regime Dynamics: The Rise and Fall of International Regimes." In Stephen Krasner (Ed.). *International Regimes.* Ithaca: Cornell University Press.

Index

127, 154

Womens's suffrage, 24–5

"Garbage can politics," 4, 13, 16,

Gaudet, Michel, 27

Gender gap, 43

Germany
Article 119 adoption, 26–7, 69
EU membership, xiv, xv, xvi, 10, 24, 41

Globalism, 3–6, 18

Greece, xiv, xxi, 6, 25, 43, 49, 73, 83, 96–7, 102, 109, 112, 119, 125

Guigou, Elizabeth, 109

Helfferich, Barbara, 57–9, 115–6, 146

Herstal strike, 33, 36, 38

Historical institutionalism, xviii, xix, xx, 12–4, 18, 21, 27, 44, 62, 67–9, 152
Unanticipated consequences, 14, 18, 63, 69–73, 87, 152–3

Hoskyns, Catherine, 30–1, 33, 36, 63 n.6

Hubert, Agnès, 28, 33, 42, 51, 55, 59, 63 n.4, 75, 114

Incrementalism, 22, 40, 44, 47–8, 61, 151

Intergovernmentalism, xviii, xx, 4, 8, 13, 15, 18, 44, 54, 61–2, 67–8, 69, 73, 78, 87, 88–9, 107, 125, 127, 154

International Governmental Organizations (IGOs), 8

International Institute for the Advancement of Women (INSTRAW), 41

International Labour Organization (ILO), 26–30, 33, 39, 41, 53, 62–3, 69, 73, 132, 134, 141,

International Labour Organization (ILO) Convention 100, 26–30, 33, 66, 69, 134

International relations theory, xviii, xxiii, 3, 7, 26

International Women's Year (IWY), 39, 42

Liberal intergovernmentalism, 10–3, 19 n.2

Luxembourg process, 53–4, 58,

Mainstreaming, 23, 48, 54–61

Major, John, 78–9

Medium Term Economic Programme (MTEP), 32

Members of the European Parliament (MEP), 13, 46, 49–50, 59

Monnet, Jean, xiv,

Moravcsik, Andrew, 13, 20, 68

National Action Plan (NAP), 116, 121

Neofunctionalism, xviii, xix, 4, 8–9, 15, 18

New Opportunities for Women (NOW), xxi, xxii, 82–3, 92, 110, 112–123, 154

Non-Governmental Organizations (NGOs), 7–8, 82–4, 89, 121, 134, 143

Nonon, Jacqueline, 35, 37–8, 39, 42, 62, 68, 86, 114–5

Objective 3, see Structural Funds

Ohlin Report, 26–7, 29–30

Operational Programme (OP), 100

Organization for Economic Co-operation and Development (OECD), 34

Papandreou, Vasso, 85

Parental Leave Directive, 45, 47, 51, 75, 79, 88, 153

Part-time Work Directive, 52

Pierson, Paul, 18, 78–9

Policy communities, 16–7, 30

Policy entrepreneurs, 22, 30, 36, 61

Punctuated equilibrium, 22, 40

Qualified Majority Voting (QMV), 51, 62, 68, 75–7, 88, 153

Quintin, Odile, 46, 114–5, 123 n.15

Regimes, xx, 7–8, 38

Rational choice institutionalism, xviii, 4, 13, 15–6